NEW RELIGIOUS MOVEMENTS
and
RELIGIOUS LIBERTY IN AMERICA

New Religious Movements
and
Religious Liberty in America

Edited
by

DEREK H. DAVIS
and
BARRY HANKINS

Published by the J.M. Dawson Institute of Church-State Studies
and Baylor University Press
Baylor University
Waco, Texas 76798-7308
USA

NEW RELIGIOUS MOVEMENTS
AND RELIGIOUS LIBERTY IN AMERICA

Address correspondence to
J.M. Dawson Institute of Church-State Studies
P.O. Box 97308, Baylor University, Waco, Texas 76798 USA

FIRST EDITION 2002

Library of Congress Cataloging-in-Publication Data
Preassigned Catalog Card Number:
2002100646

International Standard Book Numbers:
ISBN 929182-64-2 (PAPER)
ISBN 929182-65-0 (CLOTH)

CONTENTS

PREFACE

All the essays in this book were presented at a symposium at Baylor University entitled "New Religious Movements and Religious Liberty in America," 12-13 February 2001. The J.M. Dawson Institute of Church-State Studies would like to thank Baylor University for its generous funding over the years that has made symposia, lectureships, and books like this one possible. We would like to thank specifically President Robert Sloan and his administration for their gracious support of our work. Chancellor Herbert Reynolds, Provost Donald Schmeltekopf, Vice-Provost Dianna Vitanza, and Arts and Sciences Dean Wallace Daniel, as always, were supportive of this project.

Several people at the Institute had a hand in bringing both the symposium and this volume to successful completion. Administrative assistant Wanda Gilbert has never left even one stone unturned in the planning of an event, while Janice Losak takes on all tasks with great aplomb. Editorial assistant Pat Cornett seems at times capable of working miracles with computerized text. She has been at the center of this project every step of the way. It would be impossible to plan and execute symposia, conferences, and lectureship without the assistance of these three individuals. Doctoral Fellow Marshall Johnston was a great help in organizing and planning for the conference that spawned this book. Graduate student Hui Fui performed the tedious yet important task of compiling the index. Also, a special word of thanks is due to those Baylor faculty who serve on our Church-State Studies Faculty Committee and *Journal of Church and State* Editorial Board. They regularly give of their time and expertise in order to keep the work of the Institute and *Journal* moving forward.

Finally, thanks to all of the contributors. In both symposium planning and the editing of this book, you have been most accommodating. Your dedication and commitment to religious liberty for people everywhere and of every religious persuasion has been humbling, and has reassured us that publishing books like this one is a worthwhile endeavor.

Derek H. Davis
Barry Hankins

Baylor University
March 2002

Introduction

BARRY HANKINS

It has been said that the measure of healthy and civilized society is how well it treats its elderly and indigent. Perhaps it should be said also that the measure of the health of religious liberty in a society is the degree to which minority, nontraditional faiths are protected. This book is a collection of essays on the subject of religious liberty and new religious movements (NRMs). The chapters were first delivered as papers at a conference sponsored by the J.M. Dawson Institute of Church-State Studies at Baylor University in March 2001. NRMs are often called "cults" by popular media commentators and the public at large, but scholars eschew that term because it is so pejorative that it skews the argument from the very beginning. By contrast, the term "new religious movements" attempts to place NRMs squarely in the mix with older, more traditional forms of religion. This is due in part to the fact that in America there should be no correlation between the level of social approval a group has achieved and the degree of religious liberty it enjoys. As the Supreme Court itself averred famously in the 1872 case *Watson v. Jones*, "The Law knows no heresy and is committed to the support of no dogma, the establishment of no sect." While often falling short of this ideal, the United States Constitution, specifically the First Amendment, is interpreted by the courts to mean that all groups should enjoy religious liberty, not just those who adhere to longstanding and traditional variations of the Christian faith. Make no mistake from the outset; each author represented in this volume believes that NRMs should enjoy the same liberties as more mainstream religions. If the book has a bias, it is a bias in favor of religious liberty. The authors believe that if the First Amendment is applied to protect the newest, nontraditional, seemingly unusual religions (by the standards of the majority of the population), then nearly everyone is safe as far as religious liberty is concerned.

The book begins with Timothy Miller setting the historical context by showing that in a sense NRMs have been a longstanding part of western history. In centuries past, the majority viewed Christian sectarian groups much as the public views NRMs today. They were not only unusual but also threatening to the social order. Sectarian groups from the Middle Ages and Early Modern Period were at least as radical and controversial as many of today's NRMs, but we tend to be much more tolerant of groups that are safely in the past. Only the NRMs of our own time threaten us.

These supposed threats are sometimes so alarming that anti-cult groups resort to rather extreme measures to combat the influence of NRMs. This is the subject of chapter two. Anson Shupe et al.'s meticulously researched findings concerning the Cult Awareness Network (CAN) raise the age-old question as to whether the proposed solution to a perceived social problem can be worse than the problem itself. This is not to say that NRMs never engage in spurious behavior. No one would make that claim for either NRMs or other, more traditional, religious groups. Clearly, religious groups of all kinds must obey the law. The flip-side of this dictum, however, is that as long as they are compliant with the law, religious liberty requires that they be free to make their cases to the wider public, which includes the right to discredit and refute competing religious groups and win converts for themselves. In addition to its financial irregularities, the problem with CAN, as Shupe and his team show, was that the organization engaged in kidnapping that violated the liberty of those who adhere to the teachings of various NRMs. This was possible because of an assumption that somehow NRMs operate outside the normal procedures of "acceptable" religious groups, which is a notion that is highly questionable in light of Miller's historical overview.

Following Miller's line of thinking, Gordon Melton shows how the highly developed Sea Org community of the Church of Scientology is much like older religious orders from the Christian faith and from eastern religions. The Sea Org, like the others, is an "ordered religious community." While to outsiders the rigor appears oppressive, for participants the community life is experienced as both voluntary and liberating. Even some ex-members of the Sea Org, whose views are rather negative, still reject the more extreme charges made by ex-Scientology members who were not in the Sea Org.

On the other hand, however, Melton also shows that the worst abuses in Scientology, those often cited by disillusioned ex-members, were indeed committed by Guardian Office (GO) officials of the Sea Org in the 1970s. Since that time, the GO was first reformed, with offending members expelled, and then the office was disbanded after leaders determined that it was unsalvageable. Melton, like Miller, makes comparisons with the history of Christianity, specifically with the sixteenth-century Catholic Reformation. Much like the Roman Catholic Church of that time, the Church of Scientology has had to come to grips with its own internal problems and abuses and reform itself.

The point of Melton's essay is not to make an apologia for Scientology. He takes no position on the truth or falsity of the group's claims. Rather, he seeks to show that its practices are not all that different from other ordered religious communities. The upshot, though not argued explicitly, is that Scientology should be treated in the legal domain just as more mainstream groups are. Unfortunately, this is not the case, especially in some European countries where Scientology is considered a dangerous cult that must be highly regulated or shut down.

It is often difficult to pinpoint what facet of NRMs appears as most dangerous to the wider community. Susan Palmer, however, may have identified such a feature in her chapter on gender and sex roles. Again, as Miller's essay shows, there is nothing new about the phenomenon whereby NRMs present a frontal challenge to traditional sex, gender, marital, and familial norms. Shaker founder Mother Ann Lee taught absolute celibacy, even within marriage, and came to be seen by her followers as the female manifestation of Christ. John Humphrey Noyes, by contrast, led his Oneida community into "complex marriage" whereby nearly all the community's males were simultaneously married to all the females. Working from a sociological perspective, Palmer steps back from contemporary NRMs to find patterns in gender roles and sexual relationships. She also finds that the longer an NRM exists, the more it tends to move toward the mainstream. As has been shown so many times in American religious history, American culture has a seemingly inexhaustible capacity to co-opt radical groups and pull them into the mainstream of American life, which is instructive for those who are concerned that NRMs will distort and possibly help destroy American culture. It is more likely that the reverse will happen.

Along with groups practicing nontraditional sex and gender roles, those practicing Satanism and witchcraft have contended for status as most controversial of the NRMs. James Richardson, like Palmer, utilizes the tools of modern sociology to analyze Wicca and Satanism, both of which consist of, as Richardson writes, "small numbers of people doing things that are usually quite harmless to themselves and others," but nevertheless "are defined as major social problems by many in the U.S. and elsewhere." Fostered by "claims makers," such social problems, which by definition must be dealt with and overcome, can lead to a "moral panic" and "perceived danger" that is out of proportion to the actual threat. Richardson traces the recent moral panic that has arisen as a result of Satanism and Wicca and concludes that the anti-cult movement combined with the penchant for melding the identities of Satanism and Wicca will likely continue to foster difficulties for both movements into the foreseeable future.

Perhaps the most disturbing chapter of the book is Stuart Wright's brief exposition of the trial of the Branch Davidians who survived the 1993 siege outside of Waco, just ten miles from the campus where these chapters were first delivered as scholarly papers and from where I write this introduction. Most disturbing is that Wright shows what can happen, in an extreme case to be sure, when a non-traditional NRM is considered as a matter of law to be fundamentally different from more traditional groups. No one excuses the illegal activities David Koresh was involved in—firearms and other weapons violations, alleged child sex abuse, etc.—but the disaster at Waco was a horrific and unacceptable response that resulted in part from recklessness stemming from the Bureau of Alcohol, Tobacco, and Firearms's (ATF) views of NRMs. The ATF used measures that directly violated its own hostage-barricade protocols. Was this the result of an assumption that Koresh and his followers, because they were non-traditional, would not respond rationally or normally to the protocols? Do government officials assume that unusual religious groups are fundamentally different in their rational capabilities and responses? Both Miller and Melton argue that throughout history there are vast similarities in the ways that religious groups of all kinds tend to organize themselves and respond to outside hostility and internal abuses; Wright shows what can happen when authorities ignore the similarities and assume that NRMs are radically different and irrational.

Closely associated with Wright's analysis, Catherine Wessinger offers a way forward that may help American law enforcement agencies avoid such tragedies in the future. Based on her long-standing concern and in-depth research, Wessinger presents a compelling argument that often law enforcement agencies, because of their lack of understanding of NRMs, actually develop a self-fulfilling prophecy. In conflicts between NRMs and law enforcement, both sides often participate in rituals of violence that can escalate into horrific consequences. Sometimes, as was the case with Jim Jones and the People's Temple, the NRM itself engages in such rituals, but in other instances, as with the Weaver family at Ruby Ridge and the Branch Davidians outside of Waco, the NRM and the law enforcement agents enter into a symbiotically destructive pattern of ritualized violence that ends in disaster. From this part of Wessinger's wider research, she hones in specifically on the role that millennialism plays in contests between NRMs and law enforcement. As with the other sociological analyses presented in this volume, she seeks to discover patterns, specifically types of millennialism, and then demonstrates how violence can escalate when law enforcement agents disregard the worldview of an NRM. In a haunting section of her chapter, Wessinger shows how close the Branch Davidians were to negotiating an acceptable surrender scenario that David Koresh could make sense of within the group's own millennial framework. The inability of the ATF to take that framework seriously had tragic consequences. Wessinger concludes that religious groups are usually able to reinterpret and adjust their views in response to events. A group's potential to be violent can, therefore, escalate or deescalate depending on their interaction with law enforcement agents. This being the case, agents should seek to understand the worldview of the group in an effort to provide the believers with a way out that fits with the adapted version of their theology. "The manner in which all of us interact with members of new religious movements helps to determine the potential for volatility," Wessinger writes.

Moving from Wright and Wessinger's discussion of the tragic consequences that can result when government authorities misunderstand NRMs, chapter eight outlines the sordid history of attacks on Scientology. While the editors cannot vouch for every charge Heber Jentzsch makes in this essay, it is widely known that the U.S. government does have a history of harassment of Scientology. Much as was the case with Jehovah's Witnesses in the 1940s and 1950s, Scientology's efforts to combat such harassment have resulted in wider protection of religious liberty. The differences are that the Jehovah's Witnesses fought their battles most visibly in the arena of constitutional law, the result being a string of important cases. The Church of Scientology's battles have been against governmental bureaucracy, and they have resulted in quieter victories, though significant nevertheless.

Adam English raises an interesting question as to whether Christian Reconstructionism should be considered an NRM. Like many other groups, Reconstructionists have a millennial message, but, unlike those Wessinger discusses, they are postmillennial. That is, they believe not in an imminent end to history but in a long process whereby eventually America will be ruled by Old Testament law. Unlike David Koresh and others, Reconstructionists are for the most part content to wait patiently for Americans to become so distraught with the moral decline of a libertine society that they will actually embrace a theocratic alternative that will come to pass in a peaceful and evolutionary way. In the mean time, Reconstructionists write books (tomes, really) advocating their position. As Adam English's chapter shows, the coming of the new millennium loomed large for Reconstructionist Gary North but in a very different way than it did for some premillennialist Christians. For him, the impending crash of computers and resulting chaos were anticipated as the opportunity to start rebuilding a new theocratic society based on God's divine law. The new millennium was to be a new beginning, not the end. Of course, as I write this introduction on a computer and ready it to be e-mailed to a colleague for further editing, we are all reminded of the failure of North's anticipated great failure, but he is sure that ultimately Christian Reconstructionism will triumph.

Finally, in a chapter where the stakes are considerably lower than was the case at Mount Carmel or in the millennial predictions of North, Derek Davis addresses the many church-state problems inherent in President George W. Bush's initiative to fund Faith-Based Organizations (FBO's). While neither western civilization nor the lives of American citizens are threatened, this is nevertheless an important topic for the landscape of church-state relations and religious liberty. Davis focuses specifically on how such a program might affect NRMs. He shows that NRMs are as divided as the rest of America in their responses to the Bush initiatives, but even more instructive is his argument that if discrimination lurks in the details of government funding for FBO's, NRMs will be the most likely victims. This brings us back to the thread that holds this book together and the reason it is being published. The health of religious liberty cannot be measured by how well traditional, mainstream religions are protected. Religious liberty should be evaluated by how well things are going on the margins of the religious landscape. The majority hardly needs the protection of the Free Exercise clause of the First Amendment; legislatures will see to it that the interests of the mainstream are well served. NRMs have little or no voice and must be protected by constitutional provisions that treat them fairly and equally alongside the traditional groups that make up the majority.

Controversial Christian Movements: History, Growth, and Outlook

TIMOTHY MILLER

We humans have a tendency to think that we are living in unique times, and often we are disinclined to look at our past as a help in understanding the present. In the case of new religions, their appeal, and the controversy surrounding them, some might locate their origins in the frantic pace of modern life, or in the access to the exotic that modern communications and transportation afford, or, from a more theological point of view, in the chaos that precedes the great millennial events that many anticipate in the very near future. From a historian's point of view, however, what we see is neither new nor particularly unusual. Religious innovation and the controversy surrounding it goes as far back as history can see. Some of the controversies that have accompanied the rise of new religions in the past, especially in the American context. I am restricting my focus to variant forms of Christianity that have caused great stress among the mainstream faithful who are not at all happy to see the rise of heresy and heterodoxy.

Historic Christianity

Such a survey of Christian history might do well to begin with Christianity itself. Like any religion, it was new and controversial in its first three centuries or so, to say the least. The early church was troubling to both of the relevant prevailing centers of power, the Jewish temple leadership, whose authority was diminished by the Christian precept that the Kingdom of God was at hand and would replace the current order, and the Roman government, which always faced insurrections in its outlying provinces and viewed radical movements of all kinds with considerable suspicion. Such movements at worst were regarded as treasonous, and at best as ignorant superstitions. The very term "Christian" was at first used derisively by the movement's opponents who scorned the contention that this Jesus fellow had actually been the Jewish Messiah.

We all know well that the church suffered persecution for hundreds of years, until a great reversal occurred in the early fourth century by the edict of Constantine. Christianity was then tolerated and soon became the official religion of the Roman Empire.

The improved official status of Christianity hardly meant the end of religious persecution. The human race, in its fallen perversity, seems to be addicted to various kinds of intolerance, and the type of Christianity that became ensconced in government was more than eager to persecute its Christian competitors. All kinds of Christian movements and points of view that have gone down officially as heresies, from Gnosticism to Montanism to Manichaeism to Arianism, could be more plausibly regarded as victims of persecution than as propagators of error, or, as the popular argot would have it today, dangerous cults. Had the ruling faction in Rome, and then Constantinople, not had considerable political and military force behind it, Christian history might have worked out quite differently.

A millennium after the time of Jesus, the Eastern and Western branches of Christianity formally separated amid excommunications and anathemas and intractable doctrinal disputes. A century or two later, the Western church undertook legendarily ghastly persecution with the establishment of the Inquisition, which sought out Albigensians and other heretics. Around 1500, the Western church saw a huge challenge erupt with the advent of Protestantism. Protestantism quickly took on variant forms in different places, with Lutherans and Calvinists and Hussites and Zwinglians all having their spheres of influence and all becoming objects of the great wrath of the Roman church. But even the dominant Protestant reformers agreed with the Catholic church that the Anabaptists, the most radical of the Protestant dissidents, needed to be eliminated. The persecution of the Anabaptists for their dissent was among the most gruesome episodes in the spotted history of Christianity. The devices used by the Inquisitors and the Anabaptist-hunters make such modern anticult techniques as deprogramming look about as serious an intrusion as a telemarketing phone call.

Seventeenth Century

It is a sad irony that those early British settlers who came to our shores for religious freedom did not themselves prove at all tolerant. The early Puritans, so called because they originally sought to "purify," meaning decatholicize, the Church of England, had themselves suffered plenty of persecution in England, particularly at the hands of William Laud, Bishop of London and later Archbishop of Canterbury, so much so that they began to flee the country, at first in small numbers to the Netherlands, and then in larger numbers to the new world. But once they had established their holy commonwealth in New England, they were as determined as any of their predecessors not to suffer the outrages of heretical doctrine and practice. The founding of Rhode Island was one outgrowth of that persecution, as refugees from Massachusetts made it their haven. Roger Williams went to Massachusetts as a minister for the church in Boston, but upon arrival refused to serve because the church had not formally separated itself from the Church of England. He compounded his problems with other heresies, including the patently outrageous idea that the settlers should not be stealing land from the Indians, as well as a set of convictions that amounted to a belief in the separation of church and state. By 1635, Williams was sentenced to deportation, and he responded by fleeing into the wilderness in 1636, heading south and eventually founding Providence. There he founded the first Baptist church in America, and, of course, he has become a great Baptist hero now that he is more than three hundred years dead and nobody actually has to deal with him any more. As an aside, one cannot help but wonder whether the current Southern Baptist leadership has ever looked at what its founding hero actually had to say, i.e., what a strong advocate he was for church-state separation.

Two years later Anne Hutchinson was similarly expelled from Massachusetts for her challenges to the Massachusetts ministers and especially for her defense, in what was essentially her heresy trial, in which she committed the cardinal error of claiming that she had received special revelation, direct communication from God. Woe be to anyone to whom God speaks directly! She and her supporters similarly found themselves starting life anew in the wilderness of Rhode Island.[1]

The early New Englanders also had an especially intense dislike of the Quakers, who in their early years were zealous promoters of their own brand of Puritanism, which differed from that of the New England majority. The Quakers were among the most radical of the Puritans, vigorously opposing hierarchy and sacraments and seeking an intensively personal and individualized spirituality. They had their origin with George Fox, who in 1648 began to speak publicly of his faith, especially of his belief that one could have a direct revelation of Christ, indeed a direct, personal connection with God. He suffered persecution, but persevered and in 1652 organized a group of spiritual seekers in Lancashire. Quakers did indeed pose a threat to the established order, what with their disdain for ritual, their minimizing of the importance of ordained clergy, their giving up of visible sacraments, and, perhaps above all, their tremendous zeal to spread their faith.

In 1656, the first Quakers landed in Massachusetts Bay Colony. Quakerism was not illegal in Massachusetts at the time, but the provincial authorities knew about this new body of belief and detained the two new arrivals, Mary Fisher and Ann Austin, searching their belongings, seizing their books, and even stripping them and inspecting them for signs of witchcraft. They were deported, but a mere two days later another ship docked, this time with eight Quakers. They were immediately imprisoned and then deported, but even as prisoners they managed to spread their message sufficiently to make one convert. The colony then adopted a series of laws against the Quakers that among other things provided that any Quaker arriving in the colony would be whipped and deported before he or she could talk with anyone. But that hardly made the Quakers give up; they simply settled in Rhode Island, which by that time had been established as a colony that would be open to people of all religious persuasions and which was a perfect beachhead for forays over the border into Massachusetts. The Bay Colony made its laws ever more stringent, and in 1658 made Quakerism a capital crime. Four Quakers were actually executed for their convictions.[2]

The story eventually ends more happily, of course. The Quaker convert William Penn established his colony in 1681 and in what was known as the "Holy Experiment" proclaimed toleration for all who believed in God. Quakers, among many others, came in droves, and eventually took the place they occupy today as a small but well-accepted religious school of thought.

Pennsylvania with its vaunted toleration attracted a host of non-mainstream believers, including various strains of Anabaptists. These most radical of the Reformation-era believers are usually traced to the early 1520s in Switzerland, where they dissented from the new Reformation Calvinist and

Zwinglian orthodoxy with such doctrines as nonresistance to evil, separation of church and state, and pacifism. The first to arrive in America came in 1683, and many more followed. Although they had their detractors, and were repeatedly persecuted, even killed, in Europe, they generally did not experience the level of persecution that many other groups suffered in America. Nevertheless, their acceptance in American society has been mixed, and they have especially suffered as pacifists in wartime. One of the most overt persecutions involved the Hutterites, the wing of the Anabaptists that practices communal living in Canada and several north central and northwestern states in America. During World War I, their pacifism was so unpopular in South Dakota, where they all lived at the time, that they closed all but one of their colonies, selling them at distressed prices, and moved to Canada. By that time they had suffered extreme verbal persecution and even occasional mob violence and vandalism. Two of their young male members, arrested and incarcerated at Fort Leavenworth, died from what may fairly be called official torture. More recently they have been the focus of legal attempts, especially in Canada, to have their ability to buy and own land restricted. Life has not always been easy for Anabaptists in North America.[3]

Eighteenth Century

More than a century after the arrival of the Quakers, another group provided a textbook case in religious persecution and eventual toleration. In 1774, a group of members of the United Society of Believers in Christ's Second Appearing, better know as the Shakers, arrived in New York under the leadership of Ann Lee. After some very quiet early years, they gathered near what is now Albany, New York, and began to live communally. From that base they undertook a series of preaching missions and began to make converts, but as their visibility increased, so did their persecution. The Revolutionary War was still going on at the time, and the Shakers, who refused military service, were suspected of being British agents. But soon other charges emerged as well. One of the first bitter anti-Shaker diatribes came from one Valentine Rathbun, who joined the movement in 1780 but later dropped out and began to accuse the Shakers of practices that might now be called deceptive recruitment and even brainwashing. They greeted visitors "with many smiles, and seeming great gladness," Rathbun wrote, and fed and entertained them. But all of their seeming goodness was actually part of their strategy of developing "absolute dependence" among members.[4]

Such criticism, and sometimes physical persecution, was to hound the Shakers for many years to come. Ann Lee and several others undertook an extensive missionary tour in New England from 1781 to 1783. Although some were persuaded by the Shaker message of holy living and millennial hope, the Shakers experienced verbal abuse and, in quite a few cases, beatings and other physical abuse everywhere they went. In Harvard, Massachusetts, in January 1782, the militia drove the Shakers out of town. Shakers were whipped and beaten repeatedly, and stones were thrown and bullets fired at the houses where they were staying. Some believe the death of Ann Lee and her brother William in 1784 was the result of the abuse they had suffered.

One inevitable part of a religious movement's growth is a growth in apostasy. New members may join, but invariably some disaffected individuals leave, and sometimes harbor great hostility toward the group to which they were formerly committed. That was certainly the case with the Shakers. Mary Dyer was the most formidable of the nineteenth-century Shaker apostates, and she made a life-long career of her activism against the believers. She had joined with her husband, who stayed behind when she left and kept their children with him in the community. Her activism, fueled by a desire to get her children back, sometimes went beyond propagandizing to participating in mob violence. She and other apostates and opponents constantly contended with the Shakers by issuing manifestoes, making public speeches, and filing lawsuits.[5] All the while the Shakers had plenty of nonapostate opponents as well, including the literary luminary Nathaniel Hawthorne, who originally had a favorable opinion of the group, but eventually denounced them bitterly. In 1851 he wrote, "The fact shows that all their miserable pretence of cleanliness and neatness is the thinnest superficiality; and that the Shakers are and must needs be a filthy set. And then their utter and systematic lack of privacy; the close function of man with man, and supervision of one man over another–it is hateful and disgusting to think of; and the sooner the sect is extinct the better–a consummation which, I am happy to hear, is thought to be not a great many years distant."[6] And so it went throughout much of Shaker history.

After the middle of the nineteenth century, Shakerism started a serious decline. By the early twentieth century, it was but a shadow of its former self. Somehow the controversies of earlier years fell by the wayside. Lovers of the arts and shrewd investors began buying up Shaker furniture, which became so renowned that one of the late-era Shakers, Mildred Barker, used to exclaim that she did not want to be remembered as a chair. Today the Shakers are remembered in the warmest and fuzziest of terms, and the few survivors in Maine have a staunch support group of loving admirers and no controversy at all. The current attitude may best be summed up in the Ken Burns film called "The Shakers," which idealizes them exquisitely. Nice pieces of Shaker furniture fetch prices in the hundreds of thousands of dollars, especially since well-heeled collectors like Oprah Winfrey can bid choice items up to astronomical levels.

Nineteenth Century

Another communal Christian group had a history that in many ways paralleled that of the Shakers, and persecution was again a major part of the story, although again it has been largely forgotten as the believers have become retrospectively idealized. The Harmony Society, created and led by George Rapp, had its origins in German Pietism in the eighteenth century. Pietists criticized the state church as coldly formal and intellectual, and instead stressed deep personal religious experience and holy Christian living. Rapp was one of the most vocal and radical of the Pietists, and he took to denouncing the established church in the strongest terms. He attracted thousands of followers, and his conflict with the state became greater and greater. In 1804, hundreds of Harmonists sailed to Pennsylvania, where they founded a communal village called Harmony north of Pittsburgh. They built up a pleasant community for a decade, then moved en masse to Indiana, where they founded New Harmony, and built it up as a truly exquisite town, one that survives as one of the country's premier museum villages today. Finally, after another decade, they undertook one last move, this time back to near where they had started in Pennsylvania. There they built the sumptuous village of Economy, where they lived for the rest of their history, gradually declining after Rapp's death in 1847 but hanging on in diminished fashion until the early years of the twentieth century.

Like other groups the Rappites underwent plenty of persecution. Groups practicing community of goods are often inherently suspect of undermining traditional American values, and the Harmonists were celibate, which did not endear them to most Americans. Their relations with their neighbors were ambivalent at best, and in 1820 a physical battle between Harmonists and their antagonists erupted right in the streets of New Harmony. There were always internal tensions as well; whatever else can be said about the society, George Rapp was a despot who ruled with an iron hand. When a charismatic visitor arrived in 1831 and was eventually rebuffed by Rapp, upon departing he took about 175 disaffected Harmonists with him. Those leaving made some bitter charges against Rapp and the Harmony Society. They alleged that Rapp believed that he was God and beyond all human rules, that community property was actually a plot by Rapp to own and control everything, that Rapp refused to let them learn English to keep them unaware of their options, and that those who left the community were forced to set out penniless.

And so it went. Like the Shakers, the Rappites had their vigorous opponents, and found themselves verbally castigated and on the receiving end of lawsuits that alleged much the same things that anticultists allege today—mind control, coercive and powerful leadership, and so forth. The Harmonists did manage to withstand the onslaughts and finally died with a whimper, after a new member joining late in the game looted the treasury and shut the movement down.[7]

Of all of the movements that have been persecuted in American history, none have been more abusively treated than the Latter-day Saints, or Mormons. From their very founding in 1830 until well into the twentieth century, they were widely regarded as outlaws, lunatics, and perverts. Although the main Mormon church has finally become well accepted in polite society, some of the fringe groups that maintain old Mormon traditions faithfully continue to feel the brunt of a great deal of public abuse today.

Mormonism was formally born in 1830 with the publication of the Book of Mormon and the organization of what was originally called the Church of Christ. The founder, a young man named Joseph Smith, Jr., had had visionary experiences since his early teenage years, and by the late 1820s was engaged in "translating" what some called Joe Smith's Golden Bible. Smith claimed that he had been directed by an angel to a buried set of golden plates on which had been inscribed the history of some of the ancient peoples of the Americas. He was miraculously given the power to translate the mysterious characters on the plates, and the translation was called the Book of Mormon, after the ancient historian who was said to have written the account that ended up on the plates.

From its beginning, Mormonism was the object of a good deal of derision, not only for its seemingly preposterous claims about the "Golden Bible," but also for the grand claims that Joseph Smith was soon making that he was a prophet of God—indeed, *the* prophet of God with a special pipeline to the divine, unique in all the world—and that his church was the one and only true church, a reconstruction of ancient apostolic Christianity. Soon the movement moved to Kirtland, Ohio, where it experienced enormous growth and began to run into its first round of serious hostility, not at the hands of outraged outsiders so much as from apostate members, who became numerous as the church grew radidly. One violent attack occurred at Kirtland, directed at Smith personally; it has been recounted thus by Fawn Brodie, Smith's biographer:

A gang of Mormon-baiters . . . fortified by a barrel of whisky . . . smashed their way into the Johnson home on the night of March 24, 1832 and dragged Joseph from the trundle bed where he had fallen asleep. . . . They stripped him, scratched and beat him with savage pleasure, and smeared his bleeding body with tar from head to foot. Ripping a pillow into shreds, they plastered him with feathers. It is said that Eli Johnson demanded that the prophet be castrated, for he suspected Joseph of being too intimate with his sister, Nancy Marinda. But the doctor who had been persuaded to join the mob declined the responsibility at the last moment, and Johnson had to be content with seeing the prophet beaten senseless. [Sidney] Rigdon [a prominent church member] likewise was beaten and dragged into unconsciousness over the frozen ground.[8]

As the account suggests, Smith may have begun practicing polygamy in Ohio, and polygamy eventually became the biggest obstacle to the Mormons' acceptance by the larger culture. Meanwhile, problems mounted and a serious financial crisis developed for the financially strapped Mormons. By the late 1830s, they moved to Missouri, where they had established an outpost as early as 1831 and where Smith announced a revelation that the town of Independence would be the site of the Second Coming of Christ, a doctrine to which all of the branches of the Latter-day Saint movement subscribe today. But life was hardly easier for the Mormons in Independence than it had been in Ohio. Indeed, it was worse, in part because Missouri was a border state dominated by pro-slavery forces who viewed with suspicion all Yankees as possible abolitionists. The saints were hounded from one county to another and suffered mob violence, incarceration, and confrontations by the local militia. Historians still refer to that episode in Missouri as the "Mormon War"; and at its worst it was something of a real war, with armed activities on both sides.

All of the persecution and violence led the Mormons to migrate yet again, this time to Illinois. There, on the banks of the Mississippi River, they took over an all-but-abandoned town called Commerce. Smith renamed it "Nauvoo," which he said meant "beautiful city" in Hebrew. There the Mormons achieved their greatest early success, building up what was for a time the largest city in Illinois with perhaps fifteen thousand inhabitants, more than Chicago in those days. They built buildings and economic institutions, and, determined to defend themselves against their seemingly intractable enemies, founded a private military unit, the Nauvoo Legion, that had two thousand soldiers by the beginning of 1842.

Nauvoo has a rich history all its own, but the beginning of the end came in 1844, when Smith suffered the most severe persecution of all when he was killed by a lynch mob. As elsewhere, the Mormons had fierce enemies in the Nauvoo area, many of whom feared that Mormonism was a dictatorial theocracy that was threatening the American way of life. They also had quite a few apostates living in the vicinity, some of whom told lurid tales of violence and corruption and sexual misbehavior among the Mormons. Polygamy, although it had not yet been publicly announced, was being practiced in Nauvoo and naturally provided sensational fodder for the Mormon antagonists.

The immediate cause of the final events of Smith's life came with the publication of the one and only issue of the *Nauvoo Expositor* on 7 June 1844. Among other things, it spoke openly of polygamy, surely information that would be sensational both among church members who had not been told about the new doctrine and among the many anti-Mormons in the vicinity. Smith responded by ordering the Nauvoo Legion to destroy the newspaper by smashing the press and scattering the type. That resulted in his arrest, and shortly thereafter, on 27 June 1844, a mob entered the jail and killed Smith and his brother Hyrum.

That was not the end of persecution of the Mormons. After Smith's death, they migrated to Utah and in 1852 finally announced publicly their practice of polygamy. That set off decades of conflict, which peaked in the 1880s with the federal government scouring the Utah countryside for the "cohabs," as polygamists were called. Church president John Taylor spent most of his term of office in hiding and remained in hiding until his death in 1887. Faced with intractable official opposition, the church finally gave up and abandoned the practice of polygamy in the 1890s and 1900s as a requirement for statehood, although as a doctrine it has never been repudiated.

However, quite a few Mormons were distressed that the church had abandoned a practice that was, after all, the will of God, a doctrine received by a divinely-inspired prophet of God. Once the church got serious about ending polygamy, the stalwarts withdrew into their own splinter organizations and continued the practice of plural marriage. And so things continue today, with tens of thousands of Latter-day Saints living in polygamous households in the intermountain West. And they, like their forebears, suffered plenty of persecution. The largest single polygamous enclave, now known as Colorado City, Arizona, has suffered three major raids by law enforcement authorities, the last in 1953. Those actions, however, have not stopped them from practicing what they believe to be the will of God. Today, Colorado City has over five thousand citizens and is a thriving desert town, its polygamy not at all hidden.[9] But a new conflict over polygamy is in the wings; anti-polygamy activists are currently trying to get new laws enacted, and old ones more stringently enforced, in order to wipe out the practice. Intense conflict seems inevitable.

The Mormons have not been the only believers whose unconventional sexual practices led to persecution. One of America's most famous historic communal societies, the Oneida Community, was finally hounded out of existence because of public opposition to its practice of free love. Oneida was founded and led by John Humphrey Noyes, who in the 1830s began preaching radical perfectionism—that he was free from sin and others could be too. Among other things, Noyes taught that the Second Coming of Christ had already occurred, and that because we were now living in the millennial dispensation, a whole new order of human society was called for. Perfect humans needed to overcome egotism and possessiveness, and that expansive spirit extended to marital relations. Simply put, the Oneida Community was the largest group marriage in American history, with nearly three hundred members at its peak and every male member considered married to every female member. The community had unusually harmonious internal relations and an excellent economic base, first with its production of the nation's best animal traps and later with silverware. It lasted for several decades, and might have gone on longer had not outside pressure intervened. It is not hard to imagine that vigorous opposition to such flagrant sexual irregularities did finally arise in Victorian America. Criticism grew, and Noyes became fearful. Eventually he fled the country, fearing criminal charges. Complex marriage, as the system was known, was discontinued, and in 1881 the community was formally dissolved.[10]

During the heyday of the Oneida Community, another religious movement arose that would suffer a good deal of persecution. The movement now known as the Jehovah's Witnesses had its beginnings in the 1870s among Christians who had been involved in William Miller's Adventist movement that had trailed off in various directions following the failure of the Second Coming to occur on 22 October 1844, as Miller had predicted. Charles Taze Russell, undeterred by the problems that date-setting had posed for the Millerites, set a date of his own: the great end of time would come in 1914. Despite the obvious problems that date has posed, the movement has managed to reinterpret things and continue to grow worldwide, but it has not done so without controversy.

What has caused opposition to the Witnesses, other than their unorthodox theology? Perhaps most prominently it has been their unwillingness to serve in the armed forces. During times when the country has had a military draft, the Witnesses have generally been unwilling to register as conscientious objectors because they are not opposed to war in any form, as conscientious objection requires. Indeed, they will be on the front lines when the climactic war of Armageddon arrives. Their objection is that they are not citizens of any earthly nation, but of the kingdom of God, and that the only army they will march for is the Lord's. Similarly, they are controversial for not saluting the flag, which, as far as they are concerned, amounts to an act of worship and fealty to an earthly government, which by definition is a false government; therefore the flag salute violates the Ten Commandments at Exodus 20:3-5. Yet another problem that has appeared repeatedly involves their unwillingness to accept blood transfusions, a position that stems from a point of biblical interpretation. We are commanded by the Levitical regulations not to eat blood, and they take that to mean any ingestion of blood. To their detractors such a position is ridiculous in any case, but especially reprehensible when it involves children. For their heartfelt beliefs and practices, the Witnesses have suffered enormous opprobrium. Thousands of them have gone to jail for refusing military service, and many more have wound up in court over their refusal to approve of blood transfusions. Their position on the flag salute went to the Supreme Court twice, and the second time they were victorious, although plenty of their detractors still condemn them for their disdain for worldly governments. In the United States and abroad, the Witnesses have been among the most controversial and persecuted of all religious movements. At the peak of their persecution, during the early years of the Second World War, they were so reviled that John T. Noonan in his book on American religious freedom has called the episode "the greatest outbreak of religious intolerance in twentieth-century America."[11]

Twentieth Century

One enduring and sad human characteristic seems to be disdain for the new, and that seems to be behind the reception that Pentecostals got when their new religion first burst upon the American scene exactly one hundred years ago. Pentecostalism had its origins in Topeka, Kansas, on 1 January 1901, when Agnes Ozman and then other students of the faith-healing Holiness minister Charles Parham began to speak in tongues. Because they believed that the outpouring of the spirit that they experienced was a sign that the millennium was at hand, they rushed headlong into missionary activities, trying to get as many people as possible on the gospel train before it pulled out of the station for the last time, so to speak.

But everywhere they faced ridicule. People were overwhelmingly not impressed with the great spiritual fervor that the fledgling Pentecostalists exhibited; they simply thought this group had gone loco. Derision and disdain met them at every turn. Gradually the movement began to sputter out, and it might well be a mere historical footnote had not William Seymour endured outrageous racism in Texas to learn about Pentecostalism and then go to Los Angeles to lead a revival there that turned the odd phenomenon into a world-wide movement. For many years, however, derision from the better-established churches continued to be the order of the day. These people who sometimes manifested physical effects in their religion were dismissed as "holy rollers." They were laughed out of their churches, and the reason that we have a series of independent Pentecostal denominations today is that the believers formed them essentially out of self-defense. For nearly two-thirds of a century the stigma remained; Pentecostals were marginalized and still often ridiculed.[12] It was not until the 1960s, when a new wave of Pentecostalism began to appear in the Episcopal, Catholic, and other churches that speaking in tongues became fairly widely accepted as a legitimate Christian alternative. Even so, some related practices remain far from general acceptance. Faith healing of the Pentecostal-revival type, for example, certainly is not regarded at all favorably by the great majority of American Christians. From the vantage point of the beginning of a new century, the birth and fantastic growth of Pentecostalism is the most significant religious story of the twentieth century, but for the majority of that century its practitioners were religious outcasts, and their full acceptance may still be in the future.

With the great historical upheaval in the 1960s came many new versions of Christianity. Several of them, like their predecessors, came in for a good deal of derision and ridicule. One group that received a great outpouring of criticism, so much that its opponents started what has become the modern anticult movement, was the Children of God, now known as the Family, founded in California in the late 1960s by David Berg. Berg was an evangelical minister who began working among the hippies and forged a movement that was in its early days best known for its dramatic denunciations of the evils of modern society. Members would dress in biblical-style robes and hurl denunciations at passers-by in public places. Soon they also began to found communes, and of course that is often suspect–people wonder, why would they want to go off by themselves? They must have something to hide–as if the monasticism of the past fifteen hundred years in Christianity represents something sinister. Eventually the controversy between members and their critics, often including their parents, became so intense that they largely withdrew, in many cases leaving the United States. For quite a time they were essentially invisible. Over time they did some unusual things, perhaps most famously "flirty fishing," in which attractive female members would essentially seduce men, telling them while making love that this act symbolized the love God had for human beings. Although flirty fishing is now a thing of the past, and in fact the group says it has outlawed all sex between members and nonmembers, a liberal sexual outlook admittedly remains, and members do have relations with members other than their spouses as the desire strikes them and they believe the circumstances warrant. It is fair to say that the Children of God had vehement critics thirty years ago, and the Family still receives plenty of criticism today. Full acceptance by mainline Christians and by society at large still seems a fair distance away.[13]

Another group roughly contemporary with the Children of God also came in for a good deal of criticism not too many years ago. The Way ministry was founded by Victor Paul Wierwille as "Vesper Chimes," a radio ministry, in 1942. Its main growth came with the grass-roots Jesus People movement of the late 1960s and early 1970s, and with growth came controversy.

Many Way members were subjected to deprogramming, but most of the complaints against the group seem pretty flimsy or just matters of opinion. Per the norm, the movement was accused of engaging in brainwashing and mind control, but it could never be discerned that it was any more intense than any number of other evangelical Christian movements. They also were accused of amassing an arsenal, but the only basis for that charge seems to be that some students at the Way College of Emporia (Kansas) once took a gun-safety course. Beyond that, one is left with only theological errors. It is true that the Way was unconventional in its Christology, denying the divinity of Christ and therefore denying the existence of the Trinity. It is also true that Wierwille believed that the original text of the New Testament was written in Aramaic, not Greek, and that, as a result, he pushed ancient-language studies. The movement was Pentecostal and members spoke in tongues, although that is hardly worth noting. But those kinds of theological and biblical ideas, while mildly unconventional, do not seem to justify the outpouring of opposition that The Way experienced. After all, denial of the Trinity occurs in quite a few bodies of Christians, the most numerous of them, like the Way, of a Pentecostal persuasion. It all may not matter much any longer, since the Way seems to be in serious decline following a good deal of internal turmoil that began in the 1980s. But it remains a rather puzzling case of persecution.[14]

Perhaps the most persecuted of all Christian-related groups of the last thirty years or so has been the Unification Church, founded in 1954 and still headed by Sun Myung Moon, who grew up in a Presbyterian home in Korea. Moon's parents had been converted by missionaries, and as often happens when a faith is exported to another country, their Presbyterianism reflected their own culture as well as that of Euroamerican Presbyterianism. Thus the religion that Moon said had been communicated to him in a series of divine revelations had a Christian core, with a strong emphasis on the biblical stories of the creation and the fall, but also had elements of Asian traditions, including Taoism and Korean shamanism.

Moon's first missionary came to the United States in 1959, but it was not until the 1970s that the movement began to get much public notice. When it did, it soon became just about the most reviled of all alternative religions, the very epitome of a "dangerous cult." Followers were depicted as glassy-eyed zombies, their minds utterly controlled by an evil genius who sought world domination. They took in hordes of new members by outright deception, and members lived in crowded housing under conditions of sleep deprivation and near-malnutrition, it was said.

Calumny was heaped upon the Moonies from all sides. Mainline churches condemned them as heretics. Jews accused them of trying to undermine Judaism by converting large numbers of Jews to membership. Parents were convinced that their children were in mortal danger and in many cases spent tens of thousands of dollars for deprogramming to get them out. When Moon was convicted of tax evasion and served a year in prison in the mid-1980s, his critics felt vindicated, although quite a few more conventional religious organizations rallied to his defense because what he was convicted of was not unlike what they were doing as well.

The controversy has settled down somewhat in recent years. Moon's early recruits have aged and had families of their own, and the zealous young bands of church members are no longer visible. Perhaps most importantly, Moon has made overtures to the American political right wing, and now has good relations with certain elements of the conservative activist community. The newspaper he underwrites, the Washington *Times*, has become a conservative favorite. The

Unificationists have not taken a regular place at the American mainstream religious table just yet, but they seem to be moving slowly toward some kind of acceptance. The enormous vituperation of the early years, in any case, has abated.[15]

One more group rooted in Christianity deserves mention for the opposition it has aroused. The International Church of Christ, also known as the Boston Movement or the Crossroads Movement, has its roots in the traditional Churches of Christ but soon developed a direction of its own. It was founded in 1979 near Boston and became visible in the 1980s and 1990s as an unusually demanding faith, one in which members had to give enormous dedication to the church and its projects, among other things making many evangelizing contacts daily. Perhaps its most controversial feature is its system of discipling, or shepherding, in which every member has a direct supervisor who has very considerable involvement in a believer's life. The discipler teaches the Bible according to the ICC's interpretation of it, and supervises the disciple's life to make sure that the disciple is living righteously. That supervision can be intense and personal, going right into a member's bedroom, in the sense that the sex life of even a married couple constitutes behavior for which one is accountable to one's discipler. The critics of the ICC are outspoken, and the church has met firm resistance, including being banned from a number of college campuses. Stay tuned, because here is a movement still very much on the front burner.[16]

There are many other Christian-derived religious groups that could be similarly included in this survey. One might look at the persecution suffered by snake handlers, who after all are merely following biblical advice given at the end of the gospel of Mark; or the Identity movement, a Christian racist school of thought that has gathered a small following over the last several decades. And let us not forget the Branch Davidians and their parent group, the Davidian Seventh Day Adventists, but since they have received sufficient attention in this book, it is not necessary to add them to my list of persecuted believers. In all, the history of persecution of Christian-related churches out of favor with the larger mainstream groups is extensive and unpleasant.

Conclusion

When alternative forms of Christianity in the American past are compared with those of more recent vintage, many

respond with skepticism. "The Shakers were just sweet,
harmless people who went off and built beautiful museum
villages and manufactured nice furniture and sang pretty
songs, but Moonies? Well, that's different. Moonies are zom-
bie slaves of a power-mad dictator." These things are actually
largely a matter of point of view and of historical perspective.
There seems to be a human tendency to idealize things safely
in the past and to demonize things that are closer to us, ideas
that are just slightly different than our own. It seems to me
that we would do well to follow the counsel provided by Ga-
maliel in Acts 5:38-39: "If this undertaking is of human origin,
it will fail; but if it is of God, you will not be able to overthrow
them. You might even be found opposing God!"

NOTES

1.   The stories of Roger Williams and Anne Hutchinson can be found in
most standard histories of American religion. See, for example, Martin E.
Marty, *Pilgrims in Their Own Land: 500 Years of Religion in America* (New
York: Penguin, 1985 [1984]), 75-82; Mark A. Noll, *A History of Christianity
in the United States and Canada* (Grand Rapids, Mich.: Eerdmans, 1992),
58-62.
2.   Sydney E. Ahlstrom, *A Religious History of the American People* (New
Haven, Conn.: Yale University Press, 1972), 176-81.
3.   The most extensive survey of Hutterite life and history is John A.
Hostetler, *Hutterite Society* (Baltimore, Md.: Johns Hopkins University
Press, 1974).
4.   Stephen J. Stein, *The Shaker Experience in America* (New Haven, Conn.:
Yale University Press, 1992), 5-16.
5.   See Elizabeth A. De Wolfe, "'So Much They have Got For Their
Folly': Shaker Apostates and the Tale of Woe," *Communal Societies* 18
(1993): 21-35.
6.   Stein, *Shaker Experience in America*, 217-18.
7.   For an overview history of the Harmony Society, see Karl J. R. Arndt,
"George Rapp's Harmony Society," in *America's Communal Utopias*, ed.
Donald E. Pitzer (Chapel Hill, N.C.: University of North Carolina Press,
1997), 57-87.
8.   Fawn M. Brodie, *No Man Knows My History: The Life of Joseph Smith
the Mormon Prophet* (New York: Knopf, 1946), 119.
9.   For a comprehensive history of Colorado City, see Martha Sonntag
Bradley, *Kidnapped from That Land: The Government Raids on the Short Creek
Polygamists* (Salt Lake City, Utah: University of Utah Press, 1993).
10.   Complex marriage is explained and analyzed in some detail in Lawrence Foster, *Religion and Sexuality: Three American Communal Experiments
of the Nineteenth Century* (New York: Oxford University Press, 1981), 72-
122. The complex events that led to the dissolution of the community are

explored by Constance Noyes Robertson, *Oneida Community: The Breakup, 1876-1881* (Syracuse, N.Y.: Syracuse University Press, 1972).

11. John T. Noonan, Jr., *The Lustre of Our Country: The American Experience of Religious Freedom* (Berkeley, Calif.: University of California Press, 1998), 243.

12. For a work that equates early Pentecostalism with pathology, see Alexander Mackie, *The Gift of Tongues: A Study in Pathological Aspects of Christianity* (New York: George H. Doran Company, 1921).

13. For a survey of the history and life of the movement, see David E. Van Zandt, *Living in the Children of God* (Princeton, N.J.: Princeton University Press, 1991); see also James D. Chancellor, *Life in the Family: An Oral History of the Children of God* (Syracuse, N.Y.: Syracuse University Press, 2000).

14. An independent book-length history of The Way has yet to be published. For a book published by the movement itself that contains some useful information, see Elena S. Whiteside, *The Way: Living in Love* (New Knoxville, Ohio: American Christian Press, 1972).

15. The standard work on the Unification Church (which contains much material on the controversies it has endured) is David G. Bromley and Anson D. Shupe, Jr., *Moonies in America: Cult, Church, and Crusade* (Beverly Hills, Calif.: Sage Publications, 1979). For a more recent work see George D. Chryssides, *The Advent of Sun Myung Moon: The Origins, Beliefs and Practices of the Unification Church* (New York: St. Martin's, 1991).

16. See Russell Paden, "The Boston Church of Christ," in *America's Alternative Religions*, ed. Timothy Miller (Albany, N.Y.: State University of New York Press, 1995), 133-40.

The Cult Awareness Network and the Anticult Movement: Implications for NRMs in America

ANSON SHUPE, SUSAN E. DARNELL,
and KENDRICK MOXON

On 23 October 1996 at 9:30 a.m., the Cult Awareness Network (CAN), a Chicago-based national anticult organization claiming to be purely a tax-exempt informational clearinghouse on new religions, closed its doors amid bankruptcy proceedings and its assets were auctioned off. The precipitating, but not lone, event that hastened its demise was a civil suit brought against both CAN and a trio of coercive deprogrammers who unsuccessfully tried to remove a legal adult, Jason Scott, from a United Pentecostal congregation. Scott was violently abducted, physically abused, and forcibly detained at a remote Washington state location for almost a week. While CAN was at the time suffering many other lawsuits for alleged deprivation of the civil rights of members of minority religions, the Scott case became its Waterloo.

The jury was quite clear in its decision to award compensatory and punitive damages to Scott.[1] CAN's primary activity, this case and others have revealed, was to provide false and/or inflammatory opinion in the guise of "information" about minority religions to the media and other inquirers. All or virtually all of such "information" was derogatory, consistent with CAN's goals of "educating" the public that various new religious movements (NRMs) are "destructive cults," that all of the members thereof are "cult victims," are "brainwashed," and are therefore at risk, possibly needing "rescue." The jury's decision, under the definitions provided in Washington law, was that CAN was truly an organized hate campaign. CAN described its activities in a euphemistic manner to make its activities seem less outrageous from a civil liberties perspective. The reason CAN even became involved in the Scott lawsuit was that, consistent with its organizational pattern, it served as a conduit for referrals to coercive deprogrammers (later termed by CAN "exit counselors") who would, for a fee, abduct and during detention harangue family members into religious apostasy.

As Philip Jenkins documents in his book, *Mystics and Messiahs: Cults and New Religions in American History*, charismatic, world-transforming-portending leaders and their attending flocks have been legion in North American history. So also have been their opponents. Jenkins emphasizes the continuities of both "cult" and "anticult" phenomena in American history, including the present era. He observes that "there is no period, including colonial times, in which we cannot find numerous groups more or less indistinguishable from the most controversial movements"[2] and, on the "normality" of NRMs, Jenkins adds, "far from being a novelty, cults and cultlike movements have a very long history on American soil. Extreme and bizarre religious ideas are so commonplace in American history that it is difficult to speak of them as fringe at all."[3]

Likewise, opposition movements are as much a predictable fixture of religious pluralism as are the NRMs themselves.[4] This fact has not always been obvious to those caught up in the fray. Each age, as Jenkins maintains, thinks it is uniquely being overrun by menacing, anti-social, questionable religious groups and, for similar reasons, "reinvents the wheel" of religious alarm.

There is an irony in this latest wave of NRM/ACM conflict that neither side would have appreciated several decades ago. Two veteran chroniclers of the controversy, looking back over a quarter century, report that neither side expected this protracted protest against new religious movements to last: either because a damaging image of the anti-cult movement as an intolerant, anti-constitutional, vigilante movement would have been successfully promoted by its opponents; or because, thanks to the ACM's mobilization of public officials and law enforcement agencies, health professionals, academics, and public opinion, the "innovative" NRMs would have been broken up, prosecuted, and deported.[5]

This report utilizes recently acquired new data on CAN in order to shed light on the maturing nature of the anticult movement since its inception in the early 1970s. For reasons of space limitation, the extensive social science literature on NRM is not reviewed. Elsewhere a detailed historical/organizational analysis of the ACM up to the end of the 1970s has been presented.[6] The chronicle is basically one of regional and local grassroots "mom-and-pop" groups' struggles to (1) acquire sufficient financial stability to allow them to spread their message of "destructive cults" subverting American society, (2) maintain a shifting membership base together long enough to lobby, publicize, and mobilize opposition to NRMs, and (3) establish a national unified organizational prominence with political clout. There were a number of false (i.e., unsuccessful) starts, but by the mid-1980s there were two prominent national-level groups—the Cult Awareness Network and the American Family Foundation.[7] In the beginning (the early 1970s), most ACM groups' membership consisted of senior family members distraught at their offsprings'/junior relatives' deviant religious choices. Over time, however, the mantle of ACM activism and leadership passed to degreed behavioral science moral entrepreneurs who made ACM involvement an important, and sometimes lucrative, part of their careers.

Methods

We rely on two sources of information. The first source consists of a large number of court transcripts and sworn testimonies in court records, depositions, and affidavits from ACM leaders, deprogrammers, ex-NRM and current NRM members, and deprogrammees gathered in the course of civil liberties litigation against primarily CAN by various attorneys (including the third author) during the legal process of "discovery."

The second source consists of approximately four hundred boxes of CAN files assigned as assets to a Chicago, Illinois bankruptcy court trustee. There is evidence that during a total of more than fifty-one pending lawsuits against CAN and its directors and during discovery inquiries (all during the early-to-mid 1990s) select documents were being destroyed by unknown persons at CAN. After the surviving boxes were secured by the court and auctioned off to a private individual, they were donated to the Foundation for Religious Freedom (based in Los Angeles, California) where they were catalogued and made available to the public (i.e., researchers such as ourselves and to representatives of a variety of NRMs) for inspection and photocopying. After the Fall of 1999, most boxes were then donated by the FRF and moved to the Special Collections section of the library at the University of California at Santa Barbara. However, a total of thirty-two boxes containing purely financial records (e.g., cancelled checks, ledgers, lists of donors and expenditures, copies of audits, and telephone files) remained until 2002 in our possession. These files are also now at the University of California, Santa Barbara.

Corporate Crime as CAN Policy

This report deals only with financial aspects of CAN and the implications thereof for religious pluralism. Thus, evidence for the existence of what criminologists refer to as *corporate crime*, i.e., performance of illegal, harmful criminal behavior as standard operating policy for administrators will be pursued. Other interesting aspects of CAN *modus operandi*—such as coercive deprogrammers' not unheard use of illegal and legal drugs before and during deprogrammings and even the use of sexual intercourse with deprogrammees, details of which can be found elsewhere, or of the 1505 NRMs and quasi-religious groups on which CAN indiscriminately kept running files—must be omitted.[8]

CAN was incorporated in 1986, originally an offshoot of the earlier Citizens Freedom Foundation—Information Services, at the time the largest ACM group in the United States. CAN claimed to be a humanitarian information clearinghouse on NRMs and publicly claimed no association with deprogrammers. This is now known to be patently false. The evidence points to coercive deprogrammers as an important lucrative source of CAN income. Deprogrammers were also regular attenders at CAN annual conferences as speakers and solicitors of clients and in regular communication with CAN leaders.[9]

Deprogrammer Kickbacks and Money-Laundering: The Inner Sanctum of NARDEC

Journalist Nora Hamerman, in writing about the Dobkowski deprogramming fiasco, referred to CAN as "a clearinghouse for kidnap-for-hire rings."[10] This is an apt description. There was a corporate crime basis for CAN's continuance and funding, as suggested earlier.

Various background informant sources speak to a deprogrammer kickback/money laundering scheme by which deprogrammers received continued referrals from CAN in exchange for "repayments" or donations (i.e., commissions) funneled back to national CAN headquarters. In one newspaper article, former deprogrammer Jonathan Nordquist "alleges that with each referral to a deprogrammer, a 'kick-back' is sent to CAN in the form of a 'donation' to ensure that the referrals continue."[11] If so, such claims would establish a financial symbiosis between CAN and coercive deprogrammers. John M. Sweeney, Jr., past head of CFF as it turned into CAN during the early-to-mid 1980s, recounting how deprogrammers charged thousands of dollars per case, testified:

Because of the large amounts of money they make due to referrals received from CFF members, deprogrammers usually kick-back money to the CFF member who gave the referral. . . The kick-backs would either be in cash or would be in the form of a tax deductible "donation" to the CFF. . . . Adrian Greek, who was the national chairman of CFF at the time that I was its national director, had an adult daughter in the Unification Church. Mr. Greek was very cheap and didn't want to pay money to have a deprogramming. He then attempted to get a deprogrammer to deprogram his daughter in exchange for Mr. Greek's future referrals of clients to the deprogrammer.[12]

Deprogrammer Mark Blocksom (see n. 9) alludes indirectly to this reciprocity. CAN's last executive director, Cynthia Kisser, gave the following evasive responses under legal examination. While vague, they are suggestive of such a corporate policy:

Q. Whether CAN National during the period of 1987 to 1989 to your knowledge received donations, pleads, or funds of any sort from deprogrammers?

A. I would say given the definition I gave of deprogramming, yes, they very well could have.

Q. To your knowledge from 1987 to 1989 have any families who to your knowledge hired deprogrammers subsequent to referrals from CAN made any donations to CAN National?

A. I would have no way of knowing on a first name basis, if that was their reason for giving.

Q. So, to your knowledge some families have given, but you don't know what their reasons were?

A. Thousands of people have given. I don't know what their reason may have been.

Q. Well, to your knowledge have families who in fact hired deprogrammers and made that known to you, made donations to CAN?

A. I don't know if specifically between '87 and '89 there were families who had hired deprogrammers who did also give money to CAN during that time period. I just do not know. It's possible they could have.[13]

The attorney in cross-examination was chipping away at the possibility that deprogrammers "discounted" the price of a deprogramming if the families (not the deprogrammers) made the donation directly to CAN. That this practice existed appears likely. Notes on donor index cards for NARDEC contributions (see below on NARDEC) in CAN desk rolodex files comment frequently on donors' family members' present or past membership in NRMs (e.g. COG, CUT, UC, HK, BCC, Alamo) and sometimes if the deprogrammings referred were successful or unsuccessful (and conducted by which deprogrammer—see CAN Box 249, "Rolodexes"). However, a more direct answer can be found in other testimony and in CAN records themselves. CAN staff member Marty Butz, who admitted to have made around five hundred deprogramming referrals, was asked in a deposition:

Q. Have any of the people that you made referrals to for deprogramming since you've been in CAN made any donations to CAN, any monetary donations?

A. I know that [deprogrammer] Carol Giambalvo has been a Nardeck [sic] member. That's the only extent of my knowledge of any contributions going CAN's way.

Q. What does "Nardeck" mean?

A. I don't know. I don't know what Nardeck represents.

Q. Nardeck members are people that make substantial monetary contributions to CAN isn't that correct?

A. Yes. [Butz suddenly remembers.]

Q. There's a—that's kind of the select people that are the primary financial supporters of CAN?

A. I believe what it is is a commitment for three years donating a thousand dollars.

Q. A year?

A. I can't say that's where CAN's primary support comes from.

Q. How much money has Miss Giambalvo donated to CAN since you've been involved in CAN?

A. I have no idea.

Q. At least $3,000?

A. If she's been a Nardeck member more than once, quite possibly more than $3,000.

Q. She's the person you've made the largest number of deprogramming referrals to, correct?

A. Yes.[14]

The court recorder had the subgroup of CAN spelled incorrectly—not Nardeck, but rather NARDEC: National Resource Development and Economic Council. This was the heart of deprogrammers' money-laundering operation and a key area of financial support for CAN. Its referral-in-exchange-for-a-kickback-of-deprogramming-fees is why CAN deprogrammer Rick Ross, in a "slump time" for business after having "paid his dues" to NARDEC, wrote CAN activist Priscilla Coates in a huff:

Have not received one really solid referral, C.A.N. included. I don't know why. Perhaps summer, "turf" issues, or lack of desire to deal with fundamentalists. Phil and Annie have called from N.Y. and Annette is trying, but some parents are so cheap they prefer to let their kids "bang the Bible" than pay.[15]

Ex-CAN executive director Cynthia Kisser acknowledged the existence of NARDEC deprogrammer contributions in a deposition:

Q. Do you know of any donations that have been made to CAN by deprogrammers?

A. Let me just take a minute to look at some of the people that you've identified as deprogrammers to let me answer that question. Yes.

Q. Who?

A. Steve Hassan, Carol Giambalvo, and . . .Randall Burkey.[16]

Formed in the mid-1980s, by 1987 NARDEC had become institutionalized as a special unit within CAN. Ronald M. Loomis, CAN president, wrote in a 26 June 1987 form letter to all CAN affiliates and newsletter subscribers:

We are grateful to those of you who responded to our appeal for contributions with the February meeting. The number of persons who have become members of the National Resource and Development Council (NaRDec) by pledging $1,000 per year for three years continues to grow, but we need that level of commitment from many more persons. Based on your generous support in 1986, we determined that we could afford to commit ourselves to the full time salary of an Executive Director for the future. A letter from our Finance and Development Chair . . . together with a pledge card, is [sic] enclosed. It will be a real challenge for us to continue in 1987 what we did in 1986. Please do what you can to sustain that effort. Remember that we cannot expect anyone to support the cult awareness effort unless we provide *the first level of support*.[17] [Italics ours.]

Apparently deprogrammers (renaming themselves "exit counselors") understood the message. Under the NARDEC aegis they began to organize within CAN. In the Preliminary Program of the Portland, Oregon 1987 annual CAN conference there was scheduled a Wednesday, 19 October special evening meeting for exit counselors (and added below that announcement: "will not post on hotel meeting sign or brochure.") On Saturday, 22 October at the same convention there was also a special NARDEC breakfast.[18] NARDEC also had special 7:30 a.m. breakfast meetings at the 1989 CAN annual conference (program noted: "NARDEC members only") and at the 1990 annual CAN conference NARDEC members met in conjunction with the CAN advisory board. Referring back to earlier sections of this chapter where CAN officials tried to distance themselves on paper and in legal testimonies that CAN in no way encouraged deprogrammings, an examination of real CAN activities belies that claim. It would appear that "exit counselors," formerly deprogrammers, were invited (literally) to sit at the CAN table.

Of course, not all contributions to CAN and NARDEC were from deprogrammers or persons who favored vigilante actions over educational goals. CAN donors each received identification numbers and were listed/enumerated in files. An inspection of such lists would include, for example, a 25 July 1988 contribution of $2,000 from the Grainger Foundation to a more modest 21 July 1995 contribution of $35.00 from evangelical Christian (counter-cult) sociologist Ronald Enroth (ID# 912). However, many were from known deprogrammers (and their sympathizers), such as Carol Giambavlo, Paul Engel, Janja Lalich, and David Clark.

Inspection of NARDEC contributions by month for 1988-95 shows a fairly stable pattern: yearly totals averaged between $40,000 and $54,000, always strongest in January (around $7,000 for that month) and then leveling off to less than $4,000 per month. (NARDEC's contribution to total CAN revenues was about one-third.) However, it appears likely that under-the-table deprogrammer referral kick-backs made up a substantial proportion of NARDEC funds. (NARDEC had its own CAN account number, 4080, as opposed to the general fund, 4000, or CAN's mail order "bookstore" selling tracts, tapes, and books, 4020.) Apparently some deprogrammers did not use this traceable account for "donations." Examining monthly NARDEC contributions for the 1990s, for example, they *rarely* approached the reported monthly total contributions in CAN and *never* approached the reported annual totals. Cash receipts for April 1992, for instance, show a total that month of one $1000 contribution. October 1992 shows the same. In other words, NARDEC fund totals in any given year cannot be explained by cash receipts or recorded individual contributions (which, as numerous boxes of rather tediously studied files show, were quite meticulously detailed).

In fact, many recorded NARDEC contributions were in "nickel-and-dime" modest amounts: $30, $50, or $150. Some donations to CAN were even split between other funds and NARDEC; for example, $50 donated by an individual in 1993, $30 to go to NARDEC and $20 into CAN's general fund. Such are the minutiae of the CAN files. There were some perennial NARDEC stalwarts who were family relatives of present or previous NRM members (and some deprogrammers). But NARDEC had a serious problem if it is assumed all monies taken in are reflected in the books eventually shown to outside auditors. There were many donors who welched on their pledges, decreasing overt NARDEC revenues: in 1992, 59 persons pledged $1000 or more, but 26 reneged; in 1993, 30 persons pledged the $1000 minimum but 14 reneged; in 1994, 23 of 27 persons reneged; and in 1995, 38 of 50 persons reneged. Towards the waning days of CAN there was a strong, last-ditch resurgence of giving to help. January 1996 checks (from a very small, "select" group of persons) of $1000 to NARDEC totalled around $10,675. But by then CAN was struggling amid many lawsuits, having lost the Jason Scott deprogramming civil suit, and had squandered an insurance settlement thereof on pointless litigation—much of which it ultimately lost or conceded.

So where did NARDEC make up the difference if recorded dollar totals do not square with meticulous, computerized receipt statements?

Two separate rolodex lists of NARDEC donors and general contacts in media, law, industry, and social sciences (marked "Major Gifts and NARDEC: comments to be included when required") include a *Who's Who* of dozens of coercive deprogrammers' names, telephone numbers, and addresses. We suggest a triangulation of evidence from: (1)

deprogrammers' testimonies; (2) former CFF/CAN officials' testimonies; (3) the obvious accounting lacunae in CAN financial records; and (4) the "Cash-only" nature of deprogramming fees. (Deprogrammers typically did not take credit cards or provide receipts, so complained families who felt taken advantage of by expensive, ineffective deprogramming interventions.) Our opinion and conclusion is that systematic records of the kick-backs that went on in CAN's offices during its last days were never kept in the first place, or were perhaps destroyed. The shoddy bookkeeping of CAN, and the likelihood of white-collar crime committed by certain CAN leaders, to which we now turn, are part of the NARDEC story.

Evidence of Mismanagement of CAN Finances and Violation of Fiduciary Responsibility

CAN president Ronald M. Loomis was especially pleased in Spring 1987 when an executive director search committee recommended Cynthia S. Kisser of Woodstock, Illinois after six months of deliberations and interviews. He wrote effusively to the CAN affiliates and newsletter subscribers about her business credentials (aside from her academic credentials): "Her professional background includes four years as a business manager with responsibility for general ledger, payroll records, tax reports, monthly billing and company financial matters. She has supervised staffs, set up computer operations and resolved hardware and software matters. . . . She has taught Business Communication for a community college."[19]

Yet, problems that had plagued the top levels of CFF-as-it-turned-into-CAN continued. Kent E. Vaughn, CFF Board of Directors member, 1982-84, had come to the disturbing conclusion that there was an "inner board" of CAN with an agenda beyond CAN's public pronouncements (see n. 8). In 1981, the earlier national director of CFFI-IS, John M. Sweeney, Jr., saw economic problems in the board's behavior. While he resigned for a number of reasons, including CFF's rejection of a deprogrammer's ethics code while simultaneously heavily involved in often illegal, coercive, expensive, and often ineffective "rescues," he was also unhappy that the group had failed to reimburse him on occasion and considered a collection suit against CFF-IS. However, his final complaint was that something untoward was occurring in CFF's management of money. He met a stonewall of silence when he called for an inspection of these issues. He voiced his frustrations: "Why has the CFF-IS Board done all in its power to prevent an audit of the corporate books? Why has over $20,000 worth of donations been buried in an interest bearing CD account (did the Board approve this action?) or in a checking account? Why was not this donation money stipulated for use in anti-cult projects? Why was money freed up so easily to finance an all expense paid trip to Dallas for the Board for an unnecessary meeting yet legitimate bills could not or would not be paid on time? I have records of threatened phone cut-off and late payment notices due to C——'s inefficient method. To protect my reputation and credit rating the WATS and SPRINT have been disconnected because they are in my name."[20]

Ironically, CAN had the same troubles during its existence and demise in 1996. For example, when CAN executive director Kisser came into office in 1987, she appears to have made some radical changes in CAN financial management. In essence, she consolidated its finances, with minimal executive office accountability to members. According to one informant knowledgeable about the group:

Kisser changed the financial lines of the Cult Awareness Network. Kisser demanded that all Cult Awareness Network chapters send all of the donations they received, including uncanceled checks, to her at the national office in Illinois. Kisser then cashed the checks, kept the amount of money that she wanted and then mailed the remaining money to the affiliated chapters as she saw fit [see n. 11].

Ex-deprogrammer Jonathan Nordquist, having met Kisser at a CAN convention, remembers:

Shortly after, [Mary] Krone told me that once Kisser fully learned how to do her new job, that Krone would no longer be working at the national offices. . . . Additionally, I recall an incident that occurred while I was riding in an elevator during the [CAN] convention in Pittsburgh. Also present in the elevator were Mary Krone, Krone's son, John, Cynthia Kisser and Rachel Andres. Mary Krone was talking about the finances of the Cult Awareness Network when Kisser stated to her: "If the cults ever get a hold of our books we'd be in trouble" [see n. 11].

Having expended its insurance money on fruitless appeals of the Jason Scott/Rick Ross/CAN deprogramming case that awarded Scott over $4 million, and having wasted funds on other lawsuits, as its income decreased CAN began to default on its phone bills (all the while continuing to pay director Cynthia Kisser $3000 per month plus lesser amounts to CAN staff).

There are several serious financial implications to these operations: All not-for-profit organizations are required to follow standard ethical and legal protocol particularly with respect to financial management. Complete detailed records must be consistently maintained, then supported by both internal and external audits to ensure both accuracy and propriety. The operations and cash flow must conform with generally accepted accounting standards. A painstakingly extensive review of the alleged complete court-ordered financial records of CAN confirms blatant impropriety. CAN was classified as a 501(c)(3), not-for-profit, tax-exempt organization with the Internal Revenue Service. To qualify and comply, certain measures of practice and accounting are required; the organization is accountable by federal law. The organizational test is a mandate that specific conditions be met and maintained for tax-exempt qualification according to the IRS code. To qualify for 501(c)(3) status the organization must be formed exclusively for literary, charitable, religious, educational, or scientific purposes; the manner of operation must be described in detail. Furthermore, the articles of the organization must appropriately limit the organization's purpose, regulate the allocation of contributions, and foster the best interests of everyone concerned. CAN's admitted affiliation with deprogrammers as confirmed in the Scott trial, among other places, appears to conflict with the IRS limited purpose constraint as well as in the express powers clause [7.8.2] 3.3.4 (02-231999), titled Express Powers that Cause Failure of Organizational Test, which provides:

An organization does not meet the organizational test if its articles expressly empower it:

To have objectives and to engage in activities which characterize it as an "action organization" (Reg. 1.501(c)(3)-1 (b)(3)(iii));

To carry on any other activities (unless they are insubstantial) which are not in furtherance of one or more exempt purposes (Reg. 1.501(c)(3)1(b)(1)(i)(a)).[21]

By affiliation, CAN cast, at minimum, a shadow on these two IRS provisions. Given the records and documented activity of this organization, it might be said that CAN acted in multiple violations of its IRS classification.

One initial and standing concern is that of missing or duplicated documents. The general condition of the financial records is deplorable. Documents are not in chronological order or in keeping with standard bookkeeping practice, making tracking a monumental feat. There are substantial gaps and pertinent items, statements, canceled checks, audits, and so forth that are missing. The list is significant. There are no itemized journals or ledgers of income or expenditures (standard accrual accounting), merely sporadic incomplete lists. The financial records are highly questionable and are at best professionally sloppy.

Cash flow is abundantly problematic and highly critical. In mere illustration, a petty cash withdrawal of $1,500 was observed. The established, acceptable norm for an organization of this size would be to maintain a generous $300 fund in total. Of greater concern, a review of cash receipts reflects numerous and substantial checks issued by CAN (National) to CAN itself with no indication or record of who received said funds, nor of the generating purpose. To illustrate, a $12,000 check issued 3/25/94 by CAN to CAN lists an account category #4250 for which there is no correlating account description. The canceled check #184 is not present among those in that series, nor is it ever listed as an expenditure. Interestingly, similar documentation and lack of canceled checks occurs with numerous other like entries.

Or another example: on 1/19/95 two checks (#5876 and #5877) were issued to J. Gordon Melton and Anson Shupe, respectively, for $600 each. Given their extensive study in this field, both men are known critics of CAN and would certainly not be on its payroll (i.e., certainly not "anti-cult apologists"). This time period ties in to the Lippmann/Scientology lawsuit against CAN with neither party involved beyond personal academic interest and neither party deposed by CAN as part of the lawsuit. (Depositional checks to professionals are rarely made out before depositions are taken.) Neither scholar has any knowledge of the existence of these checks. The checks were then processed as stop payments—Melton's the same day, Shupe's not until April—yet the funds ($1,200) were never reentered into the CAN account to offset the would-be stop payments. Both checks were physically located, reflecting stop payments, yet the bookkeeping does not appropriately correlate. Uncannily, Shupe discovered these particular en-

tries personally while examining financial data in the CAN
boxes. Why were bogus checks issued, who retained the
$1,200, and, more importantly, how many other orchestrated
entries lie within the records of CAN and to whose financial
gain?

Moreover, while not unheard of, not-for-profit CAN maintained a steady and healthy separate account with the Merrill
Lynch firm housing an extremely active money market account with no correlating income relationship and with certif-
icates of deposit averaging $40,000, far exceeding the standard
required reserve. Despite these investments, letters and audits
indicate financial distress. According to records, CAN was
unable to pay concurrent Sprint network telephone bills, net-
ting numerous final disconnect notices. These concerns led to
a recommendation issued by Virginia Hulet, CAN Treasurer
(resigned October, 1989) asking that all Sprint credit cards be
returned. From whom? Phone records indicate substantial use
by deprogrammers of CAN phone lines, calling from CAN's
national office. We ask again, was this careless mismanagement or diverted attention?

In 1987, Cynthia Kisser, CAN's executive director, directed
all chapters' funds to be generated directly to the national office. While there was noted board objection, this practice was
implemented, allowing the national office complete control of
funds with minimal accountability.

Peat Marwick (KPMG), a respected certified public accounting firm, was procured by CAN to conduct its annual
audits. Auditing correspondence consistently expressed numerous concerns regarding the need for improved accounting
principles, further suggesting accrual accounting. They cited
concern with the lack of internal audits indicating neglect of
Auditing Standards No. 50 as previously posed. In the face of
rising litigation expenses, no allotments were made to accom-
modate this clear necessity appropriately. Finally on 1 June
1994, a letter signed by KPMG Peat Marwick expressed serious concern regarding CAN's solvency. In a letter dated 8
June 1995, KPMG indicated an imbalance between the general
ledger and the bank reconciliations that had existed since July
1994. In a final communication, KPMG elected to withdraw its
affiliation with CAN in the face of growing financial concerns.

Countless fringe questions arise when analyzing the CAN
boxes: why do CAN records contain an inordinate amount of
letters of dispute (i.e., a $26,228.76 disputed conference bal-
ance with the Crown Plaza Hotel in White Plains, N.Y., No-

vember 1995)? Why were multiple financial accounts simultaneously active (i.e., 4/9/96 when Cynthia Kisser requested NBD Bank of Skokie to transfer remaining funds to an account titled Cult Awareness Network Corp AKA CAN D.I.P.)? Why would an organization of good intent be faced with fiercely escalating litigation (i.e., in 1994 there were fifty-one lawsuits in various states of settlement as presented to KPMG for completion of 1994 audit)? Finally, why did Kisser and several staff members continue to receive their salaries (Kisser $1500 every two weeks) beyond the filing of bankruptcy? More importantly, what became of CAN's final funds in the midst of dissolution?

These examples serve only as a small segment of a greater deluge of seeming impropriety currently under scrutiny within the CAN financial records. Two outside veteran auditors, when questioned regarding potential innocent explanations for these issues, stated that this appears to be a case of "money laundering" or of "looting the assets" (their words). Again we ask, is this a case of atrocious bookkeeping or instead calculated misappropriation? Neither option is acceptable per standard auditing and IRS protocol.

We have evidence of substantial malfeasance throughout the documents purportedly representing the complete fiscal records of this organization. The "why" remains yet to be addressed, the leaders and trustees are yet to be held accountable. This preliminary finding is just that: a highlighted report of what we believe to be a much darker indication than that of poor record-keeping. A Brownie troop with a naive, inexperienced leader might maintain such records and be accused of poor bookkeeping. For an organization with the capital, the influence, and the magnitude of CAN, such explanations are inexcusable and suspect.

At the time of this presentation, the exploration of CAN documents continues as additional discoveries unfold. Are these findings the result of gross negligence or of something much more untoward? Our final assessment will appear in a much more extensive book treatment forthcoming.

Conclusions About CAN Operations

This report is part of a work in progress. The CAN files will take years to thoroughly comb for data. Thus, we continue to find new evidence of CAN's criminal involvement the further we delve, despite evidence that toward the end

Kisser and/or CAN operatives deliberately shredded/destroyed important files dealing with CAN's telephone calls and likely selected cancelled checks.[22] In this chapter, we have dealt only with CAN, not its sister ACM organization, the American Family Foundation, although we will be examining that group in the future.

We offer five reasonable propositions about the operations and philosophy of America's formerly most activist anti-cult organization:

Proposition 1: Despite public claims otherwise, CAN had as its operating corporate policy the routine referrals of inquirers to coercive deprogrammers. As has been shown, this proposition is supported by a variety of sources: testimonies of deprogrammers, testimonies of CFF-CAN officials, CAN records, and Federal Bureau of Investigation wiretap surveillance.

Regarding the last source, it has recently been discovered that the FBI, learning of certain deprogrammers conspiring toward, among other things, the kidnapping of a young heir to the duPont estate who had become involved in Lyndon LaRouche's organization, and learning of those deprogrammers' involvement with CAN, in 1992 conducted wiretaps of CAN telephone conversations and certain deprogrammers' telephone conversations. FBI Special Agent Daniel Murphy presented an affidavit dated 19 July 1992 to the U. S. Federal Court, Eastern District of Pennsylvania, in which he stated:

As a result of my personal participation in this investigation, my knowledge of reports made to me by other FBI agents . . . there is probable cause to believe that Donald Moore, Galen Kelly, Edgar N. (Newbold] Smith, and others unknown, have been, or continuing to, and will be committing offenses agaĩnt the United States including conspiracy, in violation of 18 U.S.C., Section 371, and kidnapping, in violation of 18 U.S.C., Section 1201. There is probable cause to believe that communications concerning said offenses will be obtained through the interception of wire communications, authorization for which is herein applied.[23]

The transcripts of over a half dozen reels of tape reveal coercive deprogrammers in frequent (and casual) contact with CAN and CAN's executive director, Cynthia Kisser, on how to harass the LaRouche organization and simultaneously protect themselves legally from prosecution after the deprogramming. Such transcripts may be one logical reason that Cynthia

Kisser had thousands of CAN phone sheets destroyed around the 1992-93 period. For brief examples:

Edgar Newbold Smith calls former deputy sheriff-turned-deprogrammer Donald Moore about suing his own son, Lewis duPont Smith, a duPont fortune heir and a follower of Lyndon LaRouche:

But the only problem with suing Lewis, having CAN sue Lewis, is *that they know that we contributed to CAN* [italics ours.] So you're going to get the biggest bunch of goddamn bunch of squawk going on down there involving us. . . . Now maybe one of the things you ought to talk to Cynthia about is why not include Lewis in your depositions?[24]

Or: Moore's answering machine for 7/15/92:

This is Cynthia Kisser for Don Moore. I'm in Chicago. My number is 312/267/7777.

Or this conversation in early August, 1992:

Donald Moore: Hello.

Cynthia Kisser: Hi. Is Don Moore there?

Moore: Yes.

Kisser: Hi, Don. It's Cynthia.

Moore: How are you doing?

Kisser: Good. Good. Um, listen, um, I still have not talked to um—

Moore: Galen? [Galen Kelly, once head of security for CAN conferences and convicted of kidnapping in the Dubkowski case.]

Kisser: Yes.

Moore: That is, uh, you are not alone in that effort.

Kisser: Okay. Now do you think that Newbold is at his office today or at his home?

Moore: He should be at his home today. And I talked to him less than an hour ago.

Kisser: Yea. I want to give him a try. Thanks.[25]

Or a call from deprogrammer Moore to CAN headquarters in Chicago:

Moore: Yes, this is Don Moore calling from Virginia. Is Cynthia Kisser there? Female voice: No, she's on a week's vacation. Moore: Ouch. Female voice: And, uh, her assistant though comes in at nine o'clock and it's ten to nine. Maybe she can help you? Moore: All right, well, uh, I, basically I don't need help as far as that goes. I'm one of the folks that work for her as far as the LaRouche case goes.[26]

One of the FBI tapes captured a conversation between Kisser and later convicted Donald Moore on 15 July 1992.

Moore was retained by Newbold Smith to work with former private investigator-turned-deprogrammer Galen Kelly on the abduction of Smith's son. On the tape, Kisser informs Moore that she has filed her suit against [various Scientologists] and states:

Kisser: I think the timing is right for me to go back and try— even if I'm not going to hear from Galen, to go back and approach Newbold to talk to him a little bit now that I've got the suit filed. I want to get him a copy of it. I want to talk to him about it. I want to, uh, talk about it.[27]

The point of these sample bits of conversation is that (1) the FBI was very aware of CAN's involvement in coercive abductions, and (2) CAN's highest eschelon was engaged in corporate criminality, coordinating legal strategies with deprogrammers. Destruction of CAN's phone sheets permanently removed written notes and comments that we are certain contained details of CAN-deprogramming conversations:

The phone sheets contain the caller's name, address, number, subject of call, information provided to the caller, and notes regarding the call. . . .The sheets are used for the sending out of materials and tabulation of statistical information about calls. . . . [Ms. Kisser] affirmed that use of phone sheets was a standard office procedure. . . Kisser estimated that CAN received from 60,000 to 80,000 phone inquiries and 20,000 to 40,000 mail inquiries from 1987 to 1993, Between 53,000 and 56,000 total phone and mail sheets were created during 1991, 1992, and 1993, most of which are phone sheets. Thus, subtracting the 15,000 that remained in existence in March of 1994, at least 38,000 phone and mail sheets have been destroyed. . . .[28]

Rolodex files from the desks of CAN officials and staff members (Box 249 labeled "Rolodexes"), however, were not destroyed and also reveal CAN's familiar connection to deprogrammers. Along with the names, addresses, telephone numbers, and business cards of attorneys, American Family Foundation officials, xerox repair men, sympathizers like comedian Steve Allen and actor Mike Farrell, and others, are entries (apparently for referrals) for deprogrammers like Ted Patrick, Joe Szimhart, Newbold Smith, Gary Scharff, Rick Ross, Galen Kelly, Shirley Landa, Ann Greek, Carol Giambolvo, Wendy Ford, Randall Burkey, and David Clark, among others.

Proposition 2: CAN was a money-laundering scheme in that coercive deprogrammers were expected to "kick-back" or donate, directly or indirectly, portions of the fees they charged families to CAN in exchange for continued referrals. The testimonies of various CFF-CAN officials, deprogrammers, and circumstantial CAN records (i.e., the NARDEC contributions from deprogrammers and the irregular movements of cash within CAN) strongly point to this conclusion. In this sense, CAN conforms to a judgment rendered by Franklin H. Littell, president of the Philadelphia Center on the Holocaust, Genocide, and Human Rights:

CAN and its staffers encourage distraught parents to take actions that further alienate young people. CAN conspires to destroy the liberties of individuals and groups that have religious [beliefs] and worldviews different from the rest of us. It deserves to be put in the dock with the individuals the FBI has exposed and the courts are now trying for criminal acitivity.[29]

Proposition 3: There were sufficient irregularities in the handling of CAN finances and cash flows to suggest that some CAN officials may have enriched themselves significantly at the expense of the CAN organization and its mission without members' general knowledge. The CAN financial documents are grossly problematic in numerous ways. Direct examination of the records as released by CAN pose the following non-inclusive concerns: tax exempt violations, incomplete and inappropriately duplicated records, pertinent required items missing, unaccounted fund appropriations, an improper petty cash allotment, contribution discrepancies, a questionable reserve and CDs, unacceptable accounting and management of funds, and auditor findings resulting in termination of association.

Our preliminary findings of these staggering discrepancies, combined with the clear affiliation to deprogrammers, points to a cash flow from deprogrammings. Are the gaping omissions in the financial records a coverup? The systematic destruction of selective pertinent financial records seems to indicate a pointed attempt at eliminating potentially incriminating evidence. In the final days of CAN's existence, why were Kisser and other anti-cultists so frantic to purchase the CAN records, as evidenced in the bidding for such which occurred during the bankruptcy sale of goods hearing 10/23/96?[30]

A final burning question rests in the reason behind the bomb threats made towards the final shipment of the CAN documents once procured, en route to a secure storage site.

Such drastic measures only serve to arouse curiosity and to stimulate this investigative study.

Our conclusion is that a reasonable description of CAN, as it existed in the period 1986-1995, views it as a criminal organization organized against new religious movements (and other groups) in large part for profit to certain actors, and hypocritical and deceptive in its public persona.

Implications for Religious Pluralism

We may seem to have been unkind to CAN. Certainly it must be embarrassing to rank-and-file CAN supporters, and perhaps threatening to former CAN leaders, all of whom never expected to have their financial secrets and personal correspondence put on display before knowledgeable critics of the ACM. But CAN was not what it claimed to be. It was a corrupt kick-back referral scheme for coercive deprogrammers and likely an avenue of enrichment and possibily even embezzlement for some leaders.

What does the CAN example say, first, about the development of the ACM, and second, about the state of American religious pluralism? First, it seems well-nigh inevitable in hindsight that in a capitalist society whose citizens are often entrepreneurial that the grassroots familial motives of love and concern, which fueled the earliest ACM leadership, would be supplanted by persons who saw financial opportunity in the controversy. Some academics and a number of deprogrammers (most untrained in any behavioral science discipline or mental health practice) climbed on the ACM bandwagon for this reason. Just as degreed "high education" drove out "low education" among many ACM spokespersons, the profit potential of the NRM/ACM controversy occured to many who came to assist or even replace the original volunteer activists. Deprogramming and/or anticultism essentially became a growth industry for a number of persons in this movement. To put it bluntly, not only will anticultisms normally arise out of the controversies over NRMs, but almost inevitably there will also emerge persons trying to "make a buck" out of the situation. Earlier ACM examples from anti-Mormonism and anti-Catholicism can be found in American history.

Second, American religious pluralism is distinctive because it operates in a relatively unrestricted religious marketplace. Thus, with no official state religion, there are also no specific state protections for NRMs, so offenses against them (i.e., violations of religious liberty for members) take longer to receive attention by state prosecutors. Hence the task of defending any NRM or its members often falls to private attorneys in civil suits where both NRM and ACM advocates argue over such issues as NRM members' "mental stability," NRMs' alleged deceptive fundraising, and so forth. In other words, defending the religious freedoms of unconventional groups is often left to private individuals and groups, not government.

Religious pluralism, therefore, sets the context for groups like CAN to emerge and operate. But pluralism also contains the seeds of anti-ACM backlash, which in CAN's case eventually resulted in unremitting lawsuits by angry ex-deprogramming victims and their NRM advocates, on one hand, and bankruptcy, on the other.

Something similar to the current controversy, in cyclical fashion, ought to be expected again in the future.

NOTES

1.   The jury awarded Jason Scott $875,000 in compensatory damages and punitive damages in the amount of $1,000,000 against CAN, $2,500,000 against deprogrammer Rick Ross, and $250,000 each against Ross's two accomplices.
2.   Philip Jenkins, *Mystics and Messiahs: Cults and New Religions in American History* (New York: Oxford University Press, 2000).
3.   Ibid., 5.
4.   See, for several excellent examples of scholarship on these trends: David Brion Davis, "Some Themes of Counter-Subversion: An Analysis of Anti-Masonic, Anti-Catholic, and Anti-Mormon Literature," in *The Mississippi Valley Historical Society* 47 (September 1960): 205-24; Thomas F. Gossett, *Race: The History of An Idea in America* (New York: Schocken Books, 1971).
5.   See, e.g., Anson Shupe and David G. Bromley, "Introduction," in Anson Shupe and David G. Bromley, eds., *Anti-cult Movements in Cross Cultural Perspective* (New York: Garland, 1994), vii.
6.   Anson D. Shupe, Jr. and David G. Bromley, *The New Vigilantes: Deprogrammers, Anti-cultists and the New Religions* (Beverly Hills, Calif.: Sage, 1980).
7.   The symbiotic relationship between AFF and CAN is not dealt with in this report. See Anson Shupe and Susan E. Darnell, *Agents of Discord*, forthcoming.
8.   See Anson Shupe, Kendrick Moxon, and Susan E. Darnell, "CAN, We Hardly Knew Ye: Sex, Drugs, Deprogrammers' Kickbacks, and Corporate Crime in the (old) Cult Awareness Network," paper presented at the

annual meeting of the Society for the Scientific Study of Religion, Houston, Texas, 21 October 2000.

9. See, e.g., Sworn (notarized) Declaration of Eugene M. Ingram, licensed private investigator, Ingram Investigations, 30 October 1992, Los Angeles, California; Sworn (notarized) Statement of Dr. Lowell D. Streiker, 14 May 1992, San Mateo County, California; Sworn (notarized) Declaration of Mark Blocksom, 17 July 1992 (Blocksom allegedly later sought to refute his own declaration when confronted by a reporter from 60 Minutes as having signed the declaration to obtain future work.); "CAN Deprogrammers hit with Arrests," *The Bakersfield News Observer*, 12 February 1992; and Deposition of Marty Butz in *Cynthia Kisser vs. The Chicago Crusader et al.*, 26 October 1994. County of Cook, Illinois, Case No. 92 L 08593. Streiker in particular observed: "As a counselor of families disturbed by so-called cults and an opponent of forcible deprogrammings, I could estimate that 80 percent of all deprogrammings that have been reported to me were set up by CAN national headquarters, or its chapters."

10. Nora Hamerman, "Don Moore: Headed for the CAN," *The New Federalist* 8 (25 April 1994): 12.

11. Declaration of Jonathan Lee Nordquist, 26 August 1991, City of Los Angeles, Calif., 17-18.

12. (Notarized) Declaration of John M. Sweeney, Jr. on deprogramming and the Citizens Freedom Foundation, Maricopa County, Arizona, 17 March 1992.

13. Deposition of Cynthia Kisser in *Jonathan Nordquist vs. Larry Zilliox et al.*, 24 June 1992. No. 92 L1447, County of Cook, Illinois.

14. See deposition of Marty Butz in n. 9.

15. Letter of Rick Ross (Phoenix, Arizona) to Priscilla Coates (Glendale, California, 30 July 1985.

16. Deposition of Cynthia Kisser in *The Emery Wilson Corporation d/b/a Sterling Management Systems Plaintiff vs. Cult Awareness Network et al. Defendant*, Case No. BC 043028, 3 March 1994, Crystal Cove, Ill.

17. Letter of CAN president Ronald M. Loomis (on CAN letterhead) to ALL CAN Affiliates and ALL CAN Newsletter Subscribers, 26 June 1987, from Ithaca, N.Y., 4.

18. Preliminary Program for the October 1987 annual CAN Conference in Portland, Oregon.

19. Sweeney, n. 12.

20. Letter from John M. Sweeney, national director CFF-IS, from Redondo Beach, California, 18 February 1981.

21. See IRS Publication 557, Ch.3 sec. 1 (3) and IRS Express Powers that Cause Failure of Organizational Test [7.8.2] 3.3.4 (02-231999): C., D.

22. *Cynthia Kisser v. The Coalition for Religious Freedom, et al.*, Motion by Defendants Church of Scientology International, "STAND," Bagley and Jentzsch to Dismiss, Or in the Alternative for Evidentiary Preclusion Order, Case No. 92C4508, 19 April 1995, United States District Court, Northern District of Illinois.

23. FBI Special Agent Daniel Murphy, Affidavit to United States Federal Court, Eastern District of Pennsylvania, Exhibit A. "Application of

the United States of America for an Order Authorizing the Interception of Wire Communications," 19 July 1997.

24. Transcript of FBI Tape #2, T3: DMReel 6. 7/15/92; Edited by bmb, 30.

25. Transcript of FBI Tape #2, T3: DMReel 16. 8/02-3,92; Edited by bmb, 2, 6.

26. Transcript of FBI Tape #2, T3: DMReel 11. 7/21/92; Edited by ssw, 10.

27. Ibid.

28. *Kisser v. The Coalition for Religious Freedom.*

29. Franklin H. Littell, "Cult Awareness Network Preys on Parents' Anxieties," *Jewish Times* 17, no. 33 (1992): 37.

30. Correspondence in the (old) CAN boxes reveal a number of anxious letters from former CAN contributors who had sent their contributions by check or credit card numbers requesting to have the bankruptcy court trustee purge their names from CAN files before the latter were auctioned. (The trustee did not.) Likewise, there were several last minute bids and counter-bids by Cynthia Kisser, AFF's Herbert J. Rosedae, and others to purchase the records. The letters clearly reveal a range of emotion: from fear to desperation.

A Contemporary Ordered Religious Community[1]: The Sea Organization[2]

J. GORDON MELTON

Most major religious traditions have made room for and encouraged the development of organizations and associations which provide a structure in which its most committed members may give their full-time effort to the deepening of their commitment through purely religious activities and offer their life in service to humanity, the larger religious community of which they are a part, and the divine as they conceive it. These associations are usually structured as intentional and ordered communities though their actual organization varies widely from the Eastern Orthodox monastic community on Mount Athos in Greece to the wandering sanyassin ascetics in India. Many ordered communities are celibate, while others admit married members. Some reside in intimate relationships in tightly structured centers, while others are rather loosely dispersed with members engaged in various service enterprises.

Members of such committed structures have been generally known for a range of practices including the assumption of special tasks and disciplines not expected of the rest of their parent community. Entering the special status of the organization usually begins with the taking of an oath of long-term commitment analogous to marriage vows. Many members of religious communities, for example, live a scheduled existence in which obedience to earthly superiors is a high virtue. Within the Roman Catholic tradition to obedience, monastic vows generally also add poverty and chastity. The Eastern Orthodox Church selects its leadership from among its monks, as do Tibetan Buddhists. Monks and nuns commonly adopt different sexual mores, wear clothing marking their special role in the community, and form an intimate relationship with their fellow sisters and brothers that compete with, if not entirely replace, their previous familial attachments.[3] Sanyassins, for example, once having assumed their new name and status, often refuse to talk about or consider their prior life and identity.

Even among groups that largely abandoned, even denigrated, the monastic life, some accommodation to disciplined community emerged. Protestantism immediately comes to mind. Protestants rejected the celibate priesthood and during its formative period closed the monasteries and nunneries only to have them reappear several centuries later. Protestant history is replete with accounts of, for example, pietist communal groups such as the Ephrata Community and the Oneida Perfectionists, the Deaconess movement in the Lutheran[4] and Methodist[5] churches, modern experiments such as the Chicago-based Ecumenical Institute,[6] and the hippie communities associated with the Jesus People movement of the 1970s, the largest and most successful being Jesus People, U.S.A.[7] Among Protestants, intentional communities frequently became, for all intents and purposes, a new denomination with a few such as the Hutterites growing into large international organizations.[8]

Western Esotericism, the surviving remnant of the ancient Gnostic tradition that emerged in the seventeenth century as Rosicrucianism, produced a series of ordered communal expressions from the German Rosicrucian group that established itself on Wissahickon Creek in Germantown, Pennsylvania[9] in the 1690s, to the contemporary Holy Order of MANS.[10] Among theosophists, communal life flourished in the early twentieth century[11] and Gnostic bishop George Burke has built a community of monks in present-day Nebraska.[12]

Given the ubiquity of ordered religious communities, it is no surprise that various New Religions have developed their own variations on monastic life. Among the more interesting of these new ordered communities is The Way Corps, the committed community within The Way International;[13] The Esoteric Section of the Theosophical Society;[14] and the subject of this paper, the Sea Organization, founded in 1967.[15] The Sea Org took its name from its origin aboard a fleet of ships, most prominently the Apollo, where L. Ron Hubbard, the person around whose thought the Church of Scientology[16] emerged, and a number of associates had located in order to continue the development of the teachings and practices of the church, most prominently what are today known as the Operating Thetan or OT Levels. In 1971, the Sea Organization assumed responsibility for the ecclesiastical management of the

Scientology churches in addition to its other duties. In 1975, the Sea Org largely transferred its activity to church facilities on land, and Sea Org members were present and active during the reorganization of the church following the trauma it experienced in 1979-80 with the arrest and conviction of a cadre of its leaders associated with the Guardian's Office (GO). The GO was a special office established in 1966, its stated purpose being to deal with attacks upon the church so that the main body could continue with its spiritual work apart from the distraction of public controversies.

Beginnings

To understand the Sea Org, it is necessary to understand the particular belief system of the Church of Scientology and its development through its first decade.[17] Scientology is an esoteric Gnostic system based upon the belief that the true self, called the Thetan, is trapped in MEST (matter, energy, space, and time), the visible world. Freedom from that entrapped state to total freedom is accomplished in a series of steps that involve both awareness of one's state and taking action to detach oneself from the encumbrances that hold the Thetan to the material world. In Scientological terms, one crosses "The Bridge" to "total freedom" one step at a time.[18] The process of moving up The Bridge is analogous to the degrees or levels of accomplishment familiar to anyone who has studied Esotericism.[19]

Important to Scientology is a belief that the Thetan has, over the millennia, been embodied on many occasions, a belief commonly called reincarnation, though Scientologists generally avoid the term.[20] They also eschew any idea of transmigration, i.e., the belief that the Thetan would incarnate into any animal form less than human. In the first stage of Scientology, one concentrates on removing from the Thetan some encumbrances acquired both in this life and in past existences. These encumbrances called "engrams" are described as aberrations attached to the self that produce dysfunctional behavior patterns. The completion of this initial work is symbolized by the acceptance of the status known as "Clear." Once one has reached that plateau, one is now ready to begin exercising one's free life operating as a Thetan. The upper levels of Scientology offer the secret wisdom, the *gnosis*, necessary to continue removing the additional encumbrances from one's past lives and experiencing total freedom.

Scientology's essential contribution to Esotericism has been the wedding of technological precision to the process of spiritual progress. This technology is expressed most prominently in the use of an instrument called the E-meter as an assist in spiritual counseling, coupled with the demand that the processes and format of counseling, called auditing in Scientology, be followed with a high level of exactness. Technological preciseness is equivalent in Scientology to adherence to orthodox belief in conservative Christianity. Thus deviation from that precision, i.e., alteration of standard tech, is considered a serious matter within the church.

By 1966, Hubbard had largely set in place the process of reaching the state of Clear, but was aware that there was more. Through that year, he explored the first of what would become the advanced realizations of the church and released the material associated with OT I and II in August and September respectively. Then, in September 1966, he resigned his role as administrative leader of the church, and turned over its management to a number of trusted associates. This resignation did not mean abandonment of the movement and organization he had founded, but it did mean that he redirected his activity to the further development of the OT levels and the associated activities. He moved aboard a series of the ocean-going vessels, illustrative of his own love of the seafarer's life, which served as his laboratory for experiments and consideration of the implications of what he observed and the experiences reported to him by those who first shared the life of an Operating Thetan. A common element in these experiences was what was termed exteriorization, more commonly designated the out-of-body experience. According to Scientologists, the Operating Thetan begins to have short periods in which it experiences itself outside the physical body with a goal of lengthening the stay.[21]

Aboard the *Apollo*, the flagship of the Scientology ships, Hubbard attracted a cadre of older, more committed Scientologists, most of whom had no experience aboard such a ship, and who had to learn from scratch the various tasks from navigation to engine repair to cooking meals for the crew. Several structures were established to concentrate on the vocational training of the crew including the Pursers Project Force and the Stewards Project Force. The idea of on-the-job training became integral to the development of the Sea Org, which recruited only a minority of people with prior training in the various areas in which they would be called to operate. Life aboard the *Apollo,* and its sister vessels, the *Diana* and the *Athena,* became the crucible in which the Sea Org was initially tested.

The Sea Org was actually established in 1967 by a small group of Scientologists, all of whom had reached the state of Clear, and some of whom had completed the previously released OT I and II levels. (OT III was released in September 1967; OT IV, V, and VI were released in January 1968.) The Sea Org membership would soon encompass all who worked on the three ships, though these were by no means all Clears.

The impact of what was occurring quietly aboard the Apollo began to be felt within the larger community of Scientologists in 1968 when the first Sea Org members left the ships to establish the initial Advanced Organizations at which the material relative to the OT Levels were released to then relatively small number of designated Clears. At the time there were approximately five hundred such individuals, though the number was rapidly expanding. The Sea Org itself expanded through the first half of the 1970s and in 1975 experienced its first dramatic change when life aboard the ships was abandoned and what was termed the Flag Land Base was established in Clearwater, Florida, which would become the spiritual center of the faith.

Meanwhile, the leadership of the movement (the organization of the church above the local church centers) had been placed in the hands of the Executive Council Worldwide. However, in 1971, it was thus determined that the Council was not doing its job adequately. It was disbanded, and its duties (primarily the management of the church's continental and national offices and its publishing facilities around the world) were assumed by the Sea Org.

Through the end of the 1970s, the Sea Org was in charge of the administration of the church internationally and three additional Scientology structures. First, the Saint Hill Organizations (named for the center in East Grinstead where Hubbard lectured while in England) specialize in the advanced training of auditors. Thus the Saint Hill Organizations are the Scientology equivalent of seminaries and graduate schools. Saint Hill graduates are deemed the most efficient and qualified auditors within the church. While the basics of auditing training may be acquired in any local Scientology church, those who wish to pursue a career as an auditor or audit people during their more advanced sessions at the OT levels would seek Saint Hill training.

Second, the initial Advanced Organizations (AO) were established in 1968 to deliver the OT Levels. The first AOs were opened in Los Angeles and Edinburgh (the latter soon moved to London and then East Grinstead). Today, there are two additional Advanced Organizations in Copenhagen, Denmark, and suburban Sidney, Australia.

Third, the Flag Service Organization offered all of the curriculum of the AOs, but also became the first center to offer OT Levels above OT III. Following the release of the OT IV-VI Levels, OT VII was initially made available in 1970. Prior to the establishment of the Flag Land Base, these higher levels could be accessed only aboard the ships and at the two Advanced Organizations.[22]

In the process of pursuing the OT Levels, church members are given access to a set of confidential materials that include the instructions for the spiritual exercises to be followed to gain the particular benefits of that level as well as the most complete statement of the religious myth underlying all of Scientology (a myth that is required for making an overall evaluation of Scientology's place on the large religious landscape).[23] This presents an obstacle for any outsider who wishes to understand the Scientology worldview.[24] Fortunately, with the continued publication (in both audio and literary formats) of Hubbard's many lectures, all of the elements of the myth have been made available and can be accessed by anyone without reference to the confidential documents, though some diligence is required as the references are scattered in a variety of sources.[25]

The Trauma of 1979

In 1979, the church began to experience a trauma of immense proportions, analogous on a smaller scale to the Counter Reformation that hit the Roman Catholic Church in the sixteenth century. After decades of complaints that the church had become corrupt at the highest levels, and following a major schism by those seeking its reform, the Roman Catholic Church finally called a church council and instituted widespread reforms that dominated the institution into the twentieth century.[26]

The Guardian's Office (GO), once formed, was headquartered at Saint Hill Manor in England. It also began to reproduce itself and soon most local churches had one or more of its representatives on its staff. The GO operated somewhat autonomously and in addition formed an Intelligence Bureau, which operated in secret from all but the GO's higher officials. The Guardian's Office also competed with the Sea Org for hegemony within Scientology. Once the problems in the Office became known, the internal process of investigating and dealing with them took several years.[27]

As the criminal trial of the church officers in the United States proceeded, the church launched its own internal review of the GO management. Based upon its assessment, a complete reorganization of the church at the national, continental, and international level was begun in April 1981 with the first preliminary investigations of the facts. In July, Mary Sue Hubbard, the wife of L. Ron Hubbard, was asked to resign. Action in line with internal church policy was begun against eleven senior Guardian's Office officials, all of whom resigned their church posts in October. Through 1982, the investigation expanded resulting in a number of those involved in what was considered improper conduct being released from their position in the church and a few being expelled entirely from the church. Still others chose to leave the church at this time. It was eventually decided that the Guardian's Office was unsalvageable as a church agency and in 1983 it was totally disbanded and its functions assigned to a variety of new agencies.[28] Also in 1983, the international headquarters of the church was relocated to Los Angeles, where it remains.

Meanwhile, as the investigation of the Guardian's Office proceeded, three important new structures were also created. The Church of Scientology International was established as the new "mother" church (using a model not unlike the Mother Church in Christian Science) to have direct oversight of the movement's otherwise autonomous local churches. A significant part of the Guardian's Office's previous functions was assigned to the Office of Special Affairs, a division within the Church of Scientology International. A second organization, Scientology Missions International, was formed to oversee the local Scientology missions (proto-churches not yet large enough to provide all the services that a "church" provides). Both of these structures were then placed into the hands of the members of Scientology's ordered community, the Sea Organization.

The most important new organization was the Religious Technology Organization, a rather unique ecclesiastical structure. RTC was established to ensure that the "technology" of Scientology is properly administered (i.e., orthodoxy and orthopraxis is followed) and remains in its intended hands (i.e., remains in the control of Hubbard's appointed successors). Hubbard assigned all of his Scientology-related trademarks to RTC and it is through its control of and ability to license said trademarks that it exercises its authority.

The actual operation of each of these new organizations (and a few other additional organizations such as the International Hubbard Ecclesiastical League of Pastors) is an interesting subject in itself, but far beyond the scope of this essay. The important point is that all of these new organizations were placed in the hands of the Sea Org. Their creation amounted to the complete reorganization of Scientology and the assumption by Sea Org members of the leadership role at the national, continental, and international levels. Scientology's organization is thus quite analogous to the placement of the Roman Catholic Church, and especially the Eastern Orthodox Church, in the care of the clergy and the members of its ordered communities. For Scientology, the changes of 1980-81 were as significant and as far-reaching as were the reforms instituted by Pope Gregory VII were for Roman Catholicism.[29]

The reorganization of the church was not well received by all Scientologists, especially those most affected by the disbanding of the Guardian's Office. Several of those who left the church in the early 1980s went on to write of the change in authority structures in a somewhat hostile fashion, and a few who broke with Scientology at this time went on to become some of the church's most hostile and committed critics. They carried with them the knowledge of the actions of the office and have used that knowledge freely to attack the church during the last two decades. Their revelation of events was supported by the opening of the Guardian Office's files by the Federal Court.[30]

Today, two decades after the reorganization of Scientology internationally, the administration of the movement above the level of the local church remains the business of the Sea Organization. Sea Org members hold all policy and administrative posts in each of the corporations mentioned above as well as the Celebrity Centre in Los Angeles, a church established to respond to the special situation of those in the artistic and entertainment industries.[31] The new organization is the Flag Ship Service Organization based on the *Freewinds*, an ocean-going vessel that operates in the Caribbean, where members go to participate in OT VIII and other advanced course material.

The Sea Org Today

During the more than thirty years of its existence, the Sea Org has grown (as of the summer of 2000) into a dedicated community of some 5,800 members, a relatively small number of church members given the scope of Scientology's activities internationally.[32] It is the dedicated core of members who have chosen to devote their lives to the spread of Scientology. The largest number of members reside at the church complexes in Los Angeles, Clearwater, Copenhagen, London and Saint Hill (in the UK), and Sydney. Smaller Sea Org centers can be found in Johannesburg, Toronto, Budapest, Madrid, Milan, and Moscow, and individual Sea Org members can at any moment be found elsewhere as their services are needed.

The process of joining the Sea Org has become somewhat institutionalized. In most instances, it begins with a public meeting in a Scientology church facility in which a Sea Org representative presents a profile of the work of the organization and invites interested attendees to consider joining. Those who attend such meeting are usually already familiar with the Sea Org from leaflets that are freely distributed in most church facilities, as well as articles in different church periodicals.

At the close of the meeting, those who express an interest in the Sea Org are invited to consider making an initial commitment in the form of signing what has come to be known as the billion-year "commitment."[33] This brief document is actually a letter of intent of offering oneself for service in the Sea Org and to submit to its rules. To be a part of the Sea Org is not just to join the fraternity, but an agreement to enter into full-time employment by the church and to go where one is needed. However, it closes with the statement, "I commit myself to the Sea Organization for the next billion years." This symbolic commitment of the individual beyond their present earthly existence is appropriate to a community that believes in reincarnation. It is also somewhat reminiscent of Mormon sealing ceremonies during which a person is sealed to a spouse beyond this earthly life for "all eternity."

After the signing of the commitment document, which is largely of symbolic import, the individual is given a period of time to consider their decision, but more importantly, to clear up any impediments to their joining the Sea Org. For example, many new Sea Org recruits are already serving in the church at one of its local centers. In those cases, they must complete

any unfinished tasks with their current position before continuing with the process of joining. Others leave the meeting
with a belief that their destiny belongs to the Sea Org, they
may have even signed the "billion year commitment," but
they are not yet ready to actually join. I have talked to members who waited as long as three or, in one instance, even six
years before taking the next step which is to report to the Sea
Org's induction program, called the Estates Project Force
(EPF).[34] Beginning the EPF usually means a change of residence to one of the large Sea Org centers at Los Angeles,
Clearwater, East Grinstead, or Copenhagen.

The completion of the EPF program takes from two weeks
to several months, (as it includes a self-study program that is
completed at different rates by different people). Included in
the program is a rigorous daily routine of work and study
that introduces people on an experiential level to the nature of
the commitment being asked of them. It also introduces them
on a cognitive level to the various options for service, the
goals of the Sea Org's activity, and the rules by which they
must abide. As the church will invest much in the Sea Org
member's training, and in common with most ordered communities, it wishes to filter out those with a lesser or superficial commitment. The EPF attempts to ensure that each recruit
is making an informed and heartfelt assent to the overall vision of what they are entering. Integral to explaining the Sea
Org is a set of lectures given by Hubbard in 1969 to the
fledgling group of original members struggling with their
new life on a ship. Though most Sea Org members are not
working on a ship, the principles articulated are deemed to
have universal value.

Following the completion of the EPF program, the recruit
makes a final decision to continue, church personnel make a
final assessment of the recruit's worth to the organization,
and the person is accepted into the Sea Org. If the person has
not already done so, he or she now participates in a formal
swearing-in ceremony that includes the reading of the "Code
of a Sea Org Member," sentence-by-sentence, and his or her
verbal ascent to each clause. The code reads as follows:

1. I promise to help get ethics in on this planet and the
   universe, which is the basic purpose of the Sea Org.
2. I promise to uphold, forward and carry out, Command
   Intention.[35]

3. I promise to use Dianetics and Scientology for the greatest good for the greatest number of dynamics.

4. I promise to do my part to achieve the Sea Org's humanitarian objective which is to make a safe environment where the Fourth Dynamic Engram[36] can be edited out.

5. I promise to uphold the fact that duty is the Sea Org's true motivation, which is the highest motivation there is.

6. I promise to keep my own personal ethics in and uphold beyond all contemporary honor, integrity and true discipline that is the Sea Org's heritage and tradition.

7. I promise to effectively lead, care for and train those under my charge and to ensure they keep their own ethics in and if that fails to take action with fair and legal justice.

8. I promise to take responsibility for the preservation and the continued full and exact use of the technologies of Dianetics and Scientology.

9. I promise to exemplify in my conduct the belief that to command is to serve and that a being is only as valuable as he can serve others.

10. I promise to improve my worth to the Sea Org and mankind by regularly advancing my knowledge of and ability to apply the truths and technologies of Dianetics and Scientology.

11. I promise to accept and fulfill to the utmost of my ability the responsibilities entrusted to me whatever they may be and wherever they may carry me in the line of duty.

12. I promise to be competent and effective at all times and never try to explain away or justify ineffectiveness nor minimize the true power that I am.

13. I promise at all times, to set a desirable example in appearance, conduct and production to fellow Sea Org members and the area in which I operate.

14. I promise to demand that my fellow Sea Org members not fall short of the purpose, ideals and spirit of the Sea Org.

15. I promise to do my part to protect and further the image of the Sea Org.

16. I promise to come to the defense of the Sea Org and fellow Sea Org members whenever needed.

17. I promise through my actions to increase the power of the Sea Org and decrease the power of any enemy.

18. I promise to make things go right and to persist until they do.

Each Sea Org member reaffirms that acceptance in a formal ceremony annually on 12 August, the anniversary of the founding of the Organization.

Once accepted as a member, the individual is assigned to a position in the church and living quarters. Single members live in a dormitory-like facility and married couples in modest apartments. Most meals are taken communally in a Sea Org managed dining facility. Following a period of training, members work a full day (five days a week) and then have several hours each day for their own spiritual development in personal study, auditing, or course work. Sea Org recruits come from all levels of progress in the overall Scientology program.

Generally, one day a week (Saturday), members will leave their regular job (which may be anything from translating texts, writing legal briefs, or assembling E-meters) and join with the local grounds crew on the upkeep of the buildings or grounds. The Sea Org has shown a pattern of buying rundown property and refurbishing it, and the work of renovation usually involves some form of physical labor from laying brick, installing plumbing or electrical outlets, to planting shrubbery or painting walls.[37] On the other hand, at various points when the church is preparing for a major event or making a big push to accomplish a particular goal, Sea Org members may work extra long hours (overnight shifts being occasionally reported) for a short period.

It is interesting to compare the daily life of the Sea Org member with that of a Roman Catholic monk or nun. In many respects they are quite similar, in that both include a preprogrammed routine that includes work and time for spiritual development. They differ somewhat in that in many of the older Roman Catholic or semi-cloistered orders the life is much more ascetic. For example, the day of a member of the Cloistered Nuns of Perpetual Adoration begins at 5:30 each day. It is punctuated with times of prayer at 11:30 a.m. and at 2, 4, and 7:45 p.m. The sisters retire at 8:45 but rise for the Midnight Office at 12:00 a.m. and then return to their room until a new day begins at 5:30. The Carmelite Nuns of Our Lady of Divine Provence rise at 5:40 each day. Their day is marked by Morning Prayer at 6 and mass at 7:30. Their schedule then follows with prayer times at 11:40, 2, 4, 7:30, and 9:30. They retire at 11 p.m. each evening.[38] Monks/nuns integrate a variety of activities as penances as part of their spiritual growth and effort to deal with human sinfulness. These penances are frequently of a kind that an outsider might consider to be of a humiliating or degrading nature. As one writer on her observation of cloistered nuns noted, "Mortification was considered an essential part of most cloistered life, and common penances included frequent fasting, kneeling during meals, and praying for extended periods of time with arms outstretched.[39]

On Sunday, most Sea Org members attend a weekly worship service, and then perform their normal tasks for a half-day (they may take every other Sunday off). They have the rest of the day to attend to personal needs such as shopping, cleaning their personal space, and washing clothes. Members receive a modest allowance that covers their personal needs. The church also arranges for medical care. Most Sea Org members dress in uniforms mildly reminiscent of the group's origin aboard the ships in 1967, though what is considered uniform clothing has become increasingly tailored to the local environment and/or duties of the office.

Married couples in the Sea Org attempt to have a normal married life within the context of their mutual commitment to Scientology. Some choose to have children; many do not. Beginning in 1986, couples that chose to have children were granted a leave of absence from the Sea Org[40] and usually assumed a staff position at a local church until such time as the child was six years old.[41] After they return to staff, the children are raised and schooled communally, and visit with parents on the weekend until they are of age. It is currently the case that a number of children of Sea Org members have reached adulthood and have joined of their own accord. It is among the basic rules that members may not marry anyone who is not a Sea Org member nor may they engage in extra-marital sexual relationships.

The Sea Org is described as having no formal organization itself. In fact there is no person designated as head of the Sea Org, nor is there a Sea Org hierarchy as such.[42] However, concurrent with Sea Org membership, one also develops a service relationship with one of the church's organizations that requires most of its staff to be drawn from the Sea Org membership. Thus, each Sea Org member is assigned to a post with a particular structure be it CSI, one of the Advanced Organizations, a Saint Hill facility, a continental organization, one of the church's publishing or recording subsidiaries, or one of any of the additional church facilities.

From that point they develop a relationship to the church through the facility that officially engages them for the church. Each facility is run according to the general organizational structure delineated by Hubbard and each Sea Org member can locate him/herself on the prominently posted organizational chart. On a practical level, the local church corporation, rather than the entire Sea Org as such, has primary responsibility for the individual member.

After a period of time at any given post, a person may be asked to assume a new position in the church or may decide that they would rather engage in some other activity or at some different task. In the latter case, they may apply for any openings about which they have become aware, but upon acceptance must finish any incomplete tasks and find a replacement for their post before moving to the new position. In every church facility, an organizing board is posted showing every job position, and the person assigned to it. The organizing board will also show any positions that are currently unfilled.

The Role of Ethics

As the first clause of the "Code of the Sea Org Member" implies, ethics is of primary concern to the life of the fraternity, both the upholding of ethics by the individual member and the spread of ethics, as understood within Scientology, through society as a whole. That being the case, the integrating of the ethical system laid out in Hubbard's volume, *Introduction to Scientology Ethics*, is basic to becoming a Sea Org member.[43]

On an abstract level, Hubbard built his ethical system (as the whole system of Scientology) on the principle of survival. The urge to survive is, Hubbard believed, the dynamic principle of existence, and he observed, "The goal of life in this universe may be easily and generally defined as an effort to survive as long as possible and attain the most desirable state possible in that survival."[44] Hubbard also saw the universe in terms of what he described as eight urges or drives in life, the eight dynamics. That is, humans express the urge to survive in eight arenas:

Self
Creativity (including family and children)
Groups (from a circle of friends to the nation)
Species (humankind)
Life forms
Physical Universe of MEST (matter, energy, space, time)
Spiritual
Infinity[45]

Ethics refers to those actions that an individual undertakes in order to accomplish optimum survival for him/herself and others. Harking back to John Stuart Mill, he proposed that the highest ethical decisions were those that "brought the greatest benefits to the greatest number of dynamics."[46] Based upon their contribution to survival in the different arenas, one can judge actions as good or bad. Moral codes express the experience of the race as to what has proven at any given moment to be the actions that produce survival as opposed to those that counter it. Ethical conduct includes the adherence to the codes of the society in which one lives.

The person pursuing a course that is counter survival is operating "out-ethics."[47] A person who begins to operate out-ethics first becomes self-destructive, but eventually the actions will become visible on several dynamics. When the actions of an individual negatively affect the group, it will react. Justice is the name we give to the system any society develops to protect itself from the anti-survival actions of the individual.

Hubbard suggested that when an individual performs a counter-survival act, he or she attempts to correct it. However, these efforts usually fail due to a lack of knowledge about what is occurring and ignorance of the means of becoming an ethical person (i.e., unfamiliarity with the Scientology tech on ethics). At the moment, the ethics technology operates only within the Church of Scientology, and the most complete attempt to apply it has occurred in the Sea Org.

The effort to establish Hubbard's ethical system is done, of course, within the context of the overall development of the spiritual life advocated by the church. Each individual Scientologist is seen as being on a spiritual journey. Ideally, that journey involves intensive self-examination, the confrontation with and removal of all of the negative influences that are seen as having attached themselves to the Self, and the learning of a new means of operating without such influences. The new Scientologist encounters what Hubbard called "engrams" and learns that dealing with engrams at various levels of reality is considered an essential element in traveling up the Bridge to the highest levels of Scientology.

When one becomes concerned with the ethical question, a second emphasis is added, the concern with present moment acts of commission or omission that transgress the moral code of the group, in this case the Sea Org. Such acts are called *overts*. An overt is an act (or failure to act) that leads to the injury, degradation, or reduction of the self or others. Overts often lead the person committing them to cover them up. The act of not revealing or talking about an overt is called a *withhold*. The withhold is seen as an act of dishonesty to the self and one's colleagues. Within the Sea Org, a primary ethical concern is with handling overts and any resulting withholds. It is the duty of a Sea Org member to report their own overts and withholds or any committed by others of which they become aware to their unit's ethics officer. Typical overts might involve negligence at one's assigned task, theft of church funds, or illicit sexual activity.

Overts, seen as having an origin in one's past, are usually dealt with in counseling (auditing) sessions. However, if they become serious, they are seen as harming the group, and the individual has to deal with the unique justice system that operates within the Sea Org. That system is based upon other beliefs of Hubbard, possibly the most important one being that handling misdeeds by punishment is ineffective. It simply leads to a worsening of the sequence of overts while at the same time degrading the individual. Thus the Scientology justice system replaces the imposition of punishment with action that seeks to remove the cause of the overts and hence prevent them in the future. That action involves the individual's willingness to confront and accept responsibility for their life, and through the technology remove the underlying cause of the overts.[48]

When the ethics officer within the church becomes aware of serious overts committed by a person of the particular organization over which they have jurisdiction, they initiate a process of fact-finding to determine the truth of any accusations. This process may, depending on the severity of the actions under discussion, involve a Board of Investigation and a Committee of Evidence. In the more serious cases, the Committee of Evidence will weigh any mitigating circumstances in the situation and make recommendations by which the person may make restitution for any harm done and take action to prevent the repetition of such acts in the future. There is also a system of appeals by which a person who feels that the initial finding against them has been wrong, can seek redress.

In the most extreme cases, when a Sea Org member has lost faith in Scientology, has actively taken actions to harm the church, and has no desire to realign with the church, the committee may recommend expulsion from the Sea Org or even the church.[49] In several instances, individuals expelled from the Church have gone on to engage in long-term public opposition to Scientology. In other cases, also deemed severe, but in which the individual has not intended direct harm and wishes to remain a member of the Sea Org, Hubbard created a program by which the person may deal with their overts and withholds in a comprehensive manner, make restitution to the group, and return to their post in good standing. The program is called the Rehabilitation Project Force (RPF). Though founded in the 1970s, this aspect of the Sea Org was virtually unknown until the 1980s when it began to be discussed in anti-Scientology writings and was introduced into several court cases. It subsequently became one of the more controversial aspects of the Church of Scientology.

The RPF[50]

As most religions have created ordered intentional communities, so those intentional communities have created systems whereby those who break the rules may make recompense and be integrated back into the life of the community. The most famous system operating in the West is possibly that created by St. Benedict for the Benedictine order. The section on rule breaking begins:

If a brother is found to be obstinate, or disobedient, or proud, or murmuring, or habitually transgressing the Holy Rule in any point and contemptuous of the order of his seniors, the latter shall admonish him secretly a first and second time, as Our Lord commands. If he fails to amend, let him be given a public rebuke in front of the whole community. But if even then he does not reform, let him be placed under excommunication, provided that he understands the seriousness of that penalty; if he is perverse, however, let him undergo corporal punishment.[51]

Among the Trappists, anyone seen breaking the rules would be reported to the "Chapter of faults, which would in turn announce these actions at the next meal after which the

superior of the order would pronounce a suitable punishment. For example, ". . . a monk might be ordered to lie in the
doorway of the refractory while the other monks stepped over
him on their way to a meal."[52]

Within the Roman Catholic Church, there is a set of general laws that all orders follow. Each order then adopts additional rules peculiar to its special purpose and mission. Canon
law operating within the Roman Catholic Church notes that a
monk or nun under perpetual vows may be dismissed from
their order for what are termed "grave external reasons." It is
the duty of the person's immediate superiors to admonish
them in hopes of correcting the situation, and may in that endeavor impose various punishments. If the person proves incorrigible, he or she is informed that he or she risks being
terminated as a member and is asked for a defense of the
questioned behavior. If the situation remains serious, it is
presented to the proper authority, the local bishop or superior
of the order, who passes it to the Congregation of Religious in
Rome. It is ultimately the decision of the pope formally to order the dismissal.[53]

In the Eastern world, one soon runs into the *Patimokkha*
section of the *Vinaya-pitaka* that lay out the rules for Buddhist
monks.[54] Among the important admonitions for the monk or
nun are to refrain from sexual activity, avoid secular work,
and not attempt to create a schism in the sangha (monastic
community). There is also a prescribed code of etiquette,
which anyone who has been present at a Buddhist gathering
that included monks and nuns has witnessed. The Vinaya also
prescribed rules for disciplining rule breakers. There are a set
of rules that if transgressed leads to the immediate expulsion
of the member from the group. Lesser rules may be handled
through the imposition of punishments after a confession or
other determination of guilt.[55] In The Korean Chogye tradition (the majority tradition in Korean Buddhism), there are
four deeds that will lead to immediate dismissal from the monastic community, sexual relations with a woman, stealing,
killing, and telling lies, especially making a false claim about
one's state of enlightenment. The Sea Org's system differs
from that of both the Roman Catholic and Buddhist systems
in that it offers a means for those judged guilty of expulsion
offenses to redeem themselves and be reintegrated into the
community.[56]

*   The RPF, the Sea Org's program for those who have committed serious violations of ethical policy, was created in Jan-

uary 1974 while the center of the Sea Org was still aboard the ships. The program grew out of the recognition that some people either could not or did not wish to adapt to life aboard the ships. Originally such persons were put off the ship, the equivalent of being dismissed from the Sea Org. Then in 1968, Hubbard created what was termed the "Mud Box Brigade." Those on board the ship who were found slacking off their duties or misbehaving (which in some cases on board the ship could place the lives of the crew and passengers in danger) were assigned to clean the "mud boxes," the place where mud collected from the anchors, and the bilge, the rather foul water that collects in the bottom of any ocean-going vessel. While the average person looking at such a structure might see it as punishment, Hubbard understood it in terms of making retribution to the people who had been harmed by the nonperformance or incorrect performance of one's assigned tasks. This rather stop-gap measure, however, was replaced in 1974 with RPF, a more systematic structure for handling misbehavior that was more fully integrated into Hubbard's understanding of ethics. The RPF also served additional purposes beyond those served by the Mud Box Brigade.

The new Rehabilitation Project Force program was designed with multi-goals, though the basic one was providing a situation in which individuals who had been negligent in their posts could be isolated from the group (thus preventing further immediate harm). They were also assigned a period each day to work on themselves using Scientology tech, considered a necessary step to their being reintegrated into the larger group. As Hubbard described it in an early Flag Order, "The RPF is in actual fact a system of recruiting by taking people off the lines who are blocking things and then not letting them back on lines until they are a valuable operating staff member."[57] The RPF was also designed as a work force in which the members spent five hours a day working upon their own inner condition using the resources available in Scientology technology, and the rest of the day engaged in physical labor of the kind that involved coordinated work with others as a team. While learning to work with others, one could make restitution for the harm done through contributions to the physical facilities in which the Sea Org and the church are housed. As each project is completed, RPF members feel rewarded, usually with a sense of accomplishment.

Assignment to the RPF can begin in one of several ways. Often it starts with a realization by an individual that his/her behavior is out of line with expectations. With a number of people I interviewed, their realization came during or shortly after their ending an illicit extramarital affair. In some cases, the affair began to affect their work, but in others the fact that their performance at work was judged superior allowed them to keep the affair unknown to their colleagues. In most cases, however, problems with performance at their assigned work over a period of time was noticed and reported. Following an investigation, the individual was offered the option of pursuing the RPF program or leaving the Sea Org. In one case, the person I interviewed had misappropriated a considerable amount of church money for personal use.

Once a person is informed of the basics of the RPF option, understands what is involved, and chooses it, he or she signs a document noting his/her agreement to join the program. The new RPFer then generally moves quickly to one of the RPF centers that are located in the Sea Org complexes in Los Angeles, Clearwater, London, or Copenhagen. The largest number is in the LA RPF (in 2000, when this study was done, more than half of the approximately 350 currently participating in the program were in LA. Slightly less were in the Clearwater RPF, and by comparison, the RPF at Copenhagen had less than 20). Choice of location is determined by several factors including space available and the presence of another person at approximately the same level on The Bridge with whom the RPFer can work in their mutual counseling. A person, for example, who is working on his/her OT levels would not be counseled by a pre-Clear.

When the person arrives, he or she is assigned to space in a dorm-like room with others and given some orientation. That orientation includes the reading of the thirty Flag Orders pertaining to RPF. Once fully aware of the conditions under which he or she will be operating,[58] he or she chooses to proceed, and then begin a refresher course in ethics.[59] In addition, some technical training is included, especially if the new person is unfamiliar with the basics of auditing.[60] The person is also assigned to a team with whom he or she will be working. In Copenhagen, the number of options is extremely limited, while in Los Angeles and Clearwater, a variety of work assignments are available.[61]

Finally, the individual is assigned to a partner with whom she/he will work during the stay in the RPF. This partner is extremely important as one's progress in the program is tied to the partner's progress. During what will be a year or more together, the pair audit each other and are responsible for each other's success. They will finish the program together, and one criteria for graduation is the demonstration that the RPFer can help another, specifically their partner. The importance of the partner is underscored in those occasional cases in which a person drops out of the program. The person who remains will be assigned another new partner whose success now becomes his/her responsibility.

The RPF is located within the Sea Org facilities, but members dine and sleep in separate quarters. In Los Angeles, for example, the RPF space—dorm, dining hall and kitchen, and woodwork shop—are in the main AO building. In Copenhagen, they are in the basement (study space) and top floor (dorm rooms) of one of the Sea Org buildings currently undergoing renovation. In Clearwater, they are located in two separate buildings in the Sea Org residence complex. These buildings housing the RPF are on the edge of the complex and immediately outside the front door of the two buildings is a gate that opens from the inside. Any person could simply walk out of the buildings and out of the gate into the city of Clearwater.[62] Contrary to images of a concentration camp-like atmosphere, there are no locks on the doors of the RPF facilities, and at almost anytime, participants in the program could, if they decided, simply walk away.[63] In the case of the Los Angeles, Clearwater, or Copenhagen facilities, such a person could lose themselves in the city in a matter of minutes.[64]

The RPF program is rigorous by any standards. It includes eight hours of physical work six days a week that begins each day immediately after the morning muster and breakfast. Most people on the RPF come with little or no skill in the tasks required to renovate and maintain buildings (painting, plumbing, carpentry, furniture making, grounds upkeep, etc.). Thus they will be taught a trade along with being involved in numerous tasks that require little training. In Los Angeles, a number of people have been taught woodworking and the professional appearance of the walls and furniture in the church's Hollywood facilities is ample evidence of the skills that they have acquired. In fact, the overall appearance of the various Scientology buildings along Hollywood Blvd. and L. Ron Hubbard Way (off Sunset Ave.) can be credited to the RPF.

This aspect of the RPF is designed to provide a change in the usual pattern of the participant's life (which has most likely been a desk job) and involve them more immediately with what in Scientology is termed the MEST universe. It is reminiscent of the work ("chop wood, carry water") that is often integrated into Zen Buddhist retreats.[65] There, work remains an integral part of the daily life of Zen monks and nuns, and visitors to a Zen monastery for retreats or short stays will be scheduled to participate in the workday that might include cooking, chopping wood, heating water, working in the fields, and cleaning.[66] Participants learn one or more skills, and RPF graduates with whom I have talked enjoyed pointing out particular things in buildings on which they had worked. By working intimately with a small cadre of fellow participants, they learned the value of teamwork.

Participants spend five hours each day with their individual partner engaged in study or auditing. Many with whom I talked had been in the Sea Org many years, but, although they had received auditing, they had never learned to audit anyone else. They reported that as a result of learning to counsel their partner, they had gained a heightened level of sensitivity to the needs of others in general and how their lives affected everyone around them.

The dominant program used by the RPF currently (others are mentioned in the Flag Orders) is called the False Purpose Rundown.[67] It is Scientology's understanding that overts and withholds are indicative of hidden evil (i.e., counter survival) purposes, solutions to problems adopted in a moment of confusion. The auditing process includes a lengthy inventory, using the immediate overts that led to the person being assigned to the RPF, of one's life, a confrontation with and clearing-up of counter-survival purposes. The goal is to see life objectively and assume responsibility for one's present condition as the result of one's own decisions. The False Purpose Rundown is repeated until the person is considered free of evil intentions on each of the eight Dynamics. The Rundown is a lengthy process, hence the year or more required to complete it.[68]

The RPF is designed to isolate the individual and provide a time and space for total concentration on self-change. The hardest hit by the program are married couples, as they have little contact while one of them is in the program. They are encouraged to write regularly, but have only infrequent face-to-face contact. Informants in LA noted that they occasionally grabbed a few words with spouses in the brief time between the lunch and afternoon activities. The program does make allowances for family needs and a number of participants noted that they had taken a week or more break in the midst of their program to attend to different particular family obligations.

As might be expected, on occasion, the problems that landed one in the RPF can and do continue to manifest in the life of a participant during their stay in the program. In that case, there is a program, the RPF's RPF, in which people may participate for short periods of time. In this case, the offense is seen as against the RPF itself and thus the person recommended to the RPF's RPF is isolated from other participants in the program. During this time, their partner still has the task of helping the person in the RPF's RPF. The person on the RPF's RPF also performs specific tasks to benefit the RPF (the group that is considered harmed, in this case), and their manual work assignment might include such tasks as improving the RPF facilities. They may return to the RPF program only by vote of the other participants in the RPF. While in the program, their communication is further restricted and must go through the RPF ethics officer.

The RPF organization is difficult to describe, as the participants essentially run it. There is an overseer (the RPF-I/C) who is not a participant whose job is to see that the program runs smoothly. The RPF-I/C, for example, handles the money that pays for the program. Each organization of the church that assigns people to the RPF also pays for his or her stay and each month contributes a stipend to cover their food, housing, and personal needs. It is also the RPF-IC's job to liaison with those in charge of the church's facilities and to decide on the particular deployment of RPF participants by prioritizing tasks to be completed.

However, the day-to-day operation of the program is left in the hands of the participants. One of the participants who is further along in the program is designated the bosun and will have several deputies to handle various practical and technical matters, including ethics. For example, one or more people with accomplished auditing skills oversee and check the auditing as it proceeds.[69]

RPF participants are organized into work teams, and such teams proceed to their assigned tasks (and partners proceed to their auditing) without immediate and constant outside supervision. The atmosphere is much more one of an adult education class in which participants are there to get what they can out of the program than that of disgruntled individuals just putting in the time. Their success will be manifest in the finished product of their labor and in their self-reported realizations about their life acquired in auditing.[70] Testimonies of new insights and understandings concerning their life may be posted for others in the RPF to read, though they have no circulation in the Sea Org or among general church members.

Because of the relative differences in the speed that individuals work through the False Purposes Rundown, different people's stay in the program varies. One year appears to be the minimum. I interviewed one person who had been in for approximately three years.

Following completion of their program, graduates generally return to the post (or a similar post) that they held when they went into the program. Graduates indicated that they received a cordial welcome back to their post. While most of the people with whom I have talked about their previous RPF experience hold anonymous staff positions, several people have gone on to hold high positions and a few are now well known in the church internationally. People whom I have met who lead different church organizations report that staff who have completed the program become their most productive staff members.

Conclusion

As an ordered community, the Sea Organization is another doorway offering scholars of New Religions some further understanding of the manner in which innovative religious organizations fit into the broader picture of the religious life of the culture. The more that we know about them, the less distinct they appear relative to larger, more familiar groups. New Religions, with a few unique innovations, tend to rediscover successful modes of operation that have been utilized by the older groups through the centuries and to learn anew some of the same insights as these older groups. In the case of Scientology, they have rediscovered a means of channeling the enthusiasm of their more committed members as well as a means of reintegrating people who had experienced problems in adjusting to the particular pattern of behavior that accompanies their initial commitment. As with marriage, even the most informed person cannot totally predict his/her reactions to the living out of long-term personal commitments.

Understanding New Religions from the perspective of ordered communities also assists us in explaining a spectrum of phenomena, especially the high level of personal commitment shared by the members of some groups. In older ordered communities, both those formed within larger religious groups and those formed as separate religious bodies, we can see processes of formation, means of building and sustaining commitments, ways of problem-solving, and the means of channeling high levels of religious enthusiasm into activity deemed useful in the world. Each of these topics have been issues for discussion in our deliberations on New Religions.

There is a large body of literature on ordered communities both historical and ethnographical as well as sociological and psychological. This study of the Sea Org suggests that such literature would prove a fruitful source of data on New Religions. It is hypothesized that the behavior of people in the first generation of, for example, new Catholic or Eastern Orthodox orders would manifest many of the characteristics of the behavior patterns we have seen in the high-demand New Religions.

NOTES

1. This chapter has grown out of more than three decades of observation of the Church of Scientology that began in 1964 in Chicago. Since 1985, when I moved to California, I have had many opportunities to visit Sea Org facilities in Hollywood, California, talk informally with Sea Org members, and gather literature on the Church and the Sea Org, all of which has been deposited in the American Religions Collection at the Davidson Library at the University of California—Santa Barbara. That collection now houses the large collection of material published by and about the Church of Scientology accumulated during the last three decades. This particular chapter has grown directly out of the book originally published in the series edited by Massimo Introvigne of the Center for the Study of New Religions, in Turin, Italy, and originally published in Italian in 1998. An English version was recently published as *The Church of Scientology* (Salt Lake City: Signature Books, 2000). This study also included structured interviews with members of the Sea Org and more than a dozen participants in the Rehabilitation Projects Force in Copenhagen, Los Angeles, and Clearwater, Florida, during the Summer and Fall of 2000. I was assisted in this study by two small grants from the J. M. Dawson Institute of Church-State Studies located at Baylor University, and the Society for the Study of Metaphysical Religion.

2. After this chapter was originally written at the beginning of 2001, I was able to visit the Sea Organization facilities at St. Hill in England following the annual meeting of the Center for Studies on New Religions in April 2001. This chapter has been slightly revised as a result of interviews made during that visit and some changes that occurred in the Church of Scientology in the first half of 2001.

3. There is an interesting body of recent literature written by Westerners who encountered the rigors of monastic life in various Eastern locations. See, for example, Anna Grimshaw, *Servants of the Buddha: Winter in a Himalayan Convent* (Cleveland, Ohio: Pilgrim Press, 1994).

4. E. Clifford Nelson, ed., *The Lutherans of North America* (Philadelphia, Pa.: Fortress Press, 1975), 197-98, 299-300; Frederick E. Weiser, *Love's Response* (Philadelphia, Pa.: Board of Publication, United Lutheran Church in America, 1962).

5. Lucy Rider Meyer, *Deaconesses: Biblical, Early Church, European, American* (Chicago, Ill.: The Message Publishing Company, 1889).

6. Newman Cryer, "Laboratory for Tomorrow's Church," *Together* 10, no. 3 (March 1966).

7. Robert Ellwood, *One Way* (Englewood Cliffs, N.J.: Prentice-Hall, 1973).

8. For accounts of such communities, see, for example, Donald E. Pitzer, ed., *America's Communal Experiments* (Chapel Hill, N.C.: University of North Carolina, 1997); Yaacov Oved, *Two Hundred Years of American Communes* (New Brunswick, N.J.: Transaction, 1993).

9. Cf. Mark Holloway, *Heavens on Earth: Utopian Communities in America, 1680-1880* (London: Turnstile Press, 1951).

10. The Holy Order of MANS was founded in the 1960s by Earl W. Blighton. See Phillip Lucas, *The Odyssey of a New Religion* (Indianapolis, Ind.: Indiana University Press, 1995).

11. See J. Gordon Melton, "The Theosophical Communities and their Ideal of Universal Brotherhood," in Pitzer, *America's Communal Experiments*, 396-418.

12. George Burke, *An Eagle's Flight: Autobiography of a Gnostic Orthodox Christian* (Geneva, Nebr.: Saint George Press, 1994).

13. "The Way Corps: Leadership Training for Proven Disciples," *The Way Magazine*, November-December 1992, 27-28.

14. Cf. Joseph E. Ross, *Krotona of Old Hollywood, 1866-1913* (Montecito, Calif.: El Montecito Oaks Press, 1989). Members of the Esoteric section may or may not live in a theosophical community, but do make a special commitment to belief in and practice of Theosophy and receive special training. Many also work for the Society and/or hold high positions in its organizational structure.

15. Given its size and importance, the literature about the Sea Org published by the church is quite small, the primary item being a recruitment piece, *Many Are Called and Few Are Chosen* (Los Angeles, Calif.: Church of Scientology International, 1999), and a brief description in *What Is Scientology?* (Los Angeles, Calif.: Bridge Publications, 1998). Some of the history may be found in a set of lectures Hubbard gave in 1969 concerning the Sea Org.

16. Any study of the Church of Scientology encounters a number of methodological problems, not the least of which are the (1) complex organizational structure and (2) the massive literature (including an increasing amount of audio-visuals) in which the church's beliefs, practices, policies, and organizational procedures are spelled out in great detail. Added to that is a variety of important documents written by former members and critics filed as briefs or depositions in court cases, and

a slowly growing number of more objective scholarly studies. At every step of the way, one must make critical decisions about relevant materials. Unlike many New Religions about which there is almost no written material, Scientology has led to the production of a veritable mountain.

17.   For the person unfamiliar with Scientology, a helpful bibliographical guide is provided online by Marco Frenschkowski, "L. Ron Hubbard and Scientology: An annotated bibliographical survey of primary and selected secondary literature," *Marburg Journal of Religion* 4, no. 1 (July 1999). It is accessed on the Internet at http://www.uni-marburg.de/fb03/religionswissenschaft/journal/mjr/frenschkowski.html.

18.   Scientologists have focused upon the parallels between their thought world and that of various Eastern religions, parallels which exist and are shared by other Esoteric groups. See *Theology & Practice of a Contemporary Religion: Scientology* (Los Angeles, Calif.: Bridge Publications, 1998). However, many have missed the essential relationship of Scientology to the Esoteric tradition as Western Esotericism has only in the late twentieth century been defined as an academic topic worthy of concentrated study. On Western Esotericism, see Antoine Faivre's two volumes: *Access to Western Esotericism* (Albany, N.Y.: State University Press of New York, 1994) and *Theosophy, Imagination, Tradition: Studies in Western Esotericism* (Albany, N.Y.: State University Press of New York, 2000).

19.   An overall picture of The Bridge, including the OT Levels, can be put together from such readily available church publications as *Take Your Next Step to Total Freedom Now* (Los Angeles, Calif.: Church of Scientology International, 1999); *Get Trained/Go OT* (Los Angeles, Calif.: Church of Scientology International, 1998); and *Freewinds: A Complete Guide to the Freewinds-Only OT Hatting Cources* (Church of Scientology Flag Ship Service Organization, 1999). OT VIII and other courses offered only aboard the *Freewinds* are also discussed in the various issues of the periodical *Freewinds*. While published primarily as advertising items for the courses and supportive activities, they also reveal the basic outlines of the cosmology and the continuity of the OT Levels with the lower stages of The Bridge.

20.   L. Ron Hubbard, *Have You Lived Before This Life?* (East Grinstead, UK: Publications World Wide, 1968).

21.   As with all religions, Scientology has experienced individuals who have joined the church, participated in its activities, and later lost their faith in its teachings. While many former members continue to appreciate their participation in the movement, some former members rejected their former beliefs. The scope of opinion, both supportive and opposed to Scientology belief and practice and which may be expressed in highly emotive language, constitute theological assessments. As such they are outside the scope of this essay that takes no position on the truth or falsity of Scientology.

22.   Today the Advanced Organization offer OT I-V, and the Flag Land Base offers Levels I-VII. OT VIII, released in 1988, is now available only aboard the ship *Freewinds*.

23. Myth here is, of course, used in its technical meaning currently employed in the field of religious studies as a narrative that expresses the values that a community of people hold.

24. The church has gone to great lengths to prevent the publication of the confidential documents, which it made the subject of a set of court cases in the mid-1990s. These cases were especially directed toward several former members who attempted to post the materials on the Internet. A small cadre of former members who had access to the documents prior to their leaving have dedicated a significant amount of time to various attempts to publish the materials in such a way that the church could not prevent access to them. The church has continually moved against such attempts (from dumping the documents into court records to entering them into various government proceedings).

25. Those who wish to understand the cosmology of Scientology should begin with L. Ron Hubbard, *The Factors* (Los Angeles, Calif.: Bridge Publications, 1990); and the guide to the OT materials, *Ron's Legacy of OT* (Los Angeles, Calif.: Golden Era Productions, n.d.). Further definition of the cosmology is found in Ron's Journal 67 (Hubbard's annual report for 1967) and in several of his tape sets such as *The Dawn of Immortality, The Time Track of Theta, Secrets of the MEST Universe,* and *A Series of Lectures on the Whole Track.* These are available in most Scientology bookstores.

26. In carrying out the Counter-Reformation, the church relied heavily on several of its ordered communities, especially the Dominicans and the newly founded Society of Jesus, popularly known as the Jesuits. Founded to evangelize the Holy Land, the Jesuits emerged just as the Reformation was expanding from its base in Saxony. The rise of Protestantism diverted the order from its original goal and gave it a new mission as the defender of the Catholic faith in Europe. Historians have given it credit for checking Protestantism's advance in many places and reclaiming some areas where Protestantism had become prominent, including Belgium, France, Poland, and Hungary.

27. To date, the story of all that occurred in the Guardian's Office has yet to be assembled. Anti-Scientology literature has discussed many of the activities, though often in their attack upon the present Church of Scientology, they are discussed in such a way as to obscure the fact that they are talking about the GO in the 1970s. The church has naturally been less than eager to highlight what is an embarrassing part of its history. Above and beyond the attempt to gather the material from the IRS and FBI files that brought the Guardian's Office down, many of the more egregious activities are now well known. They include a spectrum of covert operations such as a plan (never implemented) to have journalist Paulette Cooper (who had written an anti-Scientology book) incarcerated in some manner; break-ins at the offices of people who opposed Scientology; and various "dirty tricks" designed to embarrass or call into question the credibility of Scientology's critics. It is hoped that a full account of the Guardian's Office can be produced in the near future, but is, unfortunately, beyond the scope of this essay.

28. Cf. Clifford Longley, "Scientology Officers Expelled," *The Times* (London), 17 August 1983.

29.   During his reign, Gregory moved to end the practice of simony (buying an ecclesiastical position) in the church and to take the selection of bishops and priests out of the hands of the king and nobles in whose lands they would work. He asserted the universality of the pope's jurisdiction and established the principal of papal elections by the College of Cardinals, a change cemented by the First Lateran Council in 1123. On Gregory, see William R. Cannon, *History of Christianity in the Middle Ages* (New York: Abingdon, 1960), 160-68. Interestingly enough, Gregory relied on his allies in the several ordered communities to accomplish his changes.

30.   It should be noted that almost all of the questionable acts mentioned in anti-Scientology literature carried out by church officials and members were instigated by the Guardians Office during the 1970s.

31.   The Celebrity Centres hearken back to previous efforts by different churches to provide space for members of the entertainment industry to develop their spiritual life apart from the glare of the media and the constant reactions by other church members to them as celebrities. Hollywood Presbyterian Church has had a program not unlike the Celebrity Centres for many years. One of its prominent members, Henrietta Mears, founded the Hollywood Christian Group to reach out to the entertainment industry. See J. Edwin Orr, *The Inside Story of the Hollywood Christian Group* (Grand Rapids, Mich.: Zondervan Publishing House, 1955). Most recently the Group has evolved into "Inter-Mission." See the Hollywood Presbyterian Church site at: http://www.fpch.org/. In the last generation, of course, various religious groups have attempted to interact with celebrities, possibly the most notable example being the Fellowship of Christian Athletes and the parallel attempts by Evangelical Christians to place "chaplains" with professional sports teams. Evangelical Christians have especially valued the testimonies of celebrities. See the FCA website at http://www.gospelcom.net/fca/index.php.

32.   The issue of how many people belongs to the Church of Scientology and the basis of counting church members remains a matter of discussion between church officials, church critics, and other knowledgeable observers of the organization. The resolution of that issue is beyond the scope of this essay.

33.   In the summer of 2001, the Church of Scientology moved to replace the famous "Billion Year Contract" with a new document, the Billion Year Commitment, the word commitment being a more descriptive term of what was actually occurring to those who signed it.

34.   As part of the training it provides to new Sea Org members, the Estates Project Force is one of the organizations that oversee the maintenance and appearance of the buildings inhabited by the Sea Org and the associated grounds. In this capacity it operates with the guidance of the Base Crew Organization that has general oversight of the building and grounds.

35.   Command Intention refers to policies set by an organization at it upper echelons. Those working in a particular organization at the lower echelons may compare what they are doing by reference to the overall policies and goals (broad targets) of the organization. The concept was

more fully explained in Flag Order 3793-8 as issued on 21 September 1980.

36.   The Fourth Dynamic Engram refers to an event in the pre-historic past according to Scientology's understanding of the evolution of the human race. A disaster befell humans some 75 million years ago and its effect is universal. Removing the negative effects of this disaster is part of the ultimate work of the Sea Org.

37.   The appearance of the Sea Org facilities in Los Angeles, Copenhagen, and Clearwater are a testimony to the proficiency that members have developed over the years.

38.   A schedule of the daily schedule of the different orders is routinely printed in the introductory brochures and informational materials given to people inquiring about the order, particularly those who might consider joining it.

39.   Julia Lieblich, "The Cloistered Life," *New York Times Magazine*, 10 July 1983, 16. See also Patricia Curran, *Grace Before Meals: Food Ritual and Body Discipline in Convent Culture* (Urbana, Ill.: University of Illinois Press, 1989); and Suzanne Cita-Malard, *Religious Orders of Women* (New York: Hawthorn Books, 1964).

40.   It had been asserted in some anti-Scientology literature that the church had, at least for a time period, demanded that any female Sea Org members who became pregnant obtain an abortion. I have been unable to find any verification of that allegation. Hubbard spoke against abortion in his seminal book *Dianetics* (Los Angeles, Calif.: Bridge Publications, 1954, 1999), and officially the church has no position on the practice. Given the nature of the church, were this ever to have become a policy of the Sea Org, there would have undoubtedly been a paper trail of documents which, if they existed, have never been produced.

41.   In 1990 the age was raised from six to ten.

42.   This lack of SO organization partially accounts for the relative paucity of material on its life and work.

43.   A more concise discussion of Scientology ethics is offered in *What Is Scientology* (Los Angeles, Calif.: Bridge Publications, 1998), 285-91.

44.   L. Ron Hubbard, *Introduction to Scientology Ethics* (Los Angeles, Calif.: Bridge Publications, 1989), 12. The 446-page current edition of the *Ethics* book is considerably expanded over the earlier editions published in the 1980s (which were less than one hundred pages). A number of Hubbard's shorter writings on ethical topics have been incorporated into the text, thus making for a more thorough and systematic approach to the subject.

45.   One also sees in Hubbard's understanding of the Dynamics, at least at a cursory level, a correlation with Abraham Maslow's levels of human need beginning with bare survival and reaching at the higher levels the needs of self-actualization. Like Hubbard, Maslow also proposed understanding the self as basically good.

46.   Ibid., 15.

47.   One of the difficulties in discussing Scientology among non-Scientologists is the massive jargon introduced by Hubbard, both in his coining of new terms and his use of words in a very different manner than that commonly understood in public discourse. The discussion of

ethics is additionally complicated by the use of a set of terms that in common discourse carry immense emotional baggage (enemy, treason, suppressive person, potential trouble source) in a technical sense in Scientology literature. As much as possible, such jargon is avoided in this essay.

48.   This discussion of Hubbard's ethics has been extremely brief and points out the need for more specialized considerations of it both as a system and in its actual operation within the Sea Org, where it appears to have functioned with some degree of success for the last three decades.

49.   The operation of the Scientology justice relative to a person who has been expelled has been the source of problems for the church due to Hubbard's use of language, which has much different meanings within the church than in common parlance. Basically, Hubbard advocated excommunication as an act of abandoning the individual to the world. The excluded individual was henceforth cut off from all of the benefits available to a church member; however, the language of the ethical texts could, upon a cursory reading, imply that the church would continue to involve themselves in the lives of former members and that Hubbard was, by his statements, giving Scientologists permission to harm them in various ways. These seeming permissions became the justification for the actions of the Guardian's Office in the 1970s. Since that debacle, the church has taken pains to state clearly that such permission is neither implied nor intended.

50.   The preparation of this part of my essay consumed a considerable portion of my total research time. I reviewed the existing literature concerning the RPF, including the set of thirty documents on the RPF written by Hubbard as Flag Orders between 1974 and 1985, as well as visits to the Sea Org and RPF facilities in Los Angeles, Clearwater, and Copenhagen in the summer and fall of 2000, and St. Hill in April 2001. During these visits, structured interviews were conducted with more than fifteen present participants of the RPF program and ten former members of the RPF who are still members of the Sea Org. In addition, of course, I reviewed a number of critical accounts of their experience written by former Sea Org members.

   I also made reference to the highly critical paper by Stephen Kent, "Brainwashing in Scientology's Rehabilitation Project Force (RPF)," based upon his survey of the reports of the hostile former Sea Org members. A revised version of the Kent paper entitled "Scientology—Is It a Religion?" was published in the online *Marburg Journal of Religion* 4, no. 1 (July 1999). This essay, originally delivered at the Society for the Scientific Study of Religion in 1998, may be found on the Internet at http:// www.uni-marburg.de/fb03/religionswissenschaft/journal/mjr/ mjr_past.html. Kent's article was completed apart from any first hand inspection of the RPF and references only a limited collection of relevant church documents. He primarily relied on the reports of ex-Scientologists. In my research, I found that he had neglected important aspects of the program, mixed accounts from the RPF's formative years with more recent accounts, and confused incidents not a part of RPF with incidents that occurred within it. He also adopted the "concentration camp" image of the RPF that had been generated with the anti-Scientology literature for use against the church in court. I have found no evidence to substantiate the use of such an extreme image either from the ex-member literature or from my examination of the sites at which the RPF is and was housed.

Kent has also found little response from his fellow social scientists for his attempt to use the RPF to revive the discarded theories of "brainwashing" as applied to new religious groups. A more detailed critique of Kent's departures from standard sociological methodology can be found in Canadian sociologist Lorne L. Dawson's "Raising Lazarus: A Methodological Critique of Stephen Kent's Revival of the Brainwashing Model," in *Misunderstanding Cults*, ed. Benjamin Zablocki and Thomas Robbins (Toronto: University of Toronto Press, 2001).

51.   "On the Excommunication for Faults," in *St. Benedict's Rules for Monasteries*, trans. by Leonard Doyle (Collegeville, Minn.: Liturgical Press, 1948), 43. On the operation of the system of rules in another setting, see Dom André Louf, *The Cistercian Alternative* (New York: Gill and Macmillan, 1985).

52.   Ivor Shapiro, "Finding Words," *Saturday Night* (May 1989): 48.

53.   Bernard van Acken, *A Handbook for Sisters* (St. Louis, Mo.: B. Herder Book Co., 1931); Adam C. Ellis, *Religious Men and Women in Church Law* (Milwaukee, Wis.: Bruce Publishing Company, 1958).

54.   The *Vinaya-pitaka* is part of the Pali Canon and is used as the monastic rule for Theravada Monks. Mahayana monastic communities have their own sets of monastic rule derived from this earlier one. For example, Pai-Chang Huai-hai (749-814 C.E.) established a set of monastic rules for Ch'an (Zen) monks in China called the *Ch'ing-Kuei* or Pure Rules. A Korean revision appeared later as *Kyech'osim hagin-mun* or Admonitions to Beginning Students. See Simon Young-suck Moon, *Korean and American Monastic Practices* (Lewiston, N.Y.: Edwin Mellen Press, 1996).

55.   See Jane Bunnag, *Buddhist Monk, Buddhist Layman* (Cambridge, Mass.: Cambridge University Press, 1973), for a discussion of the operation of the Vinaya in a modern setting in Thailand. See also Sukumar Dutt, *Early Buddhist Monachism, 600 B.C.-100 B.C.* (London: Kegan Paul, Trench, Thübner & Co., 1924) for a more detailed discussion of the system of rules and punishments actually laid down in the *Vinaya*.

56.   Moon, *Korean and American Monastic Practices*, 124-25.

57.   "The Rehabilitation Project Force," Flag Order 3434RE-1, RPF Series 1 (10 June 1974): 1.

58.   This part of the process includes a signing of documents to the effect that they understand what RPF is about and want to participate.

59.   One theme that runs through anti-Scientology writings on the Sea Org and the RPF is the lack of informed assent by the participants. This appears to be an unsubstantiated charge. At the time of joining, members of the Sea Org go through an extensive orientation process as well as a screening process by the church to determine their fitness for the organization. That orientation program is conducted by the Estates Project Force, the same structure that oversees the RPF. In like measure, entrance into the RPF program includes an explanation of options open to individuals choosing participation and at several points during the entrance process they are called upon to make a conscious decision about continu-

ing. As with the acceptance of any process of recovering one's status in a religious community whose rules one has broken, the participant can at any time choose to leave the community as an alternative to continued participation. Those who participated in the program indicated that they chose to go through the program because they wished to remain a member of the Sea Org.

60.   Individuals may join the Sea Org from any point in their progress up the Bridge. Pre-Clears who join may serve in position that have little to do with auditing, and thus while they may receive personal auditing, they never learn how to be an auditor and counsel another person. Such a person in the RPF must learn how to audit before actually beginning the program.

61.   A dozen or more accounts of life in the RPF are posted on the Internet, a few being posted in multiple sites. A selection of these postings came be found in the references to Kent, "Brainwashing." In general, these accounts offer valuable research data concerning several individual's negative experience in the RPF, as far as they go. It is the case that some abuse of authority appears to have been experienced by individuals while serving in the Sea Org or participating in the RPF. The RPF includes numerous people who were in the program for "out Tech," and that activity does not automatically stop when one enters the RPF. The church's own literature and later revisions of rules for the Sea Org and RPF indicate reactions to problems. I have, however, found no evidence of any pattern of abuse as a common element of life in the RPF.

As with accounts of present and former members who remain in Scientology, these accounts, while very useful, must be received with a critical eye. The accounts of members must be understood in light of their commitments and desires to be part of the Scientology program. Those of ex-members have a few similar problems. First, many were written as depositions for court cases and are thus quite selective in their discussion of RPF. Following a pattern also seen in accounts of former monks and nuns who have left a Roman Catholic order, they have imported later appraisals of their experience into their story. Some have incorporated the popular anti-Scientology analogy of the RPF as a prison camp, and thus, for example, they speak of their withdrawal from the program as "escaping" the RPF. As members have praise for Scientology and the auditing process, former members often include harsh opinions of Scientology belief and practice, especially the auditing process. Second, one must struggle with the significant omissions in the ex-member literature. They were not designed as complete stories of their experience in the church, but merely brief accounts of their bad experiences, usually for use in a court case. For example, almost none include any discussion of the role played by the person with whom they were paired during their stay in the RPF. That being said, if critically approached, the accounts of former members remain one valuable source of information on the operation of the Sea Org and RPF.

It should also be noted that church authorities have questioned the veracity of several of the former members. People who were present and even mentioned in the accounts of Andre Tabayoyon and Dennis Erlich have suggested that they had both distorted accounts of incidents upon which they reported and on several occasions created incidents that had never occurred.

62. The present RPF facility has been used since the mid-1980s. Prior to that time, it was in two different locations in the Fort Harrison Hotel. It was first located in what is now the bakery and later in what is now the primary ethics office. In each case, it was inside the hotel in space adjacent to the parking lot. The parking lot is completely open with no doors to lock.

63. Locks on Sea Org facilities through which a departing RPF member might have to pass are such as to prevent someone from coming into the building but not prevent an egress from it. The fences around the present Sea Org residences in Clearwater were erected after an incident in which an outsider came into the complex and discharged a firearm. They were designed to keep possible troublemakers out, not prevent anyone from leaving.

64. This is confirmed in the accounts of former members such as Lynn Froyland, Hana Whitefield, and Ann Rosenblum, all of whom simply walked away from the Clearwater RPF. The only exception to this possibility concerns the RPF at the Gilman Hot Springs center. Gilman Hot Springs is a former resort that the Church of Scientology purchased and now uses as its international dissemination headquarters. Located there are a professional level recording studio, a large building for shooting dissemination and training films, and a large auditorium. It is frequently used by people from the nearby community of Hemet, California, for non-Scientology community events. It is located in the countryside, and intermittently in the 1980s and 1990s, there was a RPF unit there. That unit was housed at a location several miles away. While it would not be difficult to walk away from either Gilman or the housing site, it would be a long walk to the next town.

65. The first observation of the Zen Buddhist rule of monastic life, attributed to the honored Buddhist monk Pai-chang (720-814 CE) stated, "A day of no work is a day of no eating." Buddhist scholar D. T. Suzuki put is thusly, "Manual labor forms one of the most essential features of the Zen life . . . Life meant to the Chinese monks to be engaged in physical labour, to move their hands and feet, to handle tools, in order to accomplish some visible and tangible ends." D. T. Suzuki, *The Training of the Zen Buddhist Monk* (New York: University Books, 1959), 33.

66. See Koji Sato, *The Zen Life* (New York: Weatherhill/Tankosha, 1977), 148-49.

67. L. Ron Hubbard. "False Purpose Rundown," *Auditing Rundowns*, vol. 3 (Los Angeles, Calif.: Bridge Publications, 1991). Over the years of Hubbard's life, he periodically introduced upgraded forms of various auditing procedures, and such new upgrades have continued to be released. As these upgrades were published, they were, as appropriate, introduced into the RPF. The method of operating the "False Purpose Rundown" is spelled out in a series of Bulletins from the Hubbard Communication Office, the "False Purpose Rundown Series, 1-7" published as *HCO Bulletin*, 5-11 June 1984; rev. January 1990.

68. In spite of Steven Kent's study of Scientology over the last decade, he continually makes fundamental errors in reporting on Scientology's

beliefs and practices. For example, his lack of knowledge of Scientology is manifest in his discussion of the False Purpose Rundown. It is one of a set of what in Scientology is called "security checks," or "sec checks." Kent asserts that "sec checks" are not covered by the same rules of confidentiality as auditing. In fact, security checks, of which the "False Purpose Rundown" is an example, are one form of auditing—the kind used to deal with overts and withholds, and is covered by all of the confidentially rules governing auditing. See Kent, "Brainwashing." On the other hand, interviews made during investigations by a Scientology official or committee to determine the facts when a person has been accused of a crime such as stealing money from the church or dishonesty on the job (sometimes called HCO security checks) are not considered auditing. In situations where someone might confuse the two, an explicit denial that the session is to be considered auditing is made. Also, all auditing sessions begin by noting the formal situation that the individual has entered.

69. "RPF Organization." Flag Order 3434RE-25, 7 January 1974; revised 8 May 1997, 1-7.

70. Quite obviously, not everyone adapts to the RPF regimen, and some people choose to leave which they are free to do at any point. Some who left the program are now quite critical of it. From the perspective of an ex-member, who no longer believes in Scientology, they have reinterpreted their life from their new perspective. These accounts bare a noticeable resemblance to similar accounts of others who have left the austerities of Roman Catholic orders. For example, Patricia Curran, who studied the rituals around food in several convents, noted that some of her informants had very different views of the behavior patterns expected of them:

They described them [particular actions they were ordered to perform] as various outdated holdovers from Europe; daily reminders of belonging to the "club" of religious life; conditioning to "perfect obedience (the instantaneous execution of the superior's command). A great number argued that the effects the practices had on them provided the best indicator of purpose. They found them humiliating, particularly when kissing the feet of the sisters, asking prayers, or making the act of reparation. The penances were constant reminders of the self-concept that was held as an ideal: to consider oneself the least, lowest, and last in importance in the community. They regarded the penances also as a negation of all that was natural in favor of all that was spiritual, when these were considered to be in conflict. One named them the tools whereby each person's spirit was broken so that she could be remolded in the new corporate image.

Once one no longer sees the purpose in their ordered life, its rules and regulations take on the appearance of a straightjacket. Life in the group no longer is seen as service to the cause and a means to nurture spiritual existence, but an oppressive existence characterized by the following of a false religion and arbitrary rules. See Curran, *Grace Before Meals*.

Women in
Controversial New Religions:
Slaves, Priestesses, or Pioneers?

SUSAN J. PALMER

New religious experiments in gender roles and relations, both their excesses and their austerities, are well publicized by the media and condemned by the anticult movement. Needless to say, these stories do not contribute to the general public's tolerance of "cults." The fact that women in NRMs participate in new, religiously motivated forms of "free love," celibacy, or polygamy—and that they may renounce marriage and even their children—certainly challenges not only traditional values, but also the more contemporary ethics of feminism and individualism. Thus, new religions, branded as "cults," tend to be portrayed in anticult literature as a backlash against the twentieth century's emancipation of women.

For the researcher who adopts a social-scientific approach to studying these movements, however, a more complex and contradictory situation emerges as he/she moves from group to group. Rather than documenting women's domestic enslavement in patriarchal enclaves or degradation in charismatic leaders' sexual experiments, the researcher begins to piece together strange, hybrid patterns of marriage, family relations, and gender politics that may combine the avant-garde ideals of feminism with traditional and fundamentalist forms of patriarchy. Thus, current standards of "political correctness" are less than useful in trying to make sense of women's participation in the fictive, spiritual "families."

How and why do NRMs tend to experiment with gender and exert control over their members' sexual and familial relationships? There seem to be at least three possible theories advanced by scholars. The first is the "leader's lab" theory. This proposes the notion that founders and prophets of new religions create new social forms to compensate for or heal their own psychic wounds and that they organize their communities so that their followers "act out" the leader's unrealized desires or participate in a utopian venture.[1]

The second is the "social change" theory, which argues that NRMs are sensitive barometers responding to upheavals, tensions, and transitions occurring in the larger society. Thus, communal groups or millenarian movements with radical new gender patterns are like summer camps or workshops where more extreme versions of the experimentation already occurring in the mainstream can occur. According to this approach, the motivations that reshape women's roles and lives do not necessarily emanate from the "charismatic cult leader's" dark psyche. Rather, these alternative patterns of gender might be influenced by counter-cultural experimentation, or the ongoing redefining of gender roles that is an ongoing process in secular society.

The third theory is the well-known "commitment mechanism" model proposed by Rosabeth Moss Kanter,[2] in which she argues that in order for a commune to "succeed" (defined as surviving twenty-five years or more), members must, among other austerities, renounce exclusive personal ties to spouses and progeny in order to strengthen their ties and commitment to the whole group.

Other explanations to account for new religious innovations in gender have been proposed, but these are variations of the three outlined above, the first focusing on the leader's needs, the second on the surrounding society's influence, and the third on the new religious community's imperatives.

A Typology of Gender Identity

Sister Prudence Allen[3] first proposed a typology of philosophical views of gender within the Christian tradition, and I have adapted it to apply to NRMs. Allen's tripart typology is based on the two variables of equality and difference.

Sex Complementarity groups regard women and men as endowed with distinctly different spiritual qualities. Marriage is strongly recommended as a means of uniting two incomplete halves of the same soul, in order to form one androgynous, balanced, and harmonious being. The individual's gender and marriage relationship are often believed to continue on in the afterworld, and ritual weddings between the living and the dead (or spirits) may be practiced. Marriage and procreation are valued as a path to salvation or a means of assisting the birth of the New Age. An androgynous godhead is often a feature of sex complementarity religions.

Sex Polarity groups, in contrast, view men and women as quite distinct and separate in their spiritual paths and qualities. They often rule that the sexes should live separately, since they cannot help, and may hinder, the other's salvation. Moreover, the sexes are not equal, since one sex is perceived as purer, more intelligent, or closer to God than the other. As one might expect, it is usually men who are held to be the superior sex, but some NRMs such as the Osho International Commune, the Raelian Movement, Dianic Wiccans, and the Brahmakumaris, consider women to be superior to men. Sexual segregation may be based on notions of spiritual danger and pollution. In some NRMs, the sexes are permitted to engage in limited, tightly controlled relationships as a necessary phase in the individual's spiritual development, or to contribute children to the group.

Sex Unity groups regard the body and its gender as a superficial crust of false identity obscuring the immortal, sexless spirit. Thus, groups believing in the essential unity of the sexes might dress unisex and foster androgynous social personae, or they might play out traditional sex roles while maintaining an inner detachment from the role. In neo-shamanic groups or neo-gnostic groups, there is often the notion that letting go of one's attachment to the body and gender is a necessary prelude to realizing one's godhood or infinite power. Sex unity groups see gender as something that can be chosen or changed through elective surgery for Raelians, through reincarnation or conscious rebirth for Scientologists, and through metamorphosis into a higher androgynous immortal extraterrestrials for the "classmates" of the notorious Heaven's Gate.

Over time, the researcher will often find that these types do not maintain their "pure" and distinct forms. A longitudinal study of a group's history often reveals a gradual transition from one type to another or to a hybrid form of two types. A quite common development found in the more mature and successful NRMs in their second generation of membership and leadership is a new, strong emphasis on traditional family values and on stable marriages and secure parent-child bonds. Former *polarity* groups, for example, will encourage families to live together under the same roof, and their literature will place a new emphasis on the (hitherto ignored) quality of the marital relationship.

This has been occurring in the Hare Krishna movement since the mid-1990s, in response to the high attrition rate among the second generation of "gurukula kids" who complained of the neglect and abuse they suffered as the result of being separated at a young age from their parents and placed in the ISKCON boarding schools or *gurukulas*. In a similar vein, since the disbanding of the international commune, the Rajneeshee (or "Friends of Osho") have abandoned their policy of placing women (seen as spiritually more advanced) in charge over men and have been offering workshops on couples rather than emphasizing short-term pluralistic sexual relationships as a viable path to "superconsciousness."[4] In general, as new religions mature in age and seek recognition as authentic religions, they tend to downplay their more startling sexual ethics and conform more closely to mainstream family values.

For this reason, in the early phases of a new religious movement, one notices that a woman's role tends to be extreme, stylized, and clearly defined. A remarkable simplicity and clarity is achieved by emphasizing only *one* role (or sometimes two) at the expense of other roles. Thus, one finds women defined by the role of "lover" or "sister" or "mother" or "wife," as one moves from group to group, to the exclusion of other roles that are perceived as profane. The disciples of Rael (prophet-founder of the largest UFO religion in the world, currently numbering around 50,000) define themselves as "lovers," but reject monogamy and marriage while tending to devalue, postpone, or even proscribe motherhood. Women in Reverend Moon's church are celibate "sisters" for many years before taking on the roles of wife and mother.[5] The Children of God, now known as The Family, have evolved a more complex role in which the normally incompatible roles of lover and mother are reconciled, and, surprisingly, a high birth rate does not interfere with women's opportunity in executive and leadership roles.[6]

Ecological and Apocalyptic Feminist Spirituality

Whether a group espouses sex unity, complementarity, or polarity, a common thread running through their rhetoric is the notion of woman as world savior. New religious movements manifest a deep concern for ecological issues such as overpopulation, pollution, deforestation, species extinction, and the nuclear threat. In forging new spiritual solutions to these contemporary problems, they often stress the notion of the androgyne. The idea is, if men and women could discard their differences, if men could stop exploiting, oppressing, and objectifying women, then the balance between the human world and the natural world could be rectified. Thus, men should cultivate feminine qualities, and women should assume leadership positions.

J.Z. Knight, the most famous and successful channeler in the U.S., is a pretty, diminutive blonde who goes into a trance so that the dynamic, masculine personality of Ramtha, an ancient warrior from Lemuria, takes over her body and vocal chords and conducts "Dialogues," instructing his students in gnostic philosophy and shamanistic powers.[7] The Reverend Chris Korda of the cyber Church of Euthenasia, is a transvestite who preaches a radical message of human extinction through suicide and cannibalism in order to bring back the diminishing species and placate the spirit of Earth, who appeared to him in a dream.

Radical prophets like Mary Daly, the "post feminist" theologian, like Bhagwan Shree Rajneesh, the late Indian-eclectic spiritual master; and Rael, the Messianic founder of the largest UFO religion in the world, predict that only if men develop the "feminine" qualities of love, receptivity, and empathy, can future holocausts be avoided. Rajneesh in his book *A New Vision of Women's Liberation* (1987) presents a utopian vision of a new society based on women's sexual, social, and spiritual liberation.[8] Rael preaches the "sex unity" view of gender—that men and women possess identical abilities—and compares them to "biological robots" that are programmed to give the other pleasure. He argues that not only gender, but human life itself is an artificial construct since extraterrestrial scientists created us in their laboratories from their own DNA when the planet was colonized. Since cloning will soon be possible, biological reproduction is considered outmoded, and for Raelians the purpose of sex is for pleasure, a panacea for man's violent impulses and a way to promote world peace. Rael urges his male followers to be more like women, for the "Age of Apocalypse is the age of women!" Homosexuals are welcomed and prominent in the Raelian community, and Raelians participate in international gay marches every year.[9]

Thus, while the sexual experimentation that is ongoing in new religious movements—whether it veers towards celibacy, free love, or polygamy—certainly raises problematic social and ethical questions, both for the individuals involved and for outside relatives. It also provides a rich source of religious symbols, new and old. These become part of a metaphysical discourse in these groups in which some of the most serious dilemmas of our era are addressed, and various spiritual solutions are proposed.

NOTES

1. See Lawrence Foster, *Religion and Sexuality* (New York: Oxford University Press, 1981), on the lives and philosophies of sexuality of Mother Ann Lee and John Humphrey Noyes.
2. Rosabeth Moss Kanter, *Commitment and Community: Communes and Utopias in Sociological Perspective* (Cambridge, Mass: Harvard University Press, 1972).
3. Prudence Allen, "Two Medieval Views of Woman's Identity," in *Studies in Religion* 16 (1985): 294.
4. Susan J. Palmer, *Moon Sisters, Krishna Mothers, Rajneesh Lovers: Women's Roles in New Religions* (Syracuse, N.Y.: Syracuse University Press, 1994).
5. Eileen Barker, *The Making of a Moonie: Choice or Brainwashing?* (New York: Basil Blackwell, 1984). See also James Grace, *Sexuality and Marriage in the Unification Church* (Toronto: The Edwin Mellen Press, 1985).
6. Ruth Wangerin, "Women in the Children of God: 'Revolutionary Women' or 'Mountain Maids'?," in *Women in Search of Utopia: Mavericks and Mythmakers*, eds. Ruby Rohrlich and Elaine Hoffman (Baruch. N.Y.: Schocken Books, 1984), 130-39.
7. J.Z. Knight, *A State of Mind, My Story* (New York: Warner Books, 1987).
8. Lewis Carter, "The New Renunciates of Bhagwan Shree Rajneesh," *Journal for the Scientific Study of Religion* 26, no.2 (1987): 148-72. See also Francis Fitzgerald, "A Reporter at Large: Rajneeshpuram I," *New Yorker*, 22 September 1986.
9. Palmer, *Moon Sisters, Krishna Mothers, Rajneesh Lovers: Women's Roles in New Religions*.

Satanism and Witchcraft: Social Construction of a Melded but Mistaken Identity

JAMES T. RICHARDSON

Theoretical Introduction

Satanism and Wicca, the latter known more popularly as witchcraft, have captured the attention of the media and the general public in recent years in the United States and elsewhere. Both are usually defined in a quite negative fashion, although there are important differences in the public definitions of the two sometimes intertwined entities. Why the current interest has developed, and the direction it has developed will be the subject of this chapter, which adopts a decidedly sociological approach in its analysis.

Before proceeding with details about Satanism and Wicca, some preliminary attention needs to be given to the theoretical perspective employed in this essay. First, one of the basic maxims of sociology, comes from W.I. Thomas: "If people define something as real, it is real in its consequences." This sociological truth seems to have special application when discussing Wicca and Satanism, both of which involve small numbers of people doing things that are usually quite harmless to themselves and others. However, the perceptions of these two entities are quite to the contrary, and both are defined as major social problems by many in the U.S. and elsewhere. Often they are quite mistakenly defined as the same social problem. This is to say that many people do not distinguish between Satanism and Wicca, although they are different in very important ways.

A social problem is something that is socially constructed, and, importantly, the construction may have little to do with objective reality or truth. The social construction is an orientation toward putative conditions, characteristics, or activities that are defined by many people in a society as inherently immoral or unjust. The emphasis here is on the putative nature of claims being made about how things are, and how they should be.[1] Thus, Nazis defined Jews as racially inferior, and Native Americans were defined as "Red Devils" by American

settlers, with both definitions leading to huge historical tragedies. Another such example of obvious relevance to this chapter is the "Burning Times," when at least a hundred thousand
and perhaps more of so-called witches were put to death in
Europe based on claims that they were a threat to Christian
society.

Social problems require promotion, and often in the development of a social problem, including Satanism and Wicca,
one can discern the actions of moral entrepreneurs who are
interested in making sure a certain definition of a situation is
accepted.[2] Scholars of deviant behavior sometimes refer to
such people as claims makers, meaning that they make claims
about certain people or groups that, if true, would place those
persons or groups beyond the pale of acceptable society.[3]
They would be outcasts, and even perhaps defined as threats
to normal society that should be dealt with harshly in order to
protect society. Moral entrepreneurs are in the business of defining evil, and helping ferret it out, for the good of the moral
order of a society.

When claims makers are especially successful, a moral
panic may develop in a society.[4] The key element of a moral
panic is that the perceived danger is considerably out of proportion to the real threat posed by whatever is of concern at
the moment. A moral panic occurs when many or all seg-
ments of a society become involved in defining something as
a social problem of major proportions, when in fact there is
little real danger. Thus we see an inordinate amount of attention paid to the putative danger in the mass media by political
figures, and in everyday conversation among the general population. The fear engendered by the particular socially constructed problem becomes widespread. Virtually everyone
accepts the definition of reality being promoted and is willing
to take action (or to allow action to be taken) based on that
hegemonic definition.

When moral entrepreneurs attempt to promote a new
moral panic in a society, it is useful to pose a few questions
about such efforts. First, who is making the claims? What
kinds of people are saying things about the reputed danger,
and what do they have in common? Second, what do the
claims makers have to gain if their claims are accepted and
whose interests are served by the claims being accepted?
Third, what exactly is the content of these specific assertions,
and what are the potential consequences if they are accepted
as true by others? These questions will guide our analysis of

the rise of Satanism and its perceived relationship to Wicca and witchcraft.

Something akin to a moral panic has existed in recent years concerning both Satanism and Wicca in the U.S. and some other western societies. Many media articles have dealt with the dangers of Satanism and witchcraft, and some key opinion leaders in society have spoken about the dangers. The general public has accepted many of the claims being made, as well as efforts by government officials and others to control these dangers. Discerning the objective facts of these developments will be the focus of the rest of this chapter. First, Satanism will be examined, using the social constructionist theory outlined above.

Historical and Structural Factors Contributing to the "Satanism Scare"

Satanism has become a major concern of many in Western societies in recent decades. Explaining why this has occurred poses a challenge for social scientists, but several scholars have made some important efforts.[5] Adopting a sociological and structural approach using the social constructionist perspective is a fruitful way to address the problem. What such an analysis reveals is that the Satanism scare movement is actually easily explained as the confluence of several related movements within a certain time, space, and cultural location.

First, it is an objective fact that some examples of Satanism do exist in contemporary society. Some small "Satanic churches" exist, especially within the U.S. Anton LaVey established the Church of Satan in San Francisco decades ago, and it received an inordinate amount of media attention from its very inception. Spin-off groups from LaVey's initial effort have also gained media attention. At least one of the "new religions," The Process, studied in detail by William Bainbridge, involved the figure of Satan, albeit a vastly redefined one from that of the LaVey tradition.[6] Media coverage of these Satan-related groups, particularly LaVey's, augmented by the involvement of some well known people such as movie stars in his group, made most people in the U.S. aware that Satanic churches existed. The inordinate amount of attention given to these groups may have made people think they were more prevalent and widespread than was actually the case.

Also, there are other activities, usually involving young people, which can be considered manifestations of Satanism.

Bill Ellis calls this behavior "ostensive traditions" in his discussion of "legend trips" of adolescents, as they find ways both to upset and garner the attention of adults.[7] Acting out rituals presumed to be a part of the Satanic tradition has become a favored way for some youth to define their own identities. Usually such activities are a passing phase of behavior, but occasionally some young people get so caught up in the legend trips that tragedy results, with people being injured or even killed, supposedly in the name of Satan. When such rare events do occur, they receive huge amounts of media attention, of course, contributing to the perception that there are dangerous Satanists everywhere. The media also contribute to the odds that other youth will notice the furor and engage in such ostensive behavior themselves.[8]

A second major factor is the rise of Christian fundamentalism as a social force in the U.S.[9] This development has had many consequences, including a major contribution to the rise of the Satanism scare. The reason for this effect is that Christian fundamentalists typically believe in, and accept the reality of, Satan and Satanism. Wherever Christian fundamentalists are taken seriously, or accepted as part of the social fabric, their beliefs about Satan are a part of the cultural baggage that they bring with them into the social arena. Thus, Satan and his alleged activities and goals may be treated as "real" (and are thus real in their consequences) by people who usually would not hold such personal beliefs.

A third element is the development of a "child saver" movement in American society and elsewhere in recent decades.[10] This is the term applied by social scientists to the broad movement concerned about the welfare of children, something that is a relatively new development in Western society. This movement has spawned new laws concerning child abuse and large governmental bureaucracies charged with enforcing the new laws in order to protect children, even if this involves the assertion of hitherto unheard of rights of ownership of said children by the state.

The child saver movement is based on the premise that there are great dangers to children afoot in the land, and that children are to be protected, at nearly any cost. One of those dangers concerns Satanism, which, according to some, is rampant in day care centers in the U.S. and elsewhere, and helps "explain" why staff members of child care centers (most of whom are female) might engage in certain kinds of ritual abuse involving their charges. Supposedly, Satanism even motivates some families to abuse their children in ways involving Satanic rituals, a claim that has been especially prevalent in some areas of the United Kingdom, as Phillip Jenkins has described, but also in the U.S. as well.[11]

When allegations of Satanic abuse arise, that is, when claims are made that Satanists are operating in day care centers or families, governmental agencies developed to protect children spring into action, sometimes without carefully checking the veracity of such claims or the motives of those making the claims.[12] Thus, we may see quite secular governmental bureaucrats acting as if the claims of anti-Satanists are true, even if they do not themselves accept the reality of Satan. And others, such as media representatives, may report on such activities as if they are true, when in fact the reporting is being done quite cynically for opportunistic reasons.

A fourth element contributing to the rise of the Satanism scare is what is called the "occult survivor" or "repressed memory" movement, which is supposedly historically related to the child saver movement, but also brings in a new major element, the involvement of the psychotherapeutic profession.[13] The occult survivor phenomenon occurs when adult women recall, usually while undergoing therapy from "believing" psychiatrists or psychologists, that they were sexually abused years ago as children. The alleged perpetrator is usually the father, but sometimes the mother or other relatives are also implicated in the claims being made by the "survivor."

What makes this phenomenon relevant to the concerns of the analysis is that the "eyewitness" claims of abuse from years before often involve alleged participation in some sort of ritual abuse associated with Satanism. Sometimes the entire family is supposedly involved in a Satanic cult that uses its children in ritual activities. The initial abuse experienced by the survivor was so horrible that memories of these events were apparently repressed, only to be dredged up years later under the helpful assistance of a psychiatrist who understands that such things do occur. Such claims are important because they supposedly demonstrate that child sex abuse associated with Satanism has been occurring for decades. Also, such claims demonstrate to those accepting them that the Satanism problem is more widespread than might have otherwise been thought, and that it affects some apparently normal families or even groups of families in society.

A fifth element germane to understanding the Satanism scare is the rise of the so-called Anti-Cult Movement (ACM), a movement that has become a major social force within the U.S. and in some other Western societies over the past three decades or so.[14] The ACM has garnered considerable attention from scholars attempting to understand how new religious movements (NRMs) have come to be defined as a major social problem within American society and elsewhere.

Some scholars have noted that the ACM predated the rise of anti-Satanism concerns, but that the ACM was quick to incorporate that concern and take advantage of the interest being shown by the media and the general public in alleged activities of Satanists. Consequently, Satanism was lumped by the ACM with other quite different groups and movements such as the Hare Krishna, the Unification Church, Scientology, the Jesus People, and many other new religious phenomena defined as dangerous by the ACM. Thus Satanism was defined as a special and virulent form of the "cult menace" in society, a development that may appear more opportunistic than real, but one that has been effective with both the general public and policymakers.[15]

A sixth related development that has contributed to the rise of concern about Satanism is the rise of feminism as a powerful social movement.[16] The contribution is not as direct as that of some other movements that have been discussed, but it is nonetheless the case that feminism has played a role in fomenting concern over Satanism, as some scholars have noted. This is mainly the result of the following line of reasoning: most of the children allegedly abused in day care centers, and most of the people making claims about being sexually abused in their childhood are female. The impetus to "believe the children" (and its corollary "believe the adult survivors") who claim sexual abuse has been promoted by some (but not all) feminists, who claim that rejecting such assertions does not take seriously the women's claims, a dismissal which only exacerbates their feelings of abuse or exploitation.

So, we have the seemingly strange situation of quite secular feminists sometimes appearing to take seriously the claims being made by anti-Satanists with whom they appear to have very little else in common. Jenkins tells of a feminist scholar writing in a Marxist journal who treats quite seriously objective claims by Christian fundamentalists about the actions of Satanists in child care centers.[17] Such occurrences are illustrative of the many forces and movements that flow together to help form the Satanism scare.

A seventh development to take into account is related to several of the ones mentioned above. I refer to the spread of anti-satanism seminars for staff in agencies established to protect children, for law enforcement personnel, and for others in the "helping professions."[18] Many professional and semi-professional staff in such occupations are required to earn continuing education credits to maintain their professional credentials. A popular way to gain such credits is to sign up for seminars offered by self-claimed experts on the Satanism threat; such offerings have been a regular part of continuing education efforts for years in the U.S. and elsewhere. These seminars thus reinforce the claims of those who say that Satanists are everywhere and gaining strength and numbers, that they are taking over the child care industry, that sex abuse was prevalent years ago in many families where children were allegedly abused by their parents in Satanic rituals, or that Satanic cults are like other cults, except maybe a little worse than most since they allegedly sacrifice and sexually abuse small children. The seminars offer a direct aura of legitimacy to those who would make such claims about Satanism. Thus they contribute to the rise of the Satanism scare.

Technology of communication and the organization of the mass media have also played a role in the spread of the Satanism scare. There has been an understandable tendency for the mass media to focus on Satanism in its normal operation involving print media and traditional television programming, because of the widespread interest in the topic within American culture and society.[19] However, the development of satellite and cable technology to transmit television more easily has exacerbated this tendency because of the increased demand for inexpensive programming to fill hours of newly-acquired airtime. The talk show motif has become prevalent in both television and radio, which means that on any given day dozens if not hundreds of different talk show hosts are looking for things to talk about that will interest potential viewers and listeners. Cults, particularly Satanic cults, meet the needs of this new media market. Self-proclaimed experts on Satanism can gain an audience on national radio or TV just by being willing to make claims about Satanism, the more colorful and audacious the better.[20]

This point was driven home to many in the media industry when Geraldo Rivera produced a television documentary on Satanism in 1988. His show, "Satanism in America," was the most watched documentary in American history with its initial showing, and was subsequently shown in a number of other countries as well. This one program demonstrated that the topic of Satanism was a powerful way to attract viewers, and many other talk show hosts soon copied it.

The outcome of these many movements and developments has been the social construction of a moral panic that scholars have dubbed the "Satanism Scare," or the "Satanic Panic." Many opinion leaders and members of the general public have accepted as objective fact some or all of the claims made about the pervasiveness of Satanic activities in society, and they have acted (or allowed others to act) accordingly. This moral panic has also been spread around the globe by anti-satanist "missionaries" from the U.S. carrying their message and materials to other countries whose traditionally Christian cultures have made it receptive to such ideas. Thus the "Satanism scare" has become globalized.[21]

Satanism and Wicca Linked

Much to the chagrin of practitioners of Wicca, there has been confusion in the minds of many about their religion, which is often linked with Satanism, although there are important differences between the two. Some in the media treat Wicca and Satanism differently, primarily (and ironically) because of the ties Wicca has with the feminist movement; the positive opinion of some in the media regarding feminism occasionally helps produce more objective coverage.[22]

Wicca has no organizational ties with the Church of Satan, and its practitioners claim historical ties with ancient Paganism, not with Christianity. Thus it is a perversion of history to claim that Wicca involves a focus on Satan, and that Wiccan rituals are Satanic. But, this claim is made and has been made for centuries, first as part of the conflict between early Christianity and Paganism, a conflict eventually won by Christianity. Later in the history of the West, claims linking Satan and allegations of witchcraft were made, to devastating effect. Hundreds of thousands of people, mostly women, were killed in horrible ways during the "Burning Times" that took place from the fifteenth through the seventeenth centuries in Europe, and also in a limited way in colonial America (recall the Salem witch trials). Today in the U.S. and elsewhere where Wicca groups have developed, opponents of Wicca claim ties between Satanism and Wicca, and many seem to accept such claims, resulting in a melding of the identities of Satanism and Wicca, much to the disadvantage of Wicca.

Wicca in Contemporary Society

Wicca exists as a separate religious or spiritual phenomenon in contemporary society. It gained new impetus in the 1950s in England with the work of Gerald Gardner, an English civil servant who claimed to have been initiated into the craft in the 1930s by an old woman named Dorothy.[23] Wicca practitioners such as Starhawk claim ties with ancient Paganism, although some dispute such claims and assert that Wicca is something new, that is, a product of contemporary ideas and movements.[24] The major themes within Wiccan beliefs include: (1) a rejection of traditional religion and dominant cultural values, and a willingness to engage in experimentation with other beliefs and values; (2) a focus on nature and ecological concerns; and (3) an acceptance of the values of feminism, including the rejection of the patriarchy of the major religions and dominant cultures. Note that Satan does not play a part in contemporary Wiccan beliefs, except for being rejected as part of the cultural baggage of Christianity. Thus the melding of Satanism with Wicca and witchcraft is especially problematic for Wiccans.

Some claim that between 200,000 and 300,000 people practice Wicca in the U.S., although other scholars dispute that claim.[25] Wiccan groups also exist in other parts of the world as well. Following the lead of Margot Adler's classic modern treatment of witchcraft in the U.S., Helen Berger and others have written about the recent development of Wicca within the U.S., offering insight into how the groups operate, what types of people participate in them, and how children of Wiccans are dealt with in such groups.[26] Lynn Hume writes of the development of Wicca in Australia, and the problems brought on by the fact that most Wiccan rituals were developed in the Northern Hemisphere, and were attuned to the seasons of that region, making them poorly suited for observance "down under."[27]

Wicca is accepted within the U.S. as a legally valid religion, having won some key court cases establishing that right. Thus Wiccan religious leaders can marry people, serve as chaplains in federal facilities, rent public facilities, buy insurance for their property and activities, and do other things any other religious group can do. Also, contributions to Wiccan

groups are tax deductible (if the specific group has applied for
and received tax exempt status). A large Wiccan group operates at Fort Hood, Texas, and does so openly and legally,
given the current legal status of Wicca in the U.S.[28]

Describing the legal status and social acceptance of Wicca
is not to say, of course, that the lot of a Wiccan group in the
U.S. is an easy one. Wiccans are not well accepted by many in
American society, in large part because of the ties that some
would claim between Wicca and Satanism.

Satanic groups and Wiccans have vastly different beliefs or
ideology, with Wicca stressing the importance of nature and
human beings being a part of nature. Also, Wiccan groups focus on the female, rejecting patriarchy in any form (including
the usually male-like figure of Satan), and being greatly influenced by the values and aims of feminism. But, in the minds
of many, Wicca and Satanism are linked, and have been since
the Middle Ages and the Burning Times. Witches have been
defined as agents of Satan, bent on destroying Christianity
and its values. This hegemonic definition justified doing terri-
ble things to those who fell within the ambit of the Catholic
Church in its crusade to establish its dominance and repress
Paganism in any form.[29]

Some of the several contributing factors to the rise of the
Satanism scare also can be applied to the growing concern in
some quarters about Wicca and witchcraft. Some Wicca
groups have attracted considerable media attention in recent
years. When it is revealed that a Wiccan group is operating in
a local area, this nearly always leads to publicity, usually, but
not always, of a negative kind.[30] Christian fundamentalists
also reject witchcraft as antithetical to Christianity. Their
claims have contributed greatly to the linking of Satanism and
witchcraft in the popular perception. Some concern about
Wicca comes from the child saver movement, especially because children are now being raised as a part of Wiccan
groups, as noted by Helen Berger. The Anti-Cult Movement
also contributes to anti-Wiccan sentiment by lumping Wicca
with other "cults" and over-generalizing about their activities
in a quite negative fashion, as is its usual practice. The anti-
Satan seminars contribute, as well, when those operating
them for professionals do not distinguish between Wicca and
Satanism. Talk show hosts on television and radio often are
not careful in making important distinctions, and indeed may
quite cynically link the two just for added interest among potential audiences. Thus, many of the same factors that contrib-

uted to the Satanism scare have also played a role in linking Satanism and witchcraft.

Conclusion

This analysis has presented a sociological explanation for the rise of concern about Satanism in the U.S. and elsewhere. A number of factors have contributed to the moral panic concerning Satanism, mainly because a proclivity exists to accept such claims within Western culture, and this tendency has been exacerbated in recent times by the several movements and developments described above. Thus, some areas of American society have major concerns about Satanism, leading to consequences beyond what would appear to be warranted by the actual facts of Satanism in contemporary society. Wicca and witchcraft, a growing "new religion" in its own right, has been linked to Satanism by some of the same movements and developments, although the linkage has not always been complete. However, the forced melding of the identities of these two movements has led to difficulties, especially for Wiccan groups. Regrettably, it would seem to be the case that this mistaken melding of identities, and the consequent difficulties, will continue for the foreseeable future.

NOTES

1. See Malcolm Spector and John I. Kituse, *Constructing Social Problems* (New York: Aldine de Gruyter, 1987), Joseph Schneider, "Social Problems Theory," *Annual Review of Sociology* 11 (1985): 209-29. See Joel Best, ed., *Images of Issues: Typifying Contemporary Social Problems* (New York: Aldine de Gruyter, 1989), for more detailed explications of social constructionism, and Peter Conrad and Joseph Schneider, *Deviance and Medicalization* (St. Louis, Mo.: Mosby, 1980), for some examples of specific problems that have been constructed in Western societies.
2. The term moral entrepreneur was added to the sociological lexicon by Howard Becker in his famous study of marijuana smoking. See Howard Becker, *Outsiders: Studies in the Sociology of Deviance* (New York: Free Press, 1963).
3. See Spector and Kituse, *Constructing Social Problems*, for delineation of the term claims making.
4. Cohen defines a moral panic as a situation, "in which a minor social problem expresses and preempts a deeper related one." See Stanley Cohen, *Folk Devils and Moral Panics* (London: Granada, 1972). For a more contemporary use of the term, see Philip Jenkins, *Intimate Enemies: Moral Panic in Britain* (Hawthorn, N.Y.: Aldine de Gruyter, 1993); and Philip

Jenkins, *Moral Panic: Changing Concepts of the Child Molester in Modern America* (New Haven, Conn.: Yale University Press, 1998).

5. See James Richardson, Joel Best, and David Bromley, *The Satanism Scare* (New York: Aldine de Gruyter, 1991) for a collection of research studies from various disciplinary perspectives, as well as Jeffrey Victor, *Satanic Panic: The Creation of a Contemporary Legend* (Chicago, Ill.: Open Court, 1993); also see Jenkins, *Intimate Enemies*. See an informative book by a law enforcement person, Robert Hicks, *In Pursuit of Satan: The Police and the Occult* (Buffalo, N.Y.: Prometheus Books, 1991).

6. William Bainbridge, *Satan's Power: A Deviant Psychotherapy Cult* (Berkeley, Calif.: University of California Press, 1978). Also see William Bainbridge, "Social Construction from Within: Satan's Process," in Richardson, Best, and Bromley, *The Satanism Scare*, 297-310.

7. Bill Ellis, "Legend Trips and Satanism: Adolescents Ostensive Traditions as 'Cult' Activity," in Richardson, Best, and Bromley, *The Satanism Scare*, 279-96.

8. Note that other youthful activities sometimes get labeled as Satanic. See David Martin and Gary Fine, "Satanic Cults, Satanic Play: Is 'Dungeons & Dragons' a Breeding Ground for the Devil?" in Richardson, Best, and Bromley, *The Satanism Scare*, 107-25. Also see James Richardson, "Satanism in the Courts: From Murder to Heavy Metal," in Richardson, Best, and Bromley, *The Satanism Scare*, 205-20, which discusses Satanist accusations associated with heavy metal music.

9. See David Bromley and Anson Shupe, *The New Christian Politics* (Macon, Ga.: Mercer University Press, 1984), and Erling Jorstad, *Holding Fast/ Pressing on: Religion in American in the 1980s* (New York: Praeger, 1990) for some descriptions of the rise of Christian fundamentalism in America.

10. The best source for the development of the child saver movement is Joel Best, *Threatened Children* (Chicago, Ill.: University of Chicago Press, 1990); also see his "Endangered Children and Antisatanist Rhetoric," in Richardson, Best, and Bromley, *The Satanism Scare*, 95-106.

11. See Jenkins, *Intimate Enemies*.

12. See Debbie Nathan, "Satanism and Child Molestation: Constructing the Ritual Abuse Scare," in Richardson, Best, and Bromley, *The Satanism Scare*, 75-94.

13. See Philip Jenkins and Daniel Maier-Katlin, "Occult Survivors: The Making of a Myth," in Richardson, Best, and Bromley, *The Satanism Scare*, 127-44, and Sherrill Mulhern, "Satanism and Psychotherapy: A Rumor in Search of an Inquisition," in Richardson, Best, and Bromley, *The Satanism Scare*, 145-74.

14. See Anson Shupe and David Bromley, *The New Vigilantes* (Beverly Hills, Calif.: Sage, 1980); Anson Shupe and David Bromley, eds., *Anti-Cult Movements in Cross Cultural Perspectives* (New York: Garland, 1994); and Marat S. Shterin and James T. Richardson, "Effects of the Western Anti-Cult Movement on Development of Laws Concerning Religion in Post-Communist Russia," *Journal of Church and State* 42 (Spring 2000): 247-71.

15. See Michael Langone and Linda Blood, *Satanism and Occult-related Violence* (Weston, Mass.: American Family Foundation, 1990).

16. See Jenkins, *Intimate Enemies*.

17. Ibid., 174-76.

18. I have attended such seminars in the U.S. and Australia, and reviewed materials from those in other countries such as New Zealand and the U.K. Jenkins's *Intimate Enemies* talks about them in Britain among social workers, and law enforcement involvement is described in Ben Crouch and Kelly Damphouse, "Law Enforcement and the Satanic Crime Connection: A Survey of 'Cult Cops'," in Richardson, Best and Bromley, *The Satanism Scare*, 191-204. Also, see Mulhern, "Satanism and Psychotherapy," for the role played by such seminars in "converting" therapists to accept the reality of repressed memories of ritual abuse.

19. See chapters by Phillips Stevens, Jeffrey Burton Russell, and David Bromley in Richardson, Best, and Bromley, *The Satanism Scare*, that analyze the historical and cultural import of Satan and Satanism in Western societies.

20. See especially Laurel Rowe and Grey Cavender, "Cauldrons Bubble, Satan's Trouble: But Witches are Okay: Media Constructions of Satanism and Witchcraft," in Richardson, Best, and Bromley, *The Satanism Scare*, 263-78. Also see other chapters in the Richardson, Best, and Bromley book (n. 5), many of which discuss the role played by media coverage in spreading concern about Satanism.

21. See James Richardson, "The Satanism Scare: Social Construction of an International Social Problem, *Australian Journal of Social Issues* 32 (1997): 61-85. Also see Jenkins, *Intimate Enemies*, and Jean La Fontaine, "The Extent and Nature of Organized Ritual Abuse: A Report to the Department of Health," (London: HMSO, 1994), on the situation in Britain; and Jenny Barnett and Michael Hill, "When the Devil Came to Christchurch," *Australian Religious Studies Review* 6 (1994): 25-30, which discusses ritual abuse claims in New Zealand, and the work of U.S. "missionaries" in spreading the concern about Satanism there.

22. See Rowe and Cavender, "Cauldrom Bubbles," for a fascinating discussion of this difference in treatment by some, but not all mass media.

23. This claim is disputed by some, but whether Gardner developed his ideas out of whole clothe or received them as he claimed, his influence has been felt in modern witchcraft on both sides of the Atlantic and beyond. See Margot Adler, *Drawing Down the Moon* (Boston, Mass.: Beacon Press, 1986); and Helen Berger, *A Community of Witches: Contemporary Neo-Paganism and Witchcraft in the United States* (Columbia, S.C.: University of South Carolina Press, 1999) for discussions of these early beginnings of Wicca in the U.S.

24. See Starhawk, *The Spiral Dance: A Rebirth of the Ancient Religion of the Great Goddess* (New York: Harper & Row, 1979) for the most influential statement of ancient origins. But also see Charlotte Allen, "The Scholars and the Goddess," *Atlantic Monthly*, January 2001, disputing these old ties.

25. See Berger, *A Community of Witches*, 9, who analyzes the methodology of estimates that have been made and suggests that a more accurate figure might be 150,000 to 200,000.

26. Adler, *Drawing Down on the Moon*; and Berger, *A Community of Witches*, 23.

27. Lynne Hume, "Exporting Nature Religions: Problems in Praxis Down Under," *Nova Religio* 2 (1999): 287-98.

28. This activity on military bases by Wiccan groups, which is growing, has been controversial, in part because they are so different from normal religions, but also because part of the belief system of Wiccan groups involves pacifism. Thus, some have claimed that Wiccans cannot make good soldiers who will follow orders, including orders to "shoot to kill."

29. There are those who take a more cynical view of the witch craze and talk about the use of this definition by the Church to accrue the property of those accused of witchcraft, and to gain political advantage using accusations and the threat of accusations as a social weapon of great power.

30. Recall the study by Rowe and Cavender, "Cauldrons Bubble," that shows some important differences between media coverage of Wicca and Satanism.

A Critical Analysis of Evidentiary and Procedural Rulings in Branch Davidian Civil Case[1]

STUART A. WRIGHT

On 14 July 2000, a jury in the Branch Davidian wrongful death lawsuit returned a verdict finding no fault with federal agents in the disastrous siege and standoff at Mt. Carmel in 1993. The federal actions precipitated the deaths of eighty sect members. Government attorneys praised the verdict, saying it was a vindication of federal law enforcement. Lead co-counsel for the government, U.S. Attorney Michael Bradford, boasted after the verdict: "What this shows is that the responsibility for the tragedy that happened at Waco is with David Koresh and the Branch Davidians." He added, "It's time to put this to rest and move on." But few scholars and observers think this verdict will put the Waco incident to rest. There are far too many lingering and disturbing questions about the civil trial.

The most troubling aspect of the trial is the discretionary authority exercised by Judge Walter Smith in limiting evidence and crafting procedural rulings that handcuffed plaintiffs' attorneys. Indeed, Davidian attorneys waged an unsuccessful battle to have Judge Smith removed from the case for over a year prior to the trial. Based on Smith's rulings in the earlier criminal trial of Davidians in 1994, the plaintiffs believed they could not receive a fair hearing in Judge Smith's court. Perhaps in response to the expressed concern, Smith empanelled an "advisory" jury in Waco, even though federal civil trials do not require a jury and the court is not bound by its verdict. Some observers suggested that by appointing an advisory jury, Smith was attempting to deflect criticism of bias arising from problems surrounding the earlier criminal trial. These concerns and criticisms appear to have some validity.

The criminal trial of eleven Branch Davidians in San Antonio in 1994 was fraught with controversy. Judge Smith took the unusual step of issuing to the initial jury pool an 80-

item questionnaire to screen potential jurors.[2] Some of the
questions appeared to be entirely inappropriate.[3] For example, there were ten items on religion, including questions on
frequency of church attendance, degree of religiosity, extent of
organizational participation, and formal religious training.
One item even asked if the respondent had ever belonged to a
"nontraditional" religious group. There were also eleven
items on gun ownership. Here, one item asked if the respondent had ever belonged to the National Rifle Association, and
another asked if the respondent had ever attended a gun
show. The questionnaire was used to eliminate 216 jurors,
leaving the attorneys with a group of 84 screened individuals
from which to choose. Smith also suppressed efforts by defense attorneys to introduce self-defense evidence. Despite
these obstacles, the jury acquitted all defendants of the more
serious charges of murder and conspiracy to murder. Five defendants were convicted on the lesser charge of aiding and
abetting manslaughter of a federal officer. Confounded by
Judge Smith's instructions, however, the jury also convicted
on a weapons count, assuming it was tied to the manslaughter
charge. Technically, the charge of carrying a firearm during
the course of a crime was tied only to the murder charge.
Faced with the inconsistent verdict, the judge set aside the
verdict, but then, at the behest of the prosecutors, changed his
mind and reinstated the convictions. Prosecutors successfully
argued that perhaps the jury was split, some wanting a murder conviction and some wanting an acquittal. Smith failed to
ask the jurors their intent (jurors later filed sworn statements
to the effect that the confusion arose from the instructions, not
a split decision). The judge ruled that the weapons used in the
commission of a crime were machine guns, and he sentenced
the five Davidians to forty years each, the maximum allowed
by federal sentencing guidelines. On appeal, the Texas Supreme Court unanimously reversed Smith on the sentence en-
hancements, finding that the district court improperly
decided during sentencing that the firearms used were machine guns. According to the court's ruling, the type of firearm used should have been determined by presentation of
evidence during the trial.

Another indication of Smith's prejudice appears in the
sentence findings and opinion in the criminal trial. Incredibly,
Smith referred to the deaths of the federal agents as "homi-
cide," and boldly asserted that the Davidians "engaged in a
conspiracy to cause the deaths of federal agents."[4] Smith's

written opinion blatantly ignored the verdict, riding rough-shod over the findings of the jury that acquitted all the defendants of murder and conspiracy to murder.

Given the history of Smith's rulings in the criminal case, it was hardly surprising that Davidian attorneys sought to have the judge removed from the civil proceeding. Actually, up until August 1999, it seemed likely that the civil lawsuit would be dismissed altogether. But things changed dramatically in early August when it was revealed that the FBI had lied about discharging pyrotechnic devices in the CS gas assault on the Davidian settlement that might have caused the conflagration. After six years of official denials about using pyrotechnic or "military" rounds, investigators for plaintiffs' attorneys discovered the devices in the evidence storage room in Austin. It was later learned that the FBI also failed to turn over audiotapes and written documentation that would have revealed the use of pyrotechnic rounds. The mishandling or concealment of evidence and the false statements made by government officials suggested a cover-up. Pressured by government missteps and the new evidence, Judge Smith was compelled to allow the Davidian lawsuit to go forward.

This promising development, however, did not mean that Davidian survivors and their kin would get a fair trial. As an observer in the courtroom during the civil trial and one who has studied the Branch Davidian tragedy for seven years,[5] I want to address some of the problems surrounding the proceedings that I believe contributed to a flawed verdict. Specifically, I contend that the federal trial in Waco failed to deliver a just verdict because evidentiary and procedural rulings handicapped the plaintiffs and prevented the jury from hearing all the evidence.

Key Evidentiary and Procedural Rulings

To begin with, Judge Smith granted a "discretionary function" exemption to federal officials granting them immunity for "bad judgments" in actions taken against the Branch Davidians. The intent of the discretionary function exemption is to protect law enforcement agents from being second-guessed in situations requiring urgent decision-making in the course of their duties. But how this exemption is applied is left to the judgment of the court and can be interpreted broadly or narrowly. Judge Smith chose the broad interpretation.

A similar claim, of course, was made by the government in the Randy Weaver case when FBI sniper Lon Horiuchi shot and killed Weaver's wife, Vicky, during a standoff which occurred less than six months before the Waco incident.[6] Horiuchi was part of the FBI's Hostage Rescue Team (HRT), the same unit that was in charge of the standoff at Waco. Mrs. Weaver was standing at the door of her cabin holding her infant child when the .308 caliber bullet pierced her neck, severed her carotid artery, then exited, ripping away most of the left side of her jaw and half of her face. The debris from the gunshot showered her children with blood and bits of skull. Prosecutors in Boundary County, Idaho filed murder charges against Horiuchi. But officials from the Justice Department filed a motion claiming that Horiuchi had immunity from prosecution based on the discretionary function exemption. The trial court agreed and in a 2-1 decision, the U.S. 9th Circuit Court of Appeals upheld the lower court's ruling. In a sharply worded dissenting opinion, however, Judge Alex Kozinski criticized the sniper's action as unprovoked and indefensible, declaring that the court's opinion "waters down the constitutional standard for the use of deadly force by giving offenders a license to kill even when there is no immediate threat to human life."[7]

In the Waco case, a Justice Department official confirmed that the government enjoyed a distinct advantage as a result of this ruling before the case ever went to trial. In an Associated Press wire service report on 15 July, Department of Justice spokesman Thom Mrozek was quoted as saying, "Even before we got to trial, the case was whittled down significantly to relatively narrow legal issues, in large part because a lot of things we did are protected by the nature of discretionary function."[8] Was this evidentiary ruling critical to the case? Did it create an uneven playing field, giving the advantage to the government? It appears that it did.

There were at least three "bad judgments" that were excluded from jury consideration. The first was the decision by ATF to engage in a dangerous, high-risk, paramilitary assault on a residence housing infants, children, pregnant women, and elderly persons in order to execute a search and arrest warrant for a single individual. It is clear that David Koresh could have been arrested away from the Mt. Carmel property, thus avoiding the reckless endangerment of 130 people who were not charged in the warrants. The second was the decision by the FBI to abandon *conciliatory negotiations* with the sect only ten days into the standoff in favor of a "psychological warfare" strategy, which according to CIA documents is a counter-terrorism tactic developed by the military designed to induce fear, emotional and psychological instability, sleep deprivation, distrust, dissension, and hopelessness in the mind of the enemy.[9] The third was the decision to assault the complex with CS gas—a chemical weapon that is banned by international treaty for use even in wartime against our worst enemies—and using tanks to crush and demolish the building. Each of these so-called bad judgments were protected by discretionary function exemptions and contributed to the disastrous outcome at Waco.

The second of the three "bad judgments" just mentioned (FBI decision to abandon conciliatory negotiations) is of particular interest. After the 1995 U.S. House of Representatives hearings on Waco, Congress mandated that the FBI overhaul the HRT to improve internal communication and give negotiators more voice and power in future hostage-barricade incidents. Following the debacle at Mt. Carmel, negotiators complained that they were ignored and undercut by the tactical unit, making the negotiations ineffective (which was then used as a rationale for the CS insertion). The FBI was told by Congress to develop an advisory group of experts on unconventional religious movements whom they could consult in similar incidents should they arise in the future. I was asked to serve on the advisory group of experts to the renamed Critical Incident Response Group (CIRG). One of the first things I sought to determine was the soundness of existing hostage-barricade protocols. Did the feds do their homework, incorporating grounded theory and research in psychology, sociology, and communications to develop crisis negotiations? To my surprise, available materials were well-grounded in scientific research. They were excellent. The only problem was that they were entirely ignored in the Waco standoff. In the 1999 summer issue of the international *Journal of Terrorism and Political Violence*, I published an extensive analysis of the FBI's crisis negotiations during the 51-day standoff.[10] Using materials culled from the FBI's own curriculum to teach law enforcement agents from all over the world how to conduct hostage-barricade incidents, sixteen violations at Mt. Carmel were identified. Space does not permit a full examination of these violations. Instead, the focus below concerns just one.

A key principle in crisis negotiations is reducing the stress of the hostage-taker or the barricaded subjects. According to a

crisis negotiations manual authored by two veteran negotiators, "one task of the negotiator is to reduce stress. . . . If the
negotiators want themselves or the hostage-taker to come up
with new ideas, they need to reduce stress levels as much as
possible."[11] "(H)igh levels of stress interfere with negotiators
performance. . . . Stress affects the hostage-taker's decision-
making skills. Stress elevates emotions, speeds physiological
processes and interferes with cognitive processing. The ability
to make decisions is hindered or even ceases."[12] If the negotiator is effective, stress levels will dissipate and provide an atmosphere conducive to a peaceful resolution: "With time, the
negotiator can reduce stress, calm the hostage-taker, improve
decision-making skills and fulfill most need states. The hostage-taker feels better and works to resolve the incident."[13]

So what did the FBI do? The HRT's response plan in Waco
after March 17 was referred to as a "stress escalation" program in the Department of Justice log.[14] By stress escalation,
the plan refers to the intensification of physiological and psychological pressures. "The constant stress overload," according to Dr. Alan Stone who was asked to review the actions of
the FBI at Waco, "is intended to lead to sleep deprivation and
psychological disorientation. In predisposed individuals, the
combination of physiological disruption and psychological
stress can also lead to mood disturbances, transient hallucina-
tions and paranoid ideation."[15] The stress escalation strategy
also entailed the alternation of conciliatory and hostile gestures to confuse the target (carrot and stick approach sending
mixed messages), the deployment of high-powered stadium
lights at night, combined with amplification of recorded
sounds of rabbits beings slaughtered, dentist drills, and chant-
ing. Stone reports that the recorded sounds deployed ex-
ceeded 105 decibels that could produce nerve deafness in
children as well as adults. The use of debilitating light and
sound were deployed as psychological irritants to induce
sleep deprivation.

Dr. Robert Cancro, another expert asked to review the
FBI's actions at Waco, was confounded by this approach. He
stated, "From a behavioral science perspective it is not clear
what benefits were expected from imposing sleep deprivation
on the members of the compound. If anything, this was likely
to make their behavior more erratic and less predictable."[16]
Nonetheless, the Justice report states that around this same
time, special agent in charge, Jeff Jamar, decided that it was

time to increase the pressure. Stone notes that "By March 21, the FBI was concentrating on tactical pressure alone."[17]

The psychological warfare program also utilized the threat of force–using tanks to demolish the children's toys (bicycles and motor bikes), crushing automobiles, driving CEVs over the graves of buried Davidians outside the complex, and encircling the buildings with tanks and helicopters to "tighten the noose" as the Justice report documents.

This is the most obvious and defiant breach of fundamental hostage and barricade protocol evidenced by the government. It is virtually impossible to reconcile a *stress escalation* strategy with the principle of *stress reduction*. No amount of government spin can erase the inexplicable and inexcusable contradiction. The only rationale for the stress escalation plan was that it would result in "driving a psychological wedge between Koresh and his followers," in the apparent hope that group fragmentation would occur. Tragically, the strategy produced the opposite effect, bonding members together against a perceived common enemy, a basic sociological axiom. All sixteen violations were of this nature. Bad judgments? More likely, it would seem, the violations were too systematic and uniform to be accidental. In any case, the jury never got to hear any of this evidence.

Judge Smith also restricted presentation of evidence to the fifty-one days between the initial ATF raid on 28 February and the final conflagration on 19 April. Why was this important? Since the jury was being asked to determine whether the ATF used excessive force in the execution of the warrants, it stands to reason that facts and events leading up to the raid were crucial to a complete understanding of the excessive force issue. The use of a high risk, "dynamic entry" is brought into relief when one considers that the ATF had less lethal and far less dangerous options that it did not exercise. Indeed, the whole plan of operation by the ATF was castigated by the Treasury Department report and Congressional investigations on Waco. Consider the summary conclusions in the final joint report by the House Committee on Government Reform and Oversight and the Committee on the Judiciary regarding the ATF raid on Mt. Carmel:

The ATF's investigation of the Branch Davidians was grossly incompetent. It lacked the minimum professionalism of a major Federal law enforcement agency. While the ATF had probable cause to obtain the arrest warrant for David Koresh and the search warrant for the Branch Davidian residence, the affidavit filed in support of the warrants contained an incredible number of false statements. The ATF agents responsible for preparing the affidavits knew or should have known that many of the statements were false. David Koresh could have been arrested outside the Davidian compound. The ATF chose not to arrest Koresh outside the Davidian residence and instead were determined to use a dynamic entry approach. In making this decision ATF agents exercised extremely poor judgement, made erroneous assumptions, and ignored the foreseeable perils of their course of action. ATF misrepresented to Defense Department officials that the Branch Davidians were involved in illegal drug manufacturing. As a result of this deception, the ATF was able to obtain some training from (military) forces which would not have otherwise provided it. . . .

The decision to pursue a military style raid was made more than 2 months before surveillance, undercover, and infiltrations efforts were (even) begun. The ATF undercover and surveillance operation lacked the minimum professionalism expected of a Federal law enforcement agency. Supervisors failed to properly monitor this operation. The ATF's raid plan for February 28 was significantly flawed. *The plan was poorly conceived, utilized a high risk tactical approach when other tactics could have been successfully used*, was drafted and commanded by ATF agents who were less qualified than other available agents, and used agents who were not sufficiently trained for the operation. Additionally, ATF commanders did not take precautions to ensure that the plan would not be discovered. The senior raid commanders, Phillip Chojnacki and Chuck Sarabyn, either knew or should have known that the Davidians had become aware of the impending raid and were likely to resist with deadly force. Nevertheless, they recklessly proceeded with the raid, thereby endangering the lives of the ATF agents under their command and the lives of those residing in the compound. *This, more than any other factor, led to the deaths of the four ATF agents killed on February 28*.[18]

The jury never heard the findings of the official report because it fell outside the time frame that Judge Smith would permit the jury to consider evidence.

Finally, Judge Smith revealed a pattern of bias against the Davidians and their attorneys in a number of bench decisions. For example, the interrogatories given to the jury were so specific and narrow that one could have found substantial fault with the government but answered in the negative to the interrogatories. In the first interrogatory, the jurors were asked to decide if excessive force was used. But jurors were only allowed to consider the question in terms of whether agents fired 1) indiscriminately into the complex, and 2) without provocation. The question, as worded, clearly ignores Texas state law that says excessive force may exist in the form of a threat, even before a shot is fired. The applicable law, cited below in its entirety, allows for a citizen to forcibly resist an arrest or search if, before any resistance is offered, he or she reasonably believes a peace officer is using or attempting to use greater force than necessary. We will return to this argument momentarily.

Smith also lumped all Davidians into a single group, not allowing the jury to consider that some sect members, such as the children, were innocent victims of aggressive government actions. This was done despite the fact that during voir dire (jury selection), Smith specifically asked potential jurors if they could consider each of the plaintiffs *individually*. Plaintiffs' attorneys were led to believe that the judge would give the jury this charge in their deliberations. The Davidian attorneys built their case on this presumption. When Smith reneged, Michael Caddell, the plaintiffs' lead counsel, was outraged and publicly accused the judge of trying to "engineer a verdict." In an eighteen-page motion filed after the trial, Caddell alleged that Smith showed a "deep seated prejudice" towards his clients.[19] In one instance, the motion stated that Smith referred to one videotaped defense witness, Livingston Fagan, as a "lying, murdering son of a bitch." Elsewhere in the motion, it stated that Smith referred to plaintiffs' transcripts of government surveillance recordings as "bullcrap," even though it was later shown that their transcripts were more accurate than those submitted by government lawyers. The motion also stated that the judge admitted that he had not read some evidence introduced by the Davidians. In one other instance, Mr. Caddell's motion said the judge acted improperly by shaking the hand of a government lawyer during a recess and congratulating him for "a good job" after a grueling cross-examination of Davidian Clive Doyle. The government attorney conducting the cross-examination, Jim Touhey, viciously attacked and ridiculed Mr. Doyle's religion and belittled his belief that Koresh was a prophet. Mr. Touhey's performance invoked frightening images of the Medieval Inquisition and the Salem witch trials. The government's challenge to the legitimacy of Davidian theology was a broadside against constitutionally protected, albeit unconventional, religious belief. Perplexing was the fact that plaintiffs' attorneys failed to object to this line of questioning. When asked later why he did not raise objections during the cross, Michael Caddell responded that he thought the tactic would backfire and that the jury would see through it. It did not, and they did not.

As an observer, I noted that Smith barked and snapped at plaintiffs' co-counsels, Ramsey Clark and James Brannon, showing notable contempt and sending less-than-subtle messages to the jury. Smith lost patience with Clark on several occasions, evidently irritated by Clark's slow and methodical style of questioning witnesses. In one exchange, Smith's face turned bright red as he yelled at Clark, demanding that he quicken his pace and "get to the point." Smith interrupted both Clark and Brannon routinely, demanding explanations for questions posed to witnesses, challenging their competency and credibility with the jury. Overall, this left me with the impression that the irascible Judge Smith harbored considerable disdain for plaintiffs' attorneys.

In the end, justice was not served in Smith's court. The finding that excessive force was not used in the initial ATF raid is particularly troubling. If Waco does not rise to the standard of excessive force, one could reasonably conclude the standard is a legal fiction. Texas state law clearly defines excessive force and the rights of citizens to protect themselves under these circumstances. The *Texas Penal Code*, in Subchapter C. Protection of Persons, section 9.31, states

The use of force to resist an arrest or search is justified: (1) if, before the actor offers any resistance, the peace officer (or person acting at his direction) uses or attempts to use greater force than necessary to make the arrest or search; and (2) when and to the degree the actor reasonably believes the force is immediately necessary to protect himself against the peace officer's (or other person's) use or attempted use of greater force than necessary.

Did the Davidians exercise reasonable belief that ATF officers in the initial raid were "using or attempting to use greater force than necessary?" Specifically, could a paramilitary assault by eighty armed agents in camouflage and full combat gear, including Kevlar helmets and flak jackets, wielding MP-5 submachine guns, semi-automatic AR-15s, Sig Sauer 9MM semi-automatic pistols, .308-caliber high power sniper rifles, shotguns, and concussion grenades rushing a residence housing infants, children, pregnant women, and elderly persons, with only an arrest and search warrant for a single individual, be grounds for a reasonable belief that the officers were using or attempting to use greater force than necessary?

If allowed to hear all the evidence, what jury would completely exonerate federal agents of such charges?

In the 1994 criminal trial of eleven Branch Davidians, Judge Smith declared that he would "not allow the government to be put on trial."[20] Judging from the proceedings of the recent civil trial, he still will not. In September 2000, Davidan Attorneys Michael Caddell and Ramsey Clark announced plans to appeal the verdict in the civil case. Based on the earlier motion filed by Caddell, it would appear that attorneys will attempt to convince an appeals court of an appearance of bias or impropriety by the trial judge. Federal courts, however, are very reticent to overturn decisions based on the alleged bias of the trial judge. The case will now go to the U.S. 5th Circuit Court of Appeals in New Orleans, thought by many to be the most conservative in the country. In all likelihood, the Davidians will not find relief in the appellate proceedings, closing the final chapter of legal redress available to the surviving sect members and their families.

Conclusion

The annals of American law will show that the government prevailed in all its legal challenges. But one must ask, at what price? Historically, no religious sect has ever been more brutally victimized by the U.S. government. Scholars have already made comparisons to the Oglala Sioux at Wounded Knee.[21] Waco is now a permanent part of our culture and serves as a symbol of raw state power and control. In the end, what was achieved in legal victory pales in comparison to what was lost in civility, confidence in public officials, and belief in our system of justice.

NOTES

1.   There is an interesting footnote here. I made a case for this charge in an editorial that appeared both in the *Houston Chronicle* and the *Beaumont Enterprise* (see Stuart A. Wright, "What the Waco Jury never Heard," *Houston Chronicle*, 23 July 2000; Stuart A. Wright, "Jurors didn't hear the whole story of Branch Davidian incident," *Beaumont Enterprise*, 23 July 2000). Mr. Bradford, whose U.S. Attorney's office is headquartered in Beaumont, responded to the editorial with a missive of his own in the *Beaumont Enterprise* (see J. Michael Bradford, "Waco critic purely biased," *Beaumont Enterprise*, 30 July 2000). Mr. Bradford attacked my scholarship and opined that my institution should not allow me to unduly influence

students in the classroom with ideas critical of the government. I found the U.S. Attorney's apparent effort to abridge free speech both ironic and revealing, particularly since his responsibility as a civil servant is to uphold the Constitution, not to advocate its violation. The spirited exchange led to a public debate on the Waco trial, organized by the Southeast Texas Press Club on 15 September 2000. The event drew a standing room only crowd at the Press Club luncheon and made headlines in the local newspaper on the local TV news the next day. We sought to have the debate televised over the Web through a local company that expressed interest. However, Mr. Bradford threatened to pull out of the debate if it were televised.

2.   Many questions had multiple parts so that the questionnaire actually consisted of over a hundred items.

3.   While these questions were relevant to issues in the case, some were entirely too invasive. As such, jurors should have been informed that they could refuse to answer. But to the contrary, the judge's instructions in the questionnaire state: "This is not a voluntary endeavor, as you are required to answer the questions." Jury questionnaire is reproduced in Jack DeVault, *The Waco Whitewash* (San Antonio, Tex.: Rescue Press, 1994), 264-82.

4.   *U.S. v. Brad Branch et al.,* U.S. District Court, Western District of Texas, W-93-CR-046, 2.

5.   See Stuart A. Wright, ed., *Armageddon in Waco: Critical Perspectives on the Branch Davidian Conflict* (Chicago, Ill.: University of Chicago, 1995).

6.   See Alan W. Bock, *Ambush at Ruby Ridge* (Irvine, Calif.: Dickens Press, 1995); Jess Walter, *Every Knee Shall Bow* (New York: Harper/Regan Books, 1995).

7.   On appeal, the U.S. 9th Circuit Court *en banc* agreed to hear the arguments for this motion.

8.   Susan Gamboa, "Immunity Helped Turn Waco Trial," Associated Press, 15 July 2000.

9.   Christopher Simpson, *Science of Coercion: Communication Research and Psychological Warfare 1945-1960* (New York: Oxford University, 1994), 12.

10.   Stuart A. Wright, "Anatomy of a Government Massacre: Abuses of Hostage-Barricade Protocols during the Waco Standoff," *Journal of Terrorism and Political Violence* 11 (1999): 39-68.

11.   Michael J. McMains and Wayman C. Mullins, *Crisis Negotiations: Managing Critical Incidents and Hostage Situations in Law Enforcement and Corrections* (Cincinnati, Ohio: Anderson, 1996), 125.

12.   Ibid., 129.

13.   Ibid.

14.   *Report to the Deputy Attorney General on the Events at Waco, Texas, February 28 to April 19, 1993* (Washington, D.C.: U.S. Department of Justice, 1993), 138.

15.   Alan A. Stone, *Report and Recommendations Concerning the Handling of Incidents Such as the Branch Davidian Standoff in Waco, Texas.* Report to the Deputy Attorney General, 8 November 1994, 28.

16.   Robert Cancro, letter to Deputy Attorney General Philip B. Heymann, *Recommendations of Experts for Improvement in Federal Law Enforcement After Waco* (Washington, D.C.: U.S. Department of Justice, 1993), 4.

17.   Stone, *Report and Recommendations*, 10.
18.   *Investigation into the Activities of Federal Law Enforcement Agencies*, 3 (emphasis added).
19.   Lee Hancock, "Davidians' attorney vents anger at judge," *Dallas Morning News*, 13 September 2000.
20.   Quoted in David B. Kopel and Paul H. Blackman, *No More Wacos: What's Wrong with Federal Law Enforcement and How to Fix It* (Amherst, N.Y.: Prometheus, 1997), 238.
21.   Michelene E. Pesantubbee, "From Vision to Violence: The Wounded Knee Massacre," in *Millenialism, Persecution, and Violence: Historical Cases*, ed. Catherine Wessinger (Syracuse, N.Y.: Syracuse University Press, 2000), 62-81.

New Religious Movements and Conflicts with Law Enforcement

CATHERINE WESSINGER

A conference at Baylor University in Waco, Texas, with its proximity to Mount Carmel Center, the site of the 1993 Branch Davidian tragedy, is a fitting place to highlight the lessons that can be learned from that case concerning conflicts between law enforcement agents and members of new religious movements. The Branch Davidian incident and the conflict involving the Randy Weaver family at Ruby Ridge, Idaho in 1992, both watershed events in the history of conflicts between American law enforcement agents and religious believers, illustrate that the *quality of the interactions* between law enforcement agents and believers is crucial in determining whether or not lives will be lost. In both cases, law enforcement agents and believers died unnecessarily. If we can understand the causes of these and other significant conflicts between law enforcement agents and religious believers, then perhaps tragic deaths can be prevented in the future.

Randy Weaver and his family were Identity Christians who had retreated to the Idaho countryside to find a refuge from the conflicts that they expected would lead to Armageddon. Federal marshals were engaged in surveillance when they got into a gunfight with Sammy Weaver, age 14, and Kevin Harris, a Weaver family friend, after the marshals shot and killed the Weavers' dog. Deputy U. S. Marshal William Degan and Sammy Weaver were killed. Subsequently, members of the FBI's Hostage Rescue Team (HRT) surrounded the Weaver cabin, but did not announce their presence and did not ask the Weavers to surrender. An FBI sniper fired upon Randy Weaver and Kevin Harris when they came out of the cabin, and one of his bullets passed through a door window striking and killing Vicki Weaver as she held her youngest child.[1]

In 1993, at Mount Carmel Center near Waco, Texas, four agents of the Bureau of Alcohol, Tobacco, and Firearms were killed, twenty ATF agents were wounded, five Branch Davidians were killed, and four Davidians were wounded during a raid carried out by seventy-six ATF agents on 28 February

1993. Interestingly, the shootout may have begun as a result of ATF agents shooting the Davidians' dogs. ATF agents killed another Davidian later that afternoon as he attempted to return to his family. The FBI's Hostage Rescue Team then arrived to preside over the 51-day siege of Mount Carmel Center. On 19 April 1993, fifty-one adult Davidians and twenty-three children died in the fire that erupted during the tank and tear gas assault launched by FBI agents.[2]

None of the deaths at Ruby Ridge or Mount Carmel Center would have occurred if law enforcement agents had been sensitive to how their activities were perceived by religious believers, if they had undertaken more ordinary measures to investigate the possibility of criminal activity, and if they had taken more moderate steps to enforce the law.

Violence involving religious groups is the result of the *interactions* between believers and people in mainstream society. The manner in which law enforcement agents, reporters, social workers, concerned family members, apostates (disgruntled former members), and citizens *interact* with members of a religious community either heightens conflict or promotes dialogue and mutual understanding.[3]

A common pattern has emerged in my comparative study of violence involving new religious movements: ritualized acts of violence can increase in scope and thus build up to a large explosion of violence in which many lives are lost. Law enforcement agents as well as religious believers can participate in rituals of violence that can escalate.[4]

Sometimes religious believers engage in acts of coercion and violence that can escalate into a large-scale culmination, such as a mass suicide or an assault against society, as in the group suicide and murders involving members of Peoples' Temple in Jonestown, Guyana, on 18 November 1978, or the release of sarin gas on the Tokyo subway by members of Aum Shinrikyo on 20 March 1995.[5]

Coercive discipline and punishments had been carried out in the Peoples' Temple both when it was a church in California and after the relocation of most of its members to Guyana in 1977. There had been suicide rehearsals in Jim Jones's inner circle since 1976. At Jonestown, the committing of a collective "revolutionary suicide" had been discussed in the community for at least a year as a means to preserve the group's ultimate concern, which was maintaining the cohesiveness of their community. The Jonestown residents had practiced carrying out group suicide in "white night" drills. The mass suicide in which 909 people died in Jonestown as a result either of drinking Fla-Vor-Aid laced with cyanide and tranquilizers or being injected with the poison included 294 children under the age of eighteen. Prior to the group suicide, men from Jonestown had opened fire on the party of Congressman Leo Ryan, which was departing with some long-time members of the Peoples' Temple, killing five people, including Ryan and wounding ten others.

Aum Shinrikyo's violence began with the coercion of devotees to follow an ascetic lifestyle by immersing themselves in extremely hot or cold water, a practice that resulted in an accidental death in 1988, and a murder in 1989 to keep that death a secret. In 1989, Aum devotees murdered an attorney, his wife, and their baby son to prevent him from revealing information about fraudulent claims made by the Aum guru, Shoko Asahara. Members of Aum Shinrikyo who wanted to leave the group were coerced, tortured, and drugged. Various individuals in Japan were attacked with poison gases because they had been identified as enemies of the group. On 27 June 1994, Aum devotees released sarin gas in the town of Matsumoto with the intention of killing three judges who were to decide an upcoming court case involving Aum. Six hundred people were injured and seven died in Matsumoto. The 20 March 1995 sarin gas attack on the Tokyo subway that injured over five thousand people and killed twelve was intended to prevent imminent police raids from being carried out on Aum communes. Aum devotees believed that their violent actions were helping to create a Buddhist utopia built by the grace of their infallible Buddha, Shoko Asahara.

The Branch Davidian tragedy illustrates that law enforcement agents can likewise engage in coercive and violent acts that can culminate in a large number of deaths and injuries. Branch Davidians who came out of Mount Carmel Center during the FBI siege were arrested and paraded in prison clothing before television cameras. Every time that adult Davidians came out, the remaining Davidians were punished by an act of coercion or psychological warfare. The electricity was cut off, bright spotlights were shone at the residence at night, and high-decibel sounds were blasted at them. The agents in the tanks made obscene gestures, mooned, and cursed the Davidians. The tanks crushed the Davidians' vehicles, which amounted to destroying evidence that was relevant to the question of whether the Davidians or the ATF agents did most of the shooting, the tanks crashed into the building from time to time, and repeatedly ran over the grave of a Davidian. These ritualized acts of violence culminated in the tank and tear gas assault on 19 April 1993, in which CS gas, which is banned for use in international warfare, was inserted into a residence containing civilians, including twenty-one children and their mothers, two pregnant women, and elderly people. The demolishing of the residence by the tanks killed Davidians, eliminated escape routes, and created conditions in which a fire could spread rapidly through the building. Regardless of whether the fire began accidentally, was ignited by pyrotechnic devices used by FBI agents to deliver the CS gas, or was set by Davidians, it would not have occurred if the FBI had relied on negotiations instead of coercion to deal with the Davidians.

Repeated acts of violence take on a ritualistic nature and can escalate into an explosion of violence. *Both* religious believers and law enforcement agents can participate in rituals of violence. In all three cases, Jonestown, Aum Shinrikyo, and the Branch Davidians, the believers were enmeshed in a net of conflicts with apostates, concerned relatives, reporters, and government and law enforcement agents of various types. The way that people in mainstream society *interact* with believers is important in determining a group's potential for volatility.

One of the most important factors in promoting conflict with a religious group is to call it a "cult." "Cult" was originally a word used to refer to an organized system of worship focused on an object of worship. Worship in a Christian denomination, according to this definition, is a "cult," and in jest we speak of people devoted to particular movies and games as "cults." Since the 1970s, "cult" has become a pejorative word to refer to religious groups that people do not like or understand, and, therefore, fear. The word "cult" now conveys a stereotype that the members are "brainwashed," whereas research has demonstrated that new religious movements typically utilize the same recruitment tactics as other evangelical and missionary religions.[6] The "cult" stereotype implies that the leader has total control over followers, although in fact no leader gains any power over people without the complicity of followers. The "cult" stereotype implies that unconventional religions are dangerous and violent, which encourages people to forget that believers in mainstream religions fight wars, torture and kill people, and often commit acts of terrorism, and that religious leaders in every tradition have emotionally, sexually, and financially abused believers. The "cult" stereotype implies that all unconventional religious groups are the same, when in fact they are vastly diverse in their characteristics, and most of them do not break the law or commit violent acts. "Cult" is a four-letter word that conveys hatred and prejudice just as much as racial, anti-Semitic slurs, and the various ugly words for women and gay people. Applying any pejorative label to a group of people can dehumanize them, make it appear to be legitimate to discriminate against them, deprive them of their civil and human rights, and kill them.

The application of the word "cult" and its corresponding stereotype to religious groups by law enforcement agents creates a situation in which law enforcement agents may be motivated to utilize excessive force. When law enforcement agents label a religious group a "cult," as was the ease with the Branch Davidians, conflict between the agents and the believers is exacerbated. Law enforcement agents can avoid falling into the trap of the anticult mindset by consulting *bona fide* experts on religion, religious studies scholars, and sociologists of religion, instead of the self-styled "cult experts" who usually have no credentials in the study of religions. Given that violence involving religious groups is determined by the *quality of the interactions* between law enforcement agents and believers, law enforcement agents have the challenge of determining the best way to proceed in enforcing the law in relation to unconventional religious groups. To assist in this task, I will offer some conceptual categories for understanding religious groups and violence, and then offer some indicators for risk assessment.

Millennialism and Violence

New religious movements are extremely diverse, ranging from Christian and Bible-based groups, to Asian and African-derived religions, to UFO believers. The leader of a new religious movement may be regarded as having access to a spiritual source of authority. Believed access to an unseen source of authority is termed "charisma" by religion scholars. Charismatic leadership of a religious group can contribute to the potential for volatility, because there are fewer checks on the whims of the leader than in a group that has institutionalized offices.[7] It must be noted that charismatic leadership is socially constructed, and if there are no believers in a person's

claimed access to an unseen source of authority, then there is
no charismatic leader. Leadership in a new religious movement may be provided by elected officers or may be shared in
some institutionalized manner. Authority in the group may be
derived from adherence to a revered body of literature. Some
believers may live in communities that are set off from mainstream society to varying degrees. Many new religious movements make very low demands on their members in terms of
time, money, associations, and commitments. They do not ask
believers to separate from their families, friends, occupations,
and ordinary lifestyles.

Religious studies scholars observe new religious movements using the same methodologies that they employ when
studying other religions. The assumption is that all of these
groups are religions, regardless of size. I define religion as
"ultimate concern," that which is the most important thing in
the world for the believers.[8] An ultimate concern is the goal
that believers wish to attain. An ultimate concern or goal is
always about well-being. An ultimate concern is about salvation from the suffering and death inherent in the human condition. Human beings want to experience well-being in their
earthly lives and continued well-being after death. Ultimate
concerns of individuals and groups can change over time, especially in response to events. Since ultimate concerns are
about well-being, many people will adjust their ultimate concerns if their well-being is threatened due to their religious
beliefs. Alternatively, people may adjust the methods that
they practice in their attempt to achieve their religious goals if
former methods prove unproductive. Some believers hold on
to their ultimate concerns so tightly that they may become
willing either to kill or die for their religious goals.

Religious groups that have come into conflict with law enforcement authorities have often been millennial movements.
Millennialism, or millenarianism, refers to certain patterns of
belief, that, strictly speaking, have nothing to do with the year
2000 and the temporal millennial period just begun, although
anticipation of the year 2000 appeared to increase millennial
religious expectations during the 1990s. Religion scholars
term these patterns of religious expression "millennialism" because the New Testament book of Revelation speaks of the
Kingdom of God on earth lasting one thousand years. Millennialism is belief in an imminent transition to a collective salvation that will be either heavenly or earthly. It is a collective
salvation because the millennial dream is that a group of peo-

ple, called the "elect" in Christianity, will enter into a state of well-being in which suffering is overcome once and for all. While millennialists expect a collective heavenly salvation, others expect that the kingdom of God will be created on Earth.[9]

I use the term "catastrophic millennialism" to refer to the belief that the transition to the millennial kingdom, the collective salvation, will occur catastrophically; the old order will be destroyed to make way for the new order. I use "apocalypticism" as a synonym for catastrophic millennialism. I use the term "progressive millennialism" to refer to the belief that the transition to the collective salvation will take place due to a progressive creation of a just society. The progressive millennial belief is that humans working according to a divine or superhuman plan will create the millennial kingdom. The study of new religious movements demonstrates that both catastrophic millennialism and progressive millennialism may or may not have a messiah, a charismatic leader who is believed to have the power to create the millennial kingdom. A messiah is a prophet, someone who is regarded as receiving divine revelation, but a prophet is not necessarily a messiah.[10]

There is a range of behaviors associated with both catastrophic millennialism and progressive millennialism. Catastrophic millennialists include the vast majority of believers who wait in faith for God's intervention to destroy this corrupt world and create the millennial kingdom. This is the position taken by many Christians in mainstream churches. Catastrophic millennialists also include those such as the Randy Weaver family and the Branch Davidians, who arm themselves for protection during the tribulation period leading to Armageddon. They live apart from mainstream society. They do not threaten society's safety, but if they are attacked, they will fight back. Catastrophic millennialists also include those who believe that they are called by God to engage in revolutionary actions to overthrow what they regard as a satanic government and to establish God's righteous kingdom. There is a contemporary right-wing Euro-American nativist millennial movement in the United States, for example, whose very extreme members resort to terrorism. They are hoping to instigate what they call the "second American Revolution" against the federal government. They know that at present they do not have a majority of Americans willing to fight against the overwhelming power of the American law enforcement establishment.[11]

My focus will not be on progressive millennialism in this chapter, but I will say briefly that the same range of behaviors is associated with progressive millennialism. Most progressive millennialists rely on social work, personal development, and ethical living to build God's kingdom on Earth. Some progressive millennialists arm themselves for protection if they feel they are under attack. In significant cases, some progressive millennialists resort to revolutionary violence to speed progress up to an apocalyptic rate. Examples of revolutionary progressive millennialism include the German Nazis, the Maoists in China, and the Khmer Rouge in Cambodia.[12] These seemingly non-religious movements were expressions of ultimate concerns to create collective salvations on Earth.

Catastrophic millennialists who live in isolated communities are inherently in tension with mainstream society. They reject the values of society that they deem to be ungodly. They withdraw to create their own god-fearing communities in anticipation of the millennial kingdom. If law enforcement agents can interact with these believers in a respectful and even friendly manner that acknowledges their right to freedom of religion, they can go a long way towards avoiding heightened conflict that might lead to violence.

A recent article in the *FBI Law Enforcement Bulletin* recommended that law enforcement agents adopt a community-oriented policing strategy when dealing with unconventional religious groups.[13] This strategy was used successfully in 1998 with Chen Tao, a Taiwanese new religious movement located in Garland, Texas, whose leader had predicted that God would appear in his front yard on 31 March 1998 as a prelude to the predicted catastrophic destruction of the world in 1999. The Garland police established friendly personal relations with the Chen Tao leaders and members. The Garland police consulted a credentialed scholar of religion, Dr. Lonnie Kliever of Southern Methodist University, enabled him to interview and observe the Chen Tao believers, listened to his advice, and permitted him to share his expertise in religious studies with news reporters.[14] They used ordinary investigative and policing measures while protecting the safety of both the Chen Tao believers and the general public. The Garland police officers were prepared to intervene in the event the group decided to take violent actions, but their humane, practical, and nonconfrontational approach to the situation contributed to the positive interactions that Chen Tao believers had with the general public and helped create a social context in which the leader could reinterpret his failed prophecy to his followers. The wise and moderate approach of the Garland police also helped to reduce sensational news coverage of Chen Tao and protect the believers from a possible hostile public. The news coverage in the *Dallas Morning News* was especially intelligent and informed.

My comparative study of catastrophic millennial groups that have become caught up in violence shows that the potential for violence is increased if catastrophic millennialists feel persecuted. A sense of being persecuted increases the intensity with which apocalyptic beliefs are held. Additionally, an apocalyptic worldview increases the possibility that a group will interpret any amount of social opposition as being persecution. An apocalyptic or catastrophic millennial worldview involves what I call "radical dualism," a rigid perspective that sees things in stark black and white, good versus evil, us versus them terms.[15] Extremely aggressive law enforcement tactics against an apocalyptic group simply confirms the group's belief that satanic agents of an evil "Babylon" will attack the true believers. Persecution by civilians and law enforcement agents, such as that of the Mormons in nineteenth-century America, only increases the believers' theological emphasis on apocalypticism.[16] Catastrophic millennial worldviews and their associated dualisms assure believers that, in end-time events, evil people will be punished and righteous people will be rewarded. When dealing with apocalyptic groups, law enforcement agents should try to avoid making believers feel persecuted.

It is important that law enforcement agents realize that they, also, are likely to possess a worldview that is dualistic. Law enforcement agents are prone to see things through the lens of radical dualism. Law enforcement agents tend to be concerned with good versus evil, us versus them, good guys versus bad guys. When two parties are in conflict, both possessing radically dualistic worldviews, what generally transpires is akin to warfare, such as the incident at Mount Carmel Center. The only way to get out of this trap of "dichotomous thinking"[17] is to promote dialogue and negotiation in which the two parties can build trust in each other's good will and humanity.

When law enforcement agents are perplexed by the unusual beliefs and practices of an unconventional religious group, they will benefit from consulting with *bona fide* scholars with academic credentials in the study of religious movements. Individuals who promote themselves as "cult experts" usually have no credentials in the academic study of religion. Religious studies scholars can help law enforcement agents by serving as information resources and as "worldview translators."[18] Trying to communicate with believers possessing an unusual religious worldview can be compared to communication with someone who speaks a foreign language. In those cases, skilled and knowledgeable translators can promote better understanding. Religious studies scholars can explain to law enforcement agents the theology of the group as well as common sociological dynamics of new religious movements and their interactions with society. Religious studies scholars can analyze religious beliefs that motivate actions.

In 1993, two Bible scholars, J. Phillip Arnold of the Reunion Institute in Houston, Texas, and James Tabor, University of North Carolina at Charlotte, made an innovative and successful attempt at intervening in the religious critical incident that involved the Branch Davidians.[19] Unfortunately, they had to do so without the cooperation of FBI agents, whose tank and gas assault on 19 April 1993 fatally undermined the progress that Arnold and Tabor had made to persuade the Davidians to come out of Mount Carmel safely. Arnold went to Waco on 7 March 1993, to offer his services to the FBI, but was ignored by agents. On 15 March, the Davidians heard Arnold on a radio program discussing biblical prophecies. Davidian Steve Schneider asked the FBI to permit Arnold to discuss the Bible with David Koresh, but this request was denied and FBI negotiators were instructed to ignore the Davidians' "Bible babble."

During the 51-day siege, the Davidians attempted to negotiate with FBI agents. The Davidians did not want to die, but they were not going to come out of Mount Carmel Center unless the exit process conformed to their understanding of biblical prophecies. Their ultimate concern was to achieve salvation by remaining faithful to God's will as expressed in biblical prophecies. Steve Schneider told an FBI negotiator that if Arnold could show the Davidians from the Bible that they should come out, they would come out no matter what David Koresh said.[20] As Seventh-day Adventists, the ultimate source of authority for the Branch Davidians was the Bible. David Koresh was open to revising his interpretation of biblical prophecies, but he could not come out without biblical sanction, because his authority as the Branch Davidian messiah was based upon what appeared to be his divinely inspired ability to interpret the Bible and its prophecies. Koresh had been wounded in the 28 February ATF raid and he was probably confused about how he could surrender and still make that scenario fit prophecies in the Bible.

On 1 April, Arnold and Tabor discussed the Bible on a radio show for the benefit of the Branch Davidians. The Davidians believed that as a result of the ATF assault they might be in the Fifth Seal of the book of Revelation, which says that after the agents of Babylon kill some members of the godly community, there will be a waiting period before the remaining believers will be martyred. The Branch Davidians were waiting to see what God had in store for them. In their radio discussion, Arnold and Tabor suggested that the waiting period would last more than a few months. They suggested that the biblical prophecies indicated that God wanted Koresh to come out to spread his message of salvation to the rest of the world.[21]

David Koresh spent Passover recuperating from his wounds and thinking over the situation. On 14 April, Koresh sent out a letter to the FBI stating that God the Father had given him permission to write a "little book" on the Seven Seals of Revelation. After the manuscript was in safekeeping with Arnold and Tabor, he and the Davidians would come out of Mount Carmel Center. The Branch Davidians' cheers at the prospect of coming out were recorded on a negotiation audiotape. On 15 April, the chief FBI negotiator at Mount Carmel Center told Justice Department officials that negotiations with the Davidians were going nowhere. On 16 April, David Koresh reported to negotiators that he had completed writing his interpretation of the First Seal, and the Davidians requested a word processor to speed up the production of Koresh's manuscript. The Davidians requested a word processor again on 17 April. On 18 April, the word processor was delivered to the Davidians, but the tanks also crushed and removed the remaining Davidian vehicles in preparation for an assault. David Koresh called a negotiator and asserted that the actions of the agents in the tanks contradicted the negotiators' claim that the FBI wanted a peaceful resolution. Koresh asked, "*What do you men really want?*" Koresh warned the negotiator that his ultimate loyalty was to God and that the actions of FBI agents were pushing him into a corner. On 19 April at 6:00 a.m., the tank and CS gas assault began that culminated in the fire which ignited at noon. The nine Davidians who escaped the fire included a woman who had a computer disk in her pocket on which was saved Koresh's interpretation of the First Seal.[22]

The intervention by Arnold and Tabor with the Branch Davidians had worked. David Koresh had been helped by these scholars to interpret the biblical prophecies in a manner that would have enabled the Davidians to come out safely from Mount Carmel Center. However, the FBI tank and CS gas assault probably convinced the Branch Davidians that God indeed intended for them to die at the hands of Babylon as predicted in the Fifth Seal as a major end-time event leading to Armageddon.

The careful reader will have noted that this chapter does *not* suggest that millennial groups cause religious violence. I have been saying that millennial groups or some new religious movements *become caught up* in violent episodes. Millennial groups involved in violence are not all the same. The comparative study of important violent incidents involving millennial groups reveals that they fall into three categories: assaulted millennial groups, fragile millennial groups, and revolutionary millennial movements.[23]

An assaulted millennial group, such as the Branch Davidians in 1993, is attacked because civilians and law enforcement agents regard the religious believers as dangerous. This often proves to be a mistaken judgment, as was the case with the Mormons in nineteenth-century America, the Lakota Sioux band massacred by American soldiers at Wounded Knee in 1890, and the police assault on a group of black Africans (Xhosa) calling themselves Israelites at Bulhoek, South Africa, in 1856.[24] Assaulted millennial groups are not rare.

Members of a fragile millennial group, such as the Jonestown residents and Aum Shinrikyo devotees, initiate violence because they perceive that they are failing to achieve their ultimate concern, the religious goal that is the most important thing in the world to them. Fragile millennial groups suffer from internal problems and external opposition that make the believers conclude that they are failing to achieve their ultimate concern, so they resort to violence to preserve their religious goal. In the instances of fragile millennial groups that initiate violence, the believers are likely to direct their violence both inwardly towards their own members and outwardly at perceived enemies in society. Always in these cases, *the quality of interactions* with people in society is crucial in creating a context in which the believers decide to take violent actions.

The exact balance of pressure from within the group and from outside the group will vary in each case. Jonestown suffered from *too much* hostile investigation and scrutiny from people in mainstream society; Aum Shinrikyo suffered from *too little* police investigation, and therefore, for a considerable period before the Tokyo subway attack, police overlooked the activities of Aum devotees in torturing and murdering people and acquiring weapons of mass destruction. The Jonestown residents had the goal of preserving the integrity of their community, which was endangered by the activities of aggressive apostates and concerned family members, sensational media coverage, and harassment by the Internal Revenue Service, the Customs Service, the U. S. Postal Service, and other federal agencies. The Jonestown community was also suffering from internal problems including the physical and mental decline of Jim Jones, financial difficulties, the challenge of supporting about a thousand people in the Guyanese jungle, disruptive dissidents, and long-term members giving up on the group's ultimate concern and leaving. The community was pushed over the edge by the unwelcome visit of Congressman Leo Ryan, whose party included representatives of Jonestown's avowed enemies, the federal government, reporters, relatives, and hostile former members. When some long-time members of Peoples' Temple decided to leave with Ryan, the Jonestown residents despaired of being able to maintain their community, their ultimate concern.[25]

Aum Shinrikyo's fragility was due primarily to internal stresses created by Shoko Asahara, who claimed to be a Buddha with the infallible ability to foretell the coming Armageddon. It was vital to the perpetuation of Aum Shinrikyo as a religion that Asahara's predictions not be disproved, because the guru's supernatural power and grace were believed to be the devotees' only means of achieving salvation. Although Asahara's inner circle of devotees was preparing to wage Armageddon against sinful society, the acts of violence committed against dissidents, people who wanted to leave, reporters, judges, and others in society who were seen as enemies, were designed to protect the religious organization from investigation and, therefore, protect the ultimate concern of creating the Buddhist millennial kingdom and the believed salvific authority of Shoko Asahara. When Aum devotees committed violence, Aum Shinrikyo was a fragile millennial group.[26]

In addition to assaulted millennial groups and fragile millennial groups, there are revolutionary millennial movements

whose adherents commit violent acts to overthrow the current
order to establish their millennial kingdom. When revolutionary millennial movements become socially dominant, they
create vast amounts of suffering as World War II and the various Communist revolutions bear out. When revolutionary
millennial movements are not socially dominant, their members resort to acts of terrorism.

It should be noted that these ideal types—assaulted millennial groups, fragile millennial groups, and revolutionary
millennial movements—are dynamic categories. Circumstances and events can cause a group to move from one type
to another. For instance, Aum Shinrikyo was preparing to become revolutionary, but police stopped its members from
their violent activities before they could initiate revolutionary
Armageddon. Twice federal agents assaulted the Branch
Davidians, but they had the potential to become revolutionary
in the future because David Koresh taught that the Davidians
would go to Israel and fight on the side of the Israelis in the
war of Armageddon that would occur in 1995. The ATF assault and the FBI psychological warfare waged against the
Davidians confirmed David Koresh's interpretations of biblical prophecies, so the Davidians were *not* a fragile millennial
group. However, it is possible that the tank and CS gas assault
on 19 April 1993 had the effect of pushing the Davidians finally over the edge to become a fragile millennial group, so
that some of its members may have intentionally set the fire to
make their situation conform to their understanding of biblical prophecies, thus enabling the Davidians to enter into
God's heavenly kingdom by remaining faithful to God and
his commands.

Evaluating the Potential for Volatility

In evaluating a religious group for its potential to become
caught up in violence, it is important that law enforcement
agents remember that the *quality of interactions* with the group
members contribute to whether or not there is potential for
volatility. Any consideration of possible indicators for the potential for violence *is not predictive*. There is always the factor
of human free will and there are many sociological, psychological, and even theological factors that may not be known at
the time of the assessment. Szubin, Jensen, and Gregg cautioned that law enforcement agents needed to become informed about the group's worldview and that they should

take their beliefs seriously.[27] The Branch Davidian tragedy illustrates what can happen if law enforcement agents disregard a group's religious beliefs. No matter how strange the beliefs appear to outsiders, the believers adhere to their religious faith sincerely because it makes sense to them. Szubin, Jensen, and Gregg advise law enforcement agents to assume that the leader sincerely believes in the doctrines that he or she teaches, even if they appear to be self-serving. It is a mistake to approach an unconventional religious group with the assumption that the leader is a con man. Likewise, law enforcement agents make a mistake if they assume that religious believers are brainwashed and cannot think for themselves. It is a *serious* mistake to rely solely on a psychological diagnosis of a religious leader when assessing a group.[28] Solely applying a psychological label to one member of a community, which may or may not be correct, does not contribute to the interdisciplinary analysis that is needed to understand fully a religious group. Insights from the disciplines of psychology, sociology, law enforcement, and religious studies, which pays particular attention to theology and worldviews, are all relevant in a good assessment of a religious group's potential to become caught up in violence.

When a religious group is suspected of breaking the law, ordinary and careful investigative measures should be taken. Whenever possible, law enforcement agents should meet with believers and cultivate positive relations with them. As long as it does not endanger law enforcement agents, it is best to give the believers the opportunity to cooperate with the investigation. David Koresh, for instance, had a record of cooperating with the investigations of law enforcement agents and social workers. David Koresh had invited ATF agents to inspect his guns and this invitation was ignored in favor of launching a no-knock, dynamic entry against Mount Carmel Center. The ATF undercover agent who had spent time inside Mount Carmel Center had reported that there was no evidence that the Davidians possessed illegal weapons.[29]

Certain characteristics of religious groups and their interactions with members of mainstream society suggest that they have the potential to become caught up in episodes of violence. A significant number of these characteristics in relation to a religious group should indicate to law enforcement agents that they should exercise even more moderate and careful methods in dealing with the group. The characteristics that cause concern can be counteracted by other characteristics that a group will not become caught up in violence.

Characteristics That Cause Concern

The characteristics that cause concern can be grouped under the three headings of "interaction factors," "internal factors," and "belief factors."[30]

Interaction Factors

1. The group is labeled with a pejorative term such as "cult" or "sect" by members of mainstream society, and it is the target of a great deal of aggressive activity on the part of the media, government and law enforcement agents, concerned relatives, and disgruntled former members.
2. The group is extremely resistant to investigation, and either aggressively battles against its perceived enemies or withdraws to an isolated refuge.
3. As a result of conflict and opposition from mainstream society, the group abandons proselytizing to gain new converts, and turns inward to preserve salvation for its members alone.
4. The group has already engaged in a violent conflict with law enforcement agents in which agents have died.

These characteristics describe a group that is in strong conflict with society. The group's opponents as well as the believers possess a rigid dualistic worldview of "us versus them," good versus evil. They are locked in a battle that can accelerate. The believers' radical dualism is expressed in their excessively combative responses to their perceived enemies, or by their withdrawal from society to an isolated refuge. Because of the social opposition that they experience, the believers may decide to stop proselytizing; they resolve that salvation is extended only to current members of their group. Their social opponents dehumanize the believers by calling them "cultists." The believers dehumanize members of mainstream society by regarding them as aligned with evil forces.

The religious group is especially prone to be caught up in further violence if it has already engaged in a violent conflict in which law enforcement agents have died, as was the case with the Weaver family at Ruby Ridge and the Branch Davidians at Mount Carmel Center. Law enforcement agents need to become aware of their propensity to take punitive violent actions against a group they deem responsible for the deaths of colleagues. Both at Ruby Ridge and Mount Carmel Center, law enforcement agents magnified the threat posed by the Weaver family and the Davidians, and they failed to consider that the actions of law enforcement agents contributed to the tragic loss of life of their colleagues.

Internal Factors

5. Believers take an extremely literal approach to interpreting scriptures and other texts that are important to the group.
6. Followers are overly dependent on a charismatic leader (who claims authority from an unseen source, such as God) as the sole means to achieve their ultimate concern (salvation).
7. The leader's charismatic authority has not yet been routinized into institutional structures and decisionmaking bodies and offices.
8. The charismatic leader has set goals for the group that is in danger of being disproven by physical events.
9. The group's leader gives new identities to the followers, including new names, and drastically rearranges the believers' family and marriage relationships.
10. Leaving the group involves very high "exit costs"[31] in terms of personal identity, family and friendship associations, and livelihood.
11. The group exists in an isolated situation, so that members are not exposed to alternative interpretations of reality.
12. Acts of violence are repeated in a ritualistic manner, so that the scale and intensity of the violence increases.

Many of the religious groups that have been involved in violence, including the Branch Davidians, Heaven's Gate, and individuals associated with Christian Identity follow a literal approach to interpreting scriptures and other texts. They think they are interpreting scripture literally, when in fact they are exercising a selective reading. Their rigid manner of reading texts is not sensitive to ambiguity and subtlety in the meaning of the texts, and they take little or no account of the historical and social circumstances that produced them. This literal approach to reading "sacred" texts appears to be related to the rigid dualism that characterizes their patterns of thinking.

There does not have to be a charismatic leader for the group to be potentially violent. For instance, the Montana Freemen who were involved in an 81-day standoff with FBI agents in 1996 were Identity Christians, who threatened violence and hoped to initiate the second American Revolution, but did not have a charismatic leader. They possessed a revolutionary ideology that contained the potential to motivate the Freemen to commit violent acts.[32] But some religious communities become overly dependent on a charismatic leader as being the sole means of attaining salvation. This gives considerable scope for a leader to abuse his or her power over followers if there are no checks on the leader's authority. Again, it is important to stress that this does not mean that followers are not able to think for themselves. They can, at any time, withdraw their allegiance and hence undermine the leader's charismatic authority. An overdependence on a charismatic leader to achieve the ultimate concern can imperil the group's ultimate concern if the leader is in danger of being removed by death or arrest, which may prompt followers to resort to violent actions in order to safeguard the ultimate concern.

Charismatic leaders often make predictions that are disconfirmed by physical events. The leader then usually provides a reinterpretation that the followers find satisfying. If the group's failure to achieve goals set by the leader calls into question whether they will achieve their ultimate concern, however, then group members may resort to violent actions to preserve their ultimate concern.

There are numerous new religious movements who make high demands on followers, which do not become involved in violence. However, I regard members permitting leaders to give them new identities and to rearrange their family relationships as giving too much authority to a leader who may turn out to be unworthy or on an ego trip.

People leave high demand groups all the time. However, if leaving the group involves high costs in terms of one's identity, friendships, family associations, and economic survival, then it is possible that members might choose to die together or attack perceived enemies rather than abandon a failing ultimate concern.

The level of isolation of a community will vary. For instance, the Branch Davidians had regular interactions with their neighbors and some had jobs outside Mount Carmel Center. The Davidians welcomed an undercover agent inside

Mount Carmel Center even though they had a good idea that he was a law enforcement agent. FBI agents imposed the isolation of the Branch Davidians during the siege. Jonestown was a community isolated in the Guyanese jungle with the news of outside events controlled and interpreted by Jim Jones. Aum Shinrikyo devotees ran businesses that catered to the general public as well as lived in communes. Their isolation was self-imposed by the worldview that they adopted. The same was true of the Montana Freemen inside Justus Township who had Internet connection with likeminded believers.

I have discussed above how ritualized acts of violence can escalate.

Belief Factors

13. The group has catastrophic millennial and dualistic beliefs that expect and promote conflict.
14. The group's millennial beliefs are related to a radical dualistic view of good versus evil that dehumanizes other people.
15. The group combines apocalyptic millennial beliefs with a conviction that the group is being persecuted.
16. Belief in reincarnation is combined with catastrophic millennialism and belief that the group is being persecuted.
17. The theology expresses the view that this Earth is not the believers' true home.
18. The group members' sense of being persecuted is expressed in strong belief in conspiracy theories.

While most millennialists never become involved in violence, many religious groups that become caught up violence have apocalyptic or catastrophic millennial worldviews. Catastrophic millennialism involves a radical dualism that expects conflict and can even promote it. This rigid dualism has the effect of dehumanizing others outside the group who are deemed to be enemies. Such dehumanization exacerbates the conflict and can sanction the murder of those who are dehumanized; they are seen as not being worthy of life.

Apocalypticism, the expectation that the world will soon be destroyed, can devalue earthly existence in the eyes of the believers. If the believers feel authorities are persecuting them, there may be greater temptation for them either to leave this sinful world through death or to commit violence against their persecutors, who in their eyes are obviously aligned with Satan. A belief in reincarnation is not usually related to violence, but the cases of Jonestown, Aum Shinrikyo, Heaven's Gate (1997), and Solar Temple (deaths in 1994, 1995, 1997 in Switzerland, France, and Quebec) suggest that the combination of belief in reincarnation with apocalypticism and a conviction that the group is being persecuted can be an especially lethal mixture, which radically devalues earthly life and can prompt some believers to commit murder, suicide, or both to prevent the failure of their ultimate concern. If the theology already emphasizes that the Earth is not the believers' true home, then this will receive heightened emphasis when there is persecution, and may be used as justification for leaving earthly life. The believers' sense of being persecuted will be expressed in a strong adherence to conspiracy theories.

Reassuring Characteristics

1. The group is not being attacked by hostile opponents such as reporters, concerned relatives, apostates, government agents, and law enforcement agents.
2. The group openly and constructively responds to questions and investigations about their beliefs and activities.
3. The believers strive to be good citizens and neighbors in their surrounding community.
4. The group is active in evangelization to extend salvation to others, but it is not preaching a hate-filled ideology.
5. The group and its leader have made clear statements against the use of violence.
6. The leader has made statements indicating a willingness to reinterpret predictions that are likely to fail, or has indicated a willingness to be flexible about the goals set for the group.

Note that the first of the reassuring characteristics involves the absence of opposition by avowed enemies of the religious group. Again, *the quality of the interactions* of people in mainstream society with members of unconventional religious groups is crucial in determining whether the group will become caught up in violence. The second reassuring characteristic is that when there is suspicion and opposition directed toward the religious group, the members respond in a healthy constructive manner to answer questions and cooperate with investigators. Correspondingly, the believers will participate as good citizens and neighbors in their surrounding context.

The believers might actively proselytize to extend salvation to others, as were the Branch Davidians, who, when their access to the public was cut off, tried to convert the FBI negotiators. This was a group that was not likely to take hostile actions against mainstream society. However, revolutionary millennialists can be very active in proselytizing, while also preaching a hate-filled ideology, such as Christian Identity or Nazism that can prompt believers to attack and kill the hated "others."

Statements against violence issued by the group and the leader need to be analyzed very carefully. For instance, Heaven's Gate posted a statement against suicide on its website, but the members defined their self-administered deaths in 1997 as an "exit" to a heavenly salvation on the mother ship instead of a group suicide.[33] It is a good sign if the group and its leader make clear statements against suicide, but it should be recalled that theological interpretations and religious methods to achieve the ultimate concern are changed in response to circumstances and events. A great deal of persecution can push the members of a peaceful group to resort to violence, either against themselves or their enemies, or both, to preserve their ultimate concern.

If the leader has made predictions that are likely to fail, it is reassuring if he or she indicates ahead of time a willingness to reinterpret. However, charismatic leaders most often make reinterpretations anyway when their predictions fail.[34] If the group is failing to achieve goals related to the ultimate concern, an expressed willingness on the part of the leader and the members to be flexible about the goal is likewise reassuring.

Conclusion

A religious group's theology is constantly being adjusted in response to events within the group, events in society, and the interactions that believers have with nonbelievers. Furthermore, members of a religious group will inevitably have different interpretations of the theology. Religious beliefs motivate people to take actions of various sorts, but those beliefs are often adjusted in response to events. A group can shift from being one that causes concern for its potential to be caught up in violence, to one that is not cause for great concern, or vice versa. Individuals and their social interactions are never static. Law enforcement agents, meanwhile, make a grave mistake if they think that the propensity to create violent religious incidents only resides with members of unconventional religions. *The manner in which all of us interact with members of religious movements helps to determine the potential for volatility.*

If a religious group is assessed to have a number of the factors that give cause for concern, that is an indication that a more thorough investigation is needed, and that law enforcement agents should deal with the group very cautiously, using moderate means. Law enforcement agents should avoid taking aggressive actions that make the believers feel persecuted and are likely to cause loss of life. Law enforcement agents have the challenging job of attempting to prevent violent acts by members of revolutionary millennial movements, while refraining from unnecessarily assaulting a religious group, or applying so much pressure to a group that it becomes fragile, prompting its members to initiate violence to preserve their ultimate concern.

NOTES

1.   Jess Walter, *Every Knee Shall Bow: The Truth and Tragedy of Ruby Ridge and the Randy Weaver Family* (New York: HarperPaperbacks, 1995).

2.   James Tabor and Eugene V. Gallagher, *Why Waco? Cults and the Battle for Religious Freedom in America* (Berkeley, Calif.: University of California Press, 1995); Stuart A. Wright, ed., *Armageddon in Waco: Critical Perspectives on the Branch Davidian Conflict* (Chicago, Ill.: University of Chicago Press, 1995); Carol Moore, *The Davidian Massacre: Disturbing Questions about Waco Which Must Be Answered* (Franklin, Tenn., and Springfield, Va.: Legacy Communications and Gun Owners Foundation, 1995); Catherine Wessinger, *How the Millennium Comes Violently: From Jonestown to Heaven's Gate* (New York: Seven Bridges Press, 2000), 56-119.

3.   Wessinger, *How the Millennium Comes Violently*; John R. Hall, "Public Narratives and the Apocalyptic Sect: From Jonestown to Mt. Carmel," in Wright, ed., *Armageddon in Waco*, 205-35; James T. Richardson, "Minority Religions and the Context of Violence: A Conflict/Interactionist Perspective," in *Terrorism and Political Violence* 3 (Spring 2001): 103-33.

4.   Wessinger, *How the Millennium Comes Violently*, 47, 121, 143, 274-75, 280-81.

5.   Wessinger, *How the Millennium Comes Violently*, 30-55, 120-57; John R. Hall, *Gone from the Promised Land: Jonestown in American Cultural History* (New Brunswick, N.J.: Transaction Books, 1987); Mary McCormick Maaga, *Hearing the Voices of Jonestown: Putting a Human Face on an American Tragedy* (Syracuse, N.Y.: Syracuse University Press, 1998); Rebecca Moore, "'American as Cherry Pie': Peoples Temple and Violence in America," in *Millennialism, Persecution, and Violence: Historical Cases*, ed.

Catherine Wessinger (Syracuse, N.Y.: Syracuse University Press, 2000), 121-37; Ian Reader, *A Poisonous Cocktail?* *Aum Shinrikyo's Path to Violence* (Copenhagen: Nordic Institute of Asian Studies Books, 1996); Ian Reader, *Religious Violence in Contemporary Japan: The Case of Aum Shinrikyo* (Richmond, Surrey, UK: Curzon Press, 2000); Robert J. Kisala and Mark R. Mullins, eds., *Religion and Social Crisis in Japan: Understanding Japanese Society through the Aum Affair* (New York: Palgrave, 2001).

6.   David G. Bromley and James T. Richardson, eds., *The Brainwashing/ Deprogramming Controversy: Sociological, Psychological, Legal and Historical Perspectives* (New York: Edwin Mellen Press, 1983).

7.   Thomas Robbins and Dick Anthony, "Sects and Violence: Factors Enhancing the Volatility of Marginal Religious Movements," in Wright, ed., *Armageddon in Waco*, 236-59.

8.   Robert D. Baird, *Category Formation and the History of Religions* (The Hague: Mouton, 1971).

9.   Wessinger, *How the Millennium Comes Violently*, 5-6. My definition of millennialism builds and expands on the definition provided by Norman Cohn, *The Pursuit of the Millennium* (London: Secker & Warburg, 1957).

10.   Catherine Wessinger, "Millennialism With and Without the Mayhem: Catastrophic and Progressive Expectations," in *Millennialism, Messiahs, and Mayhem: Contemporary Apocalyptic Movements*, eds. Thomas Robbins and Susan J. Palmer (New York: Routledge, 1997), 47-59; Wessinger, *How the Millennium Comes Violently*; Catherine Wessinger, "The Interacting Dynamics of Millennial Beliefs, Persecution, and Violence," in Wessinger, *Millennialism, Persecution, and Violence*, 3-39.

11.   Wessinger, *How the Millennium Comes Violently*, 158-217; Wessinger, "The Interacting Dynamics," 35-38.

12.   Scott Lowe, "Western Millennial Ideology Goes East: The Taiping Revolution and Mao's Great Leap Forward," in Wessinger, *Millennialism, Persecution, and Violence*, 220-40; Robert Ellwood, "Nazism as a Millennialist Movement," in Wessinger, *Millennialism, Persecution, and Violence*, 241-60; Richard C. Salter, "Time, Authority, and Ethics in the Khmer Rouge: Elements of the Millennial Vision in Year Zero," in Wessinger, *Millennialism, Persecution, and Violence*, 281-98. "Speed progress up to an apocalyptic rate" is Robert Ellwood's phrase.

13.   Adam Szubin, Carl J. Jensen, Rod Gregg, "Interacting with 'Cults': A Policing Model," *FBI Law Enforcement Bulletin* (September 2000): 16-24, <http://www.fbi.gov/library/leb/2000/sep00leb.pdf>.

14.   Szubin, Jensen, Gregg, "Interacting with 'Cults'"; Lonnie Kliever, "Meeting God in Garland: A Model of Religious Tolerance," *Nova Religio: The Journal of Alternative and Emergent Religions* 3, no. 1 (October 1999): 45-53.

15.   Wessinger, *How the Millennium Comes Violently*.

16.   Grant Underwood, "Millennialism, Persecution, and Violence: The Mormons," in Wessinger, *Millennialism, Persecution, and Violence*, 43-61.

17.   Linda E. Olds, *Fully Human: How Everyone Can Integrate the Benefits of Masculine and Feminine Sex Roles* (Englewood Cliffs, N.J.: Prentice-Hall, 1981).

18.   Phillip Lucas, "How Future Wacos Might Be Avoided: Two Proposals," in *From the Ashes: Making Sense of Waco*, ed. James R. Lewis (Lanham,

Md.: Rowman & Littlefield, 1994), 209-13; Jayne Seminare Docherty, "When the Parties Bring Their Gods to the Table: Learning Lessons from Waco," Ph.D. diss., George Mason University, 1998, published as *Learning Lessons from Waco: When the Parties Bring Their Gods to the Negotiation Table* (Syracuse, N.Y.: Syracuse Univesrsity Press, 2001).

19.   Tabor and Gallagher, *Why Waco?*; James D. Tabor, "The Waco Tragedy: An Autobiographical Account of One Attempt to Prevent Disaster," in Lewis, *From the Ashes*, 13-21.

20.   Wessinger, *How the Millennium Comes Violently*, 73-74, citing negotiation audiotape no. 129.

21.   Wessinger, *How the Millennium Comes Violently*, 75-76; James D. Tabor, "The Events at Waco: An Interpretive Log" (1995), <http://home.maine.rr.com/waco/ww.html>.

22.   Wessinger, *How the Millennium Comes Violently*, 22, 93-94; on the Davidians cheering at the prospect of coming out, see House of Representatives, *Investigation into the Activities of Federal Law Enforcement Agencies toward the Branch Davidians: Thirteenth Report by the Committee on Government Reform and Oversight Prepared in Conjunction with the Committee on the Judiciary together with Additional and Dissenting Views*, Report 104-749 (Washington, D.C.: U.S. Government Printing Office, 1996), 65; "Last Recorded Words of David Koresh, April 16-18, 1993" audiotape introduced by James Tabor, transcribed and published in Wessinger, *How the Millennium Comes Violently*, 105-12.

23.   Wessinger, "The Interacting Dynamics"; Wessinger, *How the Millennium Comes Violently*.

24.   Underwood, "Millennialism, Persecution, and Violence: The Mormons"; Michelene E. Pesantubbee, "From Vision to Violence: The Wounded Knee Massacre," in Wessinger, *Millennialism, Persecution, and Violence*, 62-81; Christine Steyn, "Millenarian Tragedies in South Africa: The Xhosa Cattle-Killing Movement and the Bulhoek Massacre," in Wessinger, *Millennialism, Persecution, and Violence*, 185-202.

25.   Maaga, *Hearing the Voices of Jonestown*; Moore, "'American as Cherry Pie,'"; Hall, *Gone from the Promised Land*; Wessinger, *How the Millennium Comes Violently*, 30-55.

26.   Wessinger, *How the Millennium Comes Violently*, 120-57; Reader, *A Poisonous Cocktail?*

27.   Szubin, Jensen, and Gregg, "Interacting with 'Cults.'"

28.   Wessinger, *How the Millennium Comes Violently*, 271.

29.   Ibid., 60-65.

30.   The following is a refinement of my discussion of characteristics that cause concern and reassuring characteristics in Wessinger, *How the Millennium Comes Violently*, 275-82.

31.   Benjamin Zablocki, "The Blacklisting of a Concept: The Strange History of the Brainwashing Conjecture in the Sociology of Religion," *Nova Religio: The Journal of Alternative and Emergent Religions* 1 (October 1997): 96-121.

32.   Wessinger, *How the Millennium Comes Violently*, 158-217; Jean E. Rosenfeld, "The Justus Freemen Standoff: The Importance of the Analysis of Religion in Avoiding Violent Outcomes," in Wessinger, *Millennialism, Persecution, and Violence*, 323-44.

33. Wessinger, *How the Millennium Comes Violently,* 229-52.
34. Lorne L. Dawson, "When Prophecy Fails and Faith Persists: A Theoretical Overview," *Nova Religio: The Journal of Alternative and Emergent Religions* 3, no. 1 (October 1999): 60-82.

Scientology: Separating Truth from Fiction

HEBER C. JENTZSCH

Introduction[1]

Scientology, the only major religion founded in the twentieth century, was born amid the controversy and turmoil of one of the most chaotic periods in mankind's history. The word "Scientology" combines the Latin "*scio*" (to know) and the Greek "*logos*" (the study of). Thus, Scientology means "the study of knowledge," or "knowing how to know." It is a religious philosophy that combines spiritual traditions from the East with a uniquely Western technology of *application* that provides people with the hope of spiritual salvation and the tools to achieve it. Scientology and its forerunner, Dianetics (from the Greek "*dia*," meaning "through," and "*nous*," meaning "soul," a spiritual healing technology that is now a sub-study of Scientology) should not themselves be controversial. The spiritual truths they provide are accessible to anyone with an average reading ability. They contain methods of application that are simple to apply. Their results are amply documented and validated by innumerable testimonials and case histories.

So why did the emergence of Dianetics and Scientology at the height of the Cold War generate such controversy? Why, in 1950, did a simple handbook on Dianetics procedure that enabled the common man to obtain relief from the sufferings of life and uncover his human potential, spark an onslaught by the combined forces of the mental health community and the U.S. government? Why did Scientology's religious philosophy, which explained mysteries plaguing mankind for millennia, and presented them in clear axioms with techniques of application that anyone could understand, provoke a vicious attack, which, in the first two years alone cost its instigators more than $2,000,000?

The promises of hope and spiritual freedom that Dianetics and Scientology brought to a world on the brink of nuclear war disturbed pre-existing plans for the literal conquest and control of mankind. This is not some mythical contest between abstract concepts of good and evil. Rather, these were the specific plans of men in key positions of influence—plans which, if successful, would have turned whole populations into something more like slaves than men.

These are harsh words, true, but in this chapter I hope to share the truth about Dianetics and Scientology and the genesis of the attacks on them. No study of these subjects is complete without at least some understanding of these matters. In this essay I hope to facilitate an understanding and appreciation of L. Ron Hubbard's life's work and what obstacles he faced in bringing that work to the public.

L. Ron Hubbard

There are only two tests of a life well lived, L. Ron Hubbard once remarked: Did one do as one intended? And were people glad one lived? In testament to the first stands the full body of his life's work, including the more than 5,000 writings and 3,000 tape-recorded lectures on Dianetics and Scientology. In evidence of the second are the tens of millions of individuals whose lives have been demonstrably bettered because he lived. They are the more than three million children now reading because of Hubbard's educational discoveries; they are the millions of men and women freed from substance abuse through his breakthroughs in drug rehabilitation; they are the more than fifty million people who have been touched by his nonreligious moral code; and they are the many millions more who hold his work to be the spiritual cornerstone of their lives.

Although widely known as the founder of Dianetics and Scientology, L. Ron Hubbard cannot be so simply categorized. If nothing else, his life was too varied, his influence too broad for classification. There are children in southern Africa, for example, who know nothing of Dianetics and Scientology, but they know him as an educator. Likewise, there are factory workers in Albania who know him only for his administrative discoveries, citizens in China who know him only as the author of their nonreligious moral code, and millions of readers in a dozen languages who know him only for his novels or his Hollywood screenplays.

Indeed, Hubbard's internationally acclaimed educational methods are utilized by thousands of educators and academic institutions, while his drug rehabilitation methods form the basis of a program acclaimed by many as the most effective in the world. Among other accomplishments, he developed and codified an administrative technology currently utilized by more than 4,000 organizations worldwide, including multinational corporations, charitable bodies, political parties, schools, youth clubs and hundreds of small businesses.

L. Ron Hubbard was a successful professional in many fields, including photography, aviation, engineering, cinematography, administration, exploration, music, philosophy, education; he was even a master mariner. Moreover, as one of the most widely read authors of our time, he was able to support his own research and development of Dianetics and Scientology.

However impressive these figures, no measure of L. Ron Hubbard is complete without some appreciation of these subjects, which became his life's work. How he came to found Dianetics and Scientology is an immense story. That research essentially consumed his entire life, and he drew from his experiences, from his early years in the back hills of Montana, through his contacts with twenty-one races and cultures including Pacific Northwest Indian tribes, Buddhist monks in inland China and Philippine Tagalogs, to, as he was wont to joke, the people of the Bronx. In the simplest terms, his research focused upon two fundamental questions. First, extending from experimentation conducted while attending university, he was searching for the long-speculated life force, i.e., the source of human consciousness. Second, he wished to determine the common denominator of life—for only with that established, he reasoned, could one effectively determine what was both true and workable as regards the human condition.

The first plateau of that search came in 1938 with an unpublished manuscript entitled *Excalibur*. That work proposed life to be much more than a random series of chemical reactions, and that some definable urge underlay all human behavior. That urge, he declared, was "Survive!" and it constituted the single most pervasive force among all people. That man was surviving was not a new idea. However, that this was the single common denominator of existence *was*, and therein lay the signpost for all research to follow.

The Second World War proved both an interruption of research and a further impetus for Hubbard. As he so succinctly put it, "Man has a madness and that madness is called war." He was also among the first to express concerns over what the advent of atomic weapons meant when unaccompanied by a corresponding understanding of human behavior.

Hubbard pursued his research, looking for ways to apply his discoveries about the fundamentals of existence. The culmination of his work to this point came in 1945, at the Oak Knoll Naval Hospital in Oakland, California. Left partially blind from injured optic nerves and lame with hip and spinal injuries, he became one of five thousand naval and Marine Corps patients under treatment at Oak Knoll. Also under treatment at the facility were several hundred former inmates of Japanese prisoner-of-war camps. Intrigued by their inexplicable failure to recover despite intensive medical care, Hubbard took it upon himself to administer an early form of Dianetics. In all, some fifteen patients received his attention as he utilized his techniques to remove what he postulated was a mental inhibition to recovery. What he eventually discovered, and what saved the lives of those patients, rested upon a key philosophic point: notwithstanding generally held scientific theory of the time, one's state of mind actually took precedence over one's physical condition. That is, our viewpoints, attitudes, and emotional condition ultimately determine our physical well being and not the reverse. Or as Hubbard himself so succinctly put it, "Function monitored structure."

After the war, Hubbard set out to further test the workability of his discoveries through intensive research on individuals from all strata of society. Included were actors from a Hollywood theater workshop, industry executives from neighboring studios, accident victims from a Pasadena hospital, and the criminally insane from a Georgia mental institution.

All told, Hubbard personally worked with some four hundred men, women and children before compiling his sixteen years of investigation into a manuscript. Entitled, *Dianetics: The Original Thesis* (published today as *The Dynamics of Life*), the work was not actually offered for publication, but rather passed to friends for review. Hundreds of copies eventually saw circulation through hand-operated duplicating machines; and so enthusiastic was the response that L. Ron Hubbard was encouraged to present a broader announcement. That paper, entitled "Terra Incognita: The Mind," appeared in the Winter/Spring 1949-1950 issue of the *Explorers Club Journal*. After this, Hubbard was deluged with requests for further information, eventually prompting his formal handbook, *Di-*

anetics: The Modern Science of Mental Health, published on 9 May 1950.

Dianetics contained L. Ron Hubbard's discovery of a previously unknown and harmful part of the mind that contains recordings of past experiences of loss, pain, and unconsciousness. These incidents of spiritual trauma are recorded along with all other experiences of one's life in sequential order on what is called the *time track.* The painful incidents recorded on this time track exist below a person's level of awareness and accumulate collectively to make up what is called the *reactive mind,* the source of all travail, unwanted fears, emotions, pains, and psychosomatic illnesses—as distinct from the *analytical mind* which thinks, observes data, remembers it, and resolves problems.

Dianetics provides a method to address this reactive mind and to erase its harmful effects on an individual. When this occurs, one has achieved a new state of spiritual awareness. One's basic and fundamental spirituality, personality, artistry, personal force and individual character, one's inherent goodness and decency are restored. This is called the state of *Clear.*

When word of Hubbard's discoveries began to spread, the response was considerable: more than thirty thousand copies of *Dianetics* sold immediately off the press, while bookstores struggled to keep the text on their shelves. As evidence of its workability grew—and the fact that Dianetics actually offered techniques anyone could apply—response was even more dramatic. The summer's headlines read: "Dianetics Taking US by Storm," and "Fastest Growing Movement in America." By the end of the year, some 750 Dianetics groups had spontaneously formed from coast to coast, and six cities boasted Dianetics foundations to help facilitate advancement of the subject.

Not everyone, however, greeted Dianetics with enthusiasm—particularly those who perceived that their livelihoods were threatened by a philosophy that gave the man in the street the ability to do something positive about his mental and emotional condition. This placed Dianetics on a collision course with the psychiatric community, some of whose members were living off of large government grants.

The Psychiatric Establishment's Reaction to Dianetics

To appreciate the threat that Dianetics posed to certain members of the psychiatric establishment, both in terms of its inherent message and its unprecedented popularity with the American public, it is necessary to examine something of their plans.

Psychiatry dates back to shortly before the turn of the twentieth century. That it promotes itself as a healing profession is arguably a misrepresentation. To a considerable degree, it has always had a mission centered on control. This purpose is exemplified in an address given to the National Council for Mental Hygiene on 18 June 1940 by then Colonel John R. Rees, who would later become the first president of the World Federation of Mental Health. In his speech entitled "Strategic Planning for Mental Health (Reese 1940)," Rees stated:

"We must aim to make it [psychiatry] permeate every educational activity on our national life: primary, secondary, university and technical education are all concerned with varying stages in the development of the child and adolescent. Those who provide the education . . . must all be objects of our interest. . . . Public life, politics and industry should all of them be within our sphere of influence.

". . . [S]ince the last world war we have done much to infiltrate the various social organizations throughout the country, and in their work one can see clearly how the principles for which this society and others stood in the past have become accepted as part of the ordinary working plan of these various bodies. . . .

"Similarly, we have made a useful attack on a number of professions. The two easiest of them, naturally, are the teaching profession and the Church: the two most difficult are law and medicine. . . .

"If we are to infiltrate the professional and social activities of other people, I think we must imitate the Totalitarians and organize some kind of fifth column activity! If better ideas on mental health are to progress and spread we as the salesmen must lose our identity. . . .

"Let us all, therefore, very secretly be "fifth columnists."[2]

Following this direction, psychiatrists used the exigencies of World War II to entrench themselves into the government via the armed forces. In England, John Rees was the prime mover at the Tavistock Clinic, where all branches of psychiatry were being developed, including family and child psychiatry as well as electroconvulsive therapy (shock treatment) and lobotomy experiments. Rees was then appointed to the War Office and by the end of the war had more than 300 psychiatrists in the British armed forces. Rees then arranged to train officers of the Office of Strategic Services (the forerunner of the American Central Intelligence Agency) in psychological warfare.[3]

Prime targets for these wartime psychiatrists were the military's desires to control large populations, and to extract information from prisoners. In a 20 November 1942 meeting, key representatives of the Office of Strategic Services, the Federal Commissioner of Narcotics, the director of the Federal Bureau of Investigation's Laboratory, and several prominent psychiatrists established a project to perform drug experiments on prisoners of war to locate substances that would make them more malleable. The psychiatrist who headed this project was Dr. Winfred Overholzer of St. Elizabeth's hospital. In a top secret meeting held on 14 December 1942, this same group of government officials and psychiatrists expanded their experiments to college students in Philadelphia.[4]

After the war, these experiments in mind control continued unbeknownst to an unsuspecting American public. As later Congressional investigations revealed, they were widespread. In fact, according to a secret document (1950) released many years later under the Freedom of Information Act, the CIA sought to recruit a Dianeticist as a "candidate for indoctrination" in its mind control programs. What made this candidate attractive in addition to his language skills and his status as a reserve officer was his training in Dianetics.[5]

Government mind control projects, such as the CIA's Project Bluebird, Project Artichoke, and the notorious MK ULTRA have been exposed in Congressional hearings and in popular literature.[6] That the scientific validity of the "brainwashing" theories developed from these experiments has come to be criticized by respected scientists[7] does not negate the fact that psychiatrists were utilizing their skills toward developing the means of implanting false personalities in people to turn them into deployable intelligence agents or even assassins. This placed these psychiatrists squarely at odds with the goals of Dianetics (and later, Scientology).

Further post-war events helped to establish psychiatry's position of influence. In October of 1945, Brock Chisholm—co-founder of the World Health Organization—refined the objective of psychiatry in his address: "The Re-Establishment of Peacetime Society: The Responsibility of Psychiatry" in which he stated:

The re-interpretation and eventual eradication of the concept of right and wrong . . . these are the belated objectives of practically all of effective psychotherapy. . . . If the race is to be freed from its crippling burden of good and evil, it must be psychiatrists who take the original responsibility.[8]

Moreover, in 1945 John Rees visited New York and proposed to the International Committee of Mental Hygiene that a world conference be held in London to unite the activities of psychiatrists. This conference began the planning of the establishment of the World Federation of Mental Health, the first meeting of which was in 1948.[9]

Finally, in 1946, the U.S. Congress passed the National Mental Health Act,[10] establishing the National Institute of Mental Health (NIMH). Robert Felix, who was instrumental in getting the Act passed, became the NIMH's first director. Since then, the NIMH has doled out billions of dollars to psychiatrists.[11]

And this is the world Dianetics entered: a world where psychiatry was entrenched among the U.S. intelligence services, living off hefty government grants, and experimenting on an oblivious public—a world where their critics were simply labeled insane and "in need of psychiatric help."

Thus, the battle lines were drawn. Dianetics offered a means to the man in the street to achieve happiness, stability, and success for himself. It gave him a method that, for the first time, he could utilize to improve his own condition. It should also be kept in mind that L. Ron Hubbard achieved something that psychiatrists have long been attempting to achieve: to write a book about the mind that was genuinely popular, that people actually wanted to read, and that was both understandable and applicable. But Dianetics did more. It labeled the latest powerful mind-altering psychiatric drugs as dangerous. And it exposed the inhuman brutalities of psychiatrists and the harm they caused with electroconvulsive therapy and lobotomies, clearly substantiating the irreparable damages these treatments caused to healthy brain tissue.

The psychiatric industry's response to Dianetics was immediate and considerable. Less than a month after the publication of *Dianetics*, psychiatrists on government payrolls were denigrating the book as a "hoax," while admitting in the same breath that they had never even read it.[12]

American Psychiatric Association (APA) medical director Dr. Daniel Blain coordinated these attacks with a handful of APA psychiatrists. Blain recognized Dianetics' potential for upsetting the *status quo*. In a paper delivered on 21 June 1950 at the annual meeting of the Canadian Medical Association, Blain described Dianetics as "a new form of therapy and treatment whereby the most serious of mental diseases can be cured in a few hours merely by getting the patient to substitute direct thinking by logic for confused thinking dominated by feelings."[13] He warned that Dianetics was becoming popular because psychiatrists "had failed in educating the public" in their theories.

Blain and his colleagues used their government connections to secretly spread lies through media and government files, escalating into an all-out attempt to close down the Dianetics foundations that had sprung up across the country and later, after its formation in 1954, the Church of Scientology. The issue was clearly financial: how long could psychiatrists continue to convince the American taxpayer to pay for multimillion dollar psychiatric appropriations when Dianetics provided a means to greater happiness and ability for only the price of a book and a willingness to apply its principles?

Dianetics also came to the attention of members of the U.S. intelligence community who tried to seize it for their own use. Shortly after the publication of *Dianetics, the Modern Science of Mental Health*, the U.S. Navy's Office of Research tried to get L. Ron Hubbard to use his discoveries on a project to make people more suggestible, threatening to reactivate his commission in the naval reserves if he refused. Hubbard was able to resign his commission before it could be reactivated, thus keeping Dianetics free from government control.

The attacks intensified after January 1951, when Hubbard published *Science of Survival*. In that book, he publicly exposed, for the first time, government-funded mind-control experiments in which psychiatrists administered drugs and electric shock to unsuspecting human guinea pigs who were then implanted, while unconscious, with hypnotic commands. Decades later, victims would receive government compensation for the injuries they suffered from such experiments. But at the time, these matters were among the best-kept secrets of the U.S. intelligence and psychiatric communities. Hubbard had unearthed these experiments while he was conducting research at St. Elizabeth's hospital and discovered that only Dianetics had the power to undo the damage and expose what these government psychiatrists were doing to people. It is not surprising, then, to find that the psychiatrists leading the charge against Dianetics were key architects of these mind control experiments. This is the plan that Dianetics crossed in 1950, and these men formed the core of all attacks against Dianetics and Scientology thereafter.[14]

From Dianetics to Scientology

L. Ron Hubbard advanced his research at a rapid pace. That advancement was continuous, methodical, and at least as revelatory as what had preceded it. At the heart of what he began to examine through late 1950 and early 1951 was yet another key philosophic point. That is, if Dianetics constituted the definitive explanation of the human mind, then what was it that utilized the mind? Or more precisely, what was it that constituted life itself?

The ensuing line of research, embarked upon some twenty years earlier, proved nothing short of momentous. As a result of his research, Hubbard discovered the essence of the life force that motivates all living things. In a critical statement on the matter, he wrote, "I have been engaged in the investigation of the fundamentals of life, the material universe and human behavior." And if many before him had "roved upon this unmapped track," he added, they had left no signposts. Nevertheless, in the early spring of 1952, through the course of a pivotal lecture in Phoenix, Arizona, the result of this research was announced: Scientology.

An applied religious philosophy, today Scientology is contained in more than forty books and more than 2,500 tape-recorded lectures. All told, these works represent the definitive statement of man's nature and potential. While culminating ten thousand years of man's search for this spiritual identity, its approach is absolutely unique and new. Among the essential tenets of the Scientology philosophy: man is an immortal spiritual being; his experience extends well beyond a single lifetime; and his capabilities are unlimited even if not presently realized. In that sense, Scientology represents what may be the ultimate definition of a religion: a means of spiritual transformation.

Yet, if Scientology represents the route to man's highest spiritual aspirations, it also means much to his more immediate existence–to his family, career, and community. This fact is critical to an understanding of Scientology philosophy and is actually what Scientology is all about: not a doctrine or dogma, but the study and handling of the human spirit in relationship to itself, to other life, and to the universe in which we live. It is a religious practice—the application of clearly defined religious principles to improve the conditions in one's life.[15]

Once again the response from the federal/psychiatric circles was considerable. By the mid-1950s, at least half a dozen federal agencies including the Federal Bureau of Investigation (FBI), the Internal Revenue Service (IRS), and the Food and Drug Administration (FDA) were brought into the psychiatric effort to suppress Dianetics and Scientology.

The APA's interest in destroying Dianetics and Scientology organizations intensified when the Church of Scientology actively opposed a bill whose introduction in Congress had been secured by the APA. That bill,[16] referred to by its opponents as "Siberia USA," would have made it possible for an individual to be involuntarily committed to a mental institution and shipped off for an indefinite time to a million-acre camp which the federal government was to furnish in Alaska. The efforts of Scientologists in exposing the true nature of this bill resulted in removal of these draconian commitment provisions. The APA was well aware of who was behind the massive response that defeated the legislation, and they never forgot, as can be seen from some of the attacks its members generated.[17]

The Food and Drug Administration

While it is not possible within the confines of this chapter to detail all of the attacks that APA psychiatrists spawned, a few examples will serve. To prevent the further undoing of their plans, the APA and its members enlisted the aid of the Food and Drug Administration (FDA).

Psychiatrist Zigmond Lebensohn of the D.C. Medical Society directed the FDA's attention to Scientology through a series of "tips." Shortly after the defeat of the "Siberia Bill," Dr. Lebensohn sent these "tips" to other members of the D.C. Medical Society, the D.C. Metropolitan Police Department, and Assistant U.S. Attorney Edward Troxell. Lebensohn alleged, among other things, that the Church of Scientology was using "illegal drugs." The substance in question was a vitamin compound called Dianazene, which consisted of a compound of the commonly available vitamins B_1, C, niacinamide, and calcium (FOIA Documents).

In May 1958, the FDA filed an action for the seizure of Dianazene from the Founding Church of Scientology in

Washington, D.C. Assistant United States Attorney Oliver Gash authorized the seizure. On 3 October 1958, the FDA conducted its first "raid" on the Founding Church of Scientology in Washington, D.C., when a U.S. deputy marshal seized a few bottles of this so-called drug. When it turned out to be a harmless vitamin compound, the case went nowhere (Court Documents).

Frustrated at their lack of success, the FDA explored other avenues of attack, such as attempting to entrap church ministers into practicing medicine without a license. A 7 January 1959 memorandum details a meeting between representatives of the U.S. Attorney's office, the FDA, the U.S. Post Office, and the U.S. Army's Criminal Investigation command, in which the participants decided that infiltration of the church was the only way to accomplish their goals. The infiltrator was "instructed to go there as an enrollee complaining of a physical ailment. . ." to entice the staff into making a medical diagnosis and offering treatment. Candidly, the author of the memo conceded, "As I view this case, we shall not have sufficient evidence with which to proceed unless and until we are able to send people to Scientology with recitations of symptoms of illness, with requests for cures and with subsequence (sic) compliance with these requests."[18]

In late January 1959, Assistant United States Attorney Edward Troxell met with the Mental Health Committee of the D.C. Medical Society, chaired by Dr. Zigmond Lebensohn. The committee suggested that AMA investigator Oliver Field would be helpful in providing a suitable plant. However, a month later, another memorandum from the U.S. Attorney's Office revealed that "after extensive discussions it was decided that the Food and Drug Administration will provide an inspector to enroll in the Scientology organization. . . ."[19]

Thus, on 19 March 1959, FDA inspector Taylor Quinn infiltrated the church, taped a religious service, and passed the information on to the U.S. Attorney's Office. On 31 March 1959, Quinn reported that "there was no evidence developed to indicate fraud or any skepticism or disbelief on the part of the operators or participants in the establishment's activities," and no indication that the church was practicing medicine without a license. Assistant U.S. Attorney Edward Troxell was dissatisfied with these findings and demanded further investigation.[20]

Having found no evidence of wrongdoing, the FDA escalated its activities. On 4 January 1963, U.S. marshals, deputized longshoremen, and armed police barged their way into the Founding Church of Scientology in Washington, D.C., threatened the staff, and left with two vans containing Electrometers,[21] books, scriptures, and other materials.

Over the next several years, the FDA, along with other government agencies, repeatedly infiltrated the church with agents and informants, employed bugging devices, placed a "cover" on church mail, planted false media stories with a willing press, and obtained confidential church bank account information. Yet, all this activity went nowhere. In 1969, the federal appellate court in Washington, D.C. held that Scientology was a bona fide religion protected by the U.S. Constitution, and "the literature setting forth the theory of auditing, including the claims for curative efficacy contained therein, is religious doctrine of Scientology. . . ."[22] Still, it was not until 1973 that a reluctant FDA finally returned the stolen church materials: 5,000 books, 2,900 booklets, and the E-Meters.

The Internal Revenue Service

With the FDA's failure to halt, or even slow down, Scientology's growth, the weight of the attacks soon fell on the shoulders of the Internal Revenue Service—more specifically, on the shoulders of an attorney in the office of the IRS's Chief Counsel, Charlotte Murphy. Of significance is Murphy's attendance at meetings of the D.C. Medical Society's Committee on Mental Health in the mid-1950s, along with the main sponsors of the Siberia bill, the psychiatrist who had falsely "tipped" the FDA that the church was involved in illegal drugs, and a number of leading psychiatrists who had been at the forefront of the attacks on Dianetics from day one. It was, therefore, not surprising that Murphy, having "left the AMA" and now working for the IRS, requested that she be the one to deal with any IRS matters regarding Scientology. Nor were her intentions surprising. She made them clear in a memo to the director of the Washington Branch of the IRS in which she asked whether there were "any local statutes or ordinances available as tools to curtail or close down the operation."

What followed was an all-out effort to harass the church by denying tax-exempt status to various Scientology churches, and issuing federal tax liens against others. The IRS provided disinformation to the Post Office to "support a charge of misrepresentation," and later sent a host of other government agencies such blatantly ludicrous statements about Scientology as: "LSD and perhaps other drugs are widely used by the members while assembled" and that the church used "electric shock" on its parishioners in an "initiation ceremony"—lies that would have been laughable if not for the consequences.

The harassment of Scientology churches and their leaders for purposes totally removed from proper enforcement of the tax laws was definitively exposed during a series of Congressional investigations and hearings in the 1970s. These hearings focused on, among other things, the infamous 1969 Nixon White House "enemies list," and revealed previously secret and illegal IRS programs against individuals and organizations, including the Church of Scientology. Of the 213 names on the Nixon list, 211 were left bankrupt, collapsed, disbanded, or dead. Indeed, of the individuals and organizations on that infamous "enemies list," only two survived intact: Hubbard and the Church of Scientology.

That these attacks continued for as long as they did serves as a study in how bureaucratic momentum can carry raw animus forward long after the initial "reason" has been forgotten. All the while, however, the church continued to expand and deliver its religious services to its growing body of parishioners. Moreover, in 1969, the church established the Citizens Commission on Human Rights (CCHR) so that the work of exposing psychiatric atrocities would continue no matter how much attention and energy the church had to commit to defending itself against unwarranted attacks. Today, CCHR is the foremost psychiatric watchdog group on the planet, with 130 chapters in thirty-one countries.[23]

The history of IRS attacks on the Church of Scientology alone would fill a book. Faced with the choice of defending itself or perishing, the church used the Freedom of Information Act (FOIA) to obtain and ultimately expose government documents that demonstrated a broad range of discriminatory conduct and illegal acts against the church and its parishioners by certain elements within the IRS. When the agency balked at releasing the information, the church was forced to litigate dozens of cases under the FOIA. These cases ultimately resulted in precedent-setting decisions and the exposure and confirmation of the very matters alleged by the church, and more. One federal judge credited the church with reforming IRS procedures that directly benefited "over 1,000 cases involving identical legal issues." An official of the U.S. Department of Justice remarked that the church's actions "significantly contributed to the preservation of democracy for everyone." Indeed, it is virtually impossible to read a page in a legal textbook about the FOIA today without finding a precedent set by the Church of Scientology.

The documents obtained under the FOIA filled scores of filing cabinets and revealed a genuinely shocking parade of dirty tricks authored by those in the IRS who hoped for the church's destruction. They tell of IRS attempts to redefine the term "church," expressly to disqualify Scientology from tax-exempt status. When that did not work, an even more incredible story unfolded: In an attempt to circumvent the absence of any wrongdoing on the church's part, rogue IRS employees engaged in a corrupt scheme of vast dimensions.

Directing this effort was the Los Angeles branch of the IRS Criminal Investigations Division (CID), a unit whose abuses of the church and countless other taxpayers eventually became the focus of extensive Congressional hearings in 1989 and 1990, and ultimately led to substantial IRS reforms. Before that, however, the Los Angeles IRS CID, with the offices of the mother Church of the Scientology religion nearby, held sway over certain key IRS matters relative to Scientology. The CID plan called for nothing short of complete destruction of the church. Yet even as attempts were made to infiltrate church premises and plots were hatched to forge and plant documents to later be "discovered" and used as evidence, church attorneys and staff exposed all.

Thus, in addition to concerns over growing public outrage resulting from this exposure, the CID now had to contend with another problem: It had spent several years investigating the church at enormous cost to taxpayers, only to find no crimes committed.[24] So, in 1985, the Los Angeles CID sought to persuade the Department of Justice to bring some kind—any kind—of prosecution to justify what it had done. The Justice Department attorneys rebuked the unit and refused to support any prosecution or even further investigation.[25]

Recognition by the United States Internal Revenue Service

Throughout this assault, the church persisted in efforts to gain fair treatment from the IRS. Finally, in 1991, senior executives of church organizations were able to find an audience with IRS officials in Washington, D.C. Once dialogue began, outside the purview and without the influence of the Los Angeles CID, the result was inevitable; on 1 October 1993, after the most extensive scrutiny of any organization applying for tax exemption as a non-profit religious organization in its history, the IRS issued a series of rulings expressly recognizing the Church of Scientology and all its subordinate churches and related charitable and educational institutions in the United States as tax-exempt organizations.

During the course of the IRS's examination, the IRS subjected the Scientology church representatives to hundreds of hours of grueling meetings where information had to be provided, over a period of two years, and under three commissioners. The church gave the IRS unrestricted access to all records reflecting the policies, structure, operations, and finances of every Scientology church and organization in the United States and around the world. IRS personnel had carte blanche to examine any and all records at their discretion, including conducting on-site inspections at the various churches of Scientology. But the results were unequivocal. The record overwhelmingly established qualification for tax-exempt recognition by the churches of Scientology.

For years, a great deal of the controversy surrounding churches of Scientology in other countries of the world stemmed from U.S. sources. That is, foreign governments would often make the claim that, "Since the Church of Scientology's headquarters are in the United States, and since the United States government has not recognized you, then why should we? After all, your policy is set in the United States and so that is where any decision should be made." Thus, obtaining religious recognition from the Internal Revenue Service was a vital step in resolving Scientology's rightful place in the world.

Shortly after IRS recognition, the International Criminal Police Organization (INTERPOL) agreed to treat Scientology in accordance with its charter prohibition against intrusion into religious organizations. This further severed a conduit used to spread the false reports about Scientology internationally.

Today, Scientology is recognized as a religion by courts and/or governments in countries such as Albania, Australia, Austria, Belgium, Canada, Costa Rica, Hungary, India, Kazakhstan, Kyrgyzstan, New Zealand, Norway, Portugal, Russia, South Africa, Switzerland, Taiwan, the United Kingdom, the United States, Venezuela, and elsewhere. These decisions and rulings involve matters of great diversity, including recognition of the right to marry, exemption from income, property and value added tax, registration as religious organizations, and immigration.

Top international scholars have also examined Scientology's religiosity and offer a unique view of its teachings. For example, Dr. Bryan Ronald Wilson, Reader Emeritus in Sociology at Oxford University and internationally respected as one of the most distinguished authorities on religious issues, has written extensively about the Scientology religion. Scientology, he wrote, "embraces features which correspond in certain respects to some of the trends evident in the mainstream of Western religion. It employs language which is contemporary, colloquial and unmystical; and it presents its dogmas as matters of objective fact. Its conception of salvation has both proximate and an ultimate dimension."[26] Similar observations have been made by other scholars throughout the world from many different academic and religious traditions. The Church of Scientology has also included several of these essays in its collection entitled *Scientology: Theology and Practice of a Contemporary Religion.*

While there are still places where prejudices are causing discrimination and harassment, at no time in our history have Scientology churches enjoyed greater governmental acceptance than now.

Scientology Today

At this writing, Scientology has grown to a worldwide religious movement comprising more than three thousand churches, missions, and groups in 153 countries, with basic texts on the subjects available in fifty-three languages. *Dianetics* has sold more than eighteen million copies and continues to be on international bestseller lists. Moreover, the international circulation of the church's informational magazines to its members has grown to more than 6.6 million copies—400 percent greater than two decades ago—and the church's World Wide Web information sites on the Internet receive approximately 200,000 visitors per week.[27]

Scientologists come from all walks of life. Demographic surveys show them to be established, productive members of their communities. Nearly 70 percent of members are over the age of thirty. More than 50 percent are married and either own or rent homes. Eighty percent of Scientologists surveyed in 1997 were earning incomes above the U.S. national average. Scientologists also tend to be well educated, with the percentage of college graduates among Scientologists 30 percent higher than the U.S. norm.

Scientologists also reported far fewer days of work missed due to illness than the average in the United States. More than half reported that, in the previous year, they did not miss any days of work due to illness, and over 85 percent missed less than the U.S. average of almost five days missed a year due to illness.

All Scientologists are drug-free, with 100 percent of Scientologists surveyed taking no street drugs at all. Indeed, with more than 250,000 people freed from the harmful effects of drug use, Scientology represents a formidable force in the war against drugs today.

Thus, the story of the attacks against Scientology is basically very simple. Dianetics and Scientology cut across vested interests that then ruthlessly attempted to destroy them. The issue was encroachment on territory claimed by a mental health industry that would stop at nothing to preserve its stake in fulfilling John R. Rees's 1940 strategy. Yet, Scientology overcame all obstacles to achieve recognition and growth.

Still, there are less enlightened countries that do not have a tradition of religious freedom, which are dominated by state religions that consider others to be competition, and which have a long and painful tradition of intolerance. In these countries, the strategy is the same as it once was in the United States. The same false reports are seeded into government files, the same types of psychiatrists and their comrades in arms make authoritative announcements, and the same kind of media blindly repeats unfounded and wild accusations. But just as in the United States where truth once again demonstrated its power by prevailing against odds that would have overwhelmed any lesser cause, so too will it in these countries. Thus, Scientology will continue to grow and to prosper.

NOTES

1. Compiled from the book *What Is Scientology?* (Church of Scientology International, 1998a); see http://www.whatisscientology.org; *L. Ron Hubbard: A Profile* (Church of Scientology International, 1995); see, http:/

/www.lronhubbard.org; Documents obtained under the Freedom of Information Act, and other references, as noted.

2. John R. Rees, "Strategic Planning for Mental Health," address given at the annual meeting of the National Council for Mental Hygiene on 18 June 1940, published in *Mental Health*, 1, no. 4 (1940).

3. A key vehicle for recruiting U.S. psychiatrists into the armed forces was the National Research Council Committee on Neuropsychiatry. Dr. Winfred Overholzer, superintendent of the federally-controlled St. Elizabeth's psychiatric hospital in Washington, D.C., chaired this committee. Those who worked on the Overholzer committee included Dr. Frank Freemont-Smith (who later became a co-founder of the World Federation of Mental Health), Dr. Daniel Blain (Medical Director of the American Medical Association), Dr. Brock Chisholm of Canada, and Dr. William Menninger. See: *Psychiatry: The Ultimate Betrayal* (Wiseman, 1995).

4. Dr. Overholzer continued his mind control experiments for the government at St. Elizabeth's hospital, seeking to develop methods to overlay a false personality on a victim that would render the subject controllable. Hubbard stumbled across victims of these experiments while researching Dianetics. Through Dianetics techniques, he was able to undo the damage. Viewing Dianetics as a threat to his efforts, Dr. Overholzer became a vociferous early attacker of Dianetics. See FOIA document, November 20, 1942.

5. FOIA Document, 1950.

6. Alan W. Scheflin and Edward Opton, Jr., *The Mind Manipulators* (New York: Paddington Press, Ltd., 1978).

7. Dick Anthony, "Religious Movements and Brainwashing Litigation: Evaluating Key Testimony," in T. Robbins and D. Anthony, eds., *In Gods We Trust* (New Brunswick, N.J.: Transaction, 1990); and his "Pseudoscience and Minority Religions: An Evaluation of the Brainwashing Theories of Jean-Marie Abgrall," *Social Justice Research* 12, no. 4 (1990); James Richardson and B. Kilbourne "Classical and Contemporary Applications of Brainwashing Models: A Critique and Comparison," in D. Bromley and J. Richardson, eds., *The Brainwashing/Deprogramming Controversy* (Lewiston, N.Y.: Edwin Mellon, 1983); G.G. James, Brainwashing: The Myth and the Actuality," in *Thought: Fordham University Quarterly* 61 ((1986): 241.

8. Brock Chisholm, "Re-Establishment of Peacetime Society: The Responsibility of Psychiatry," The William Alanson White Memorial Lectures, 2nd Series, October 1945 in *Psychiatry: Journal of the Biology and the Pathology of Interpersonal Relations*, February 1946.

9. Attending this conference from the United States were Dr. Winfred Overholzer, Dr. Robert Felix, Dr. Frank Freemont-Smith, Dr. Daniel Blain, and others.

10. The House of Representatives passed the Act (HR 4512) on 15 March 1946. The Senate passed its version of the Act (SR 4512) on 15 June. After negotiations on a combined bill, the final Act was signed into law on 3 July 1946 (PL 79-487).

11. The April 1949 edition of the newsletter of the Group for the Advancement of Psychiatry (GAP) provides further evidence of the implementation of Rees's 1940 strategy. It discusses such things as increasing

psychiatry's influence in schools, courts, lawyers, and among the clergy—the very key points of attack that Rees outlined in his 1940 strategy for psychiatry. Two excellent books that chronicle psychiatry's organized effort to degrade mankind are: Bruce Wiseman, *Psychiatry: The Ultimate Betrayal* (Los Angeles, Calif.: Freedom Publishing, 1995), and Thomas Roder, Volker Kubillus, and Anthony Burwell, *Psychiatists: The Men Behind Hitler* (Los Angeles, Calif.: Freedom Publishing, 1995), both of which are available from the Citizens Commission on Human Rights.

12.   The first to appear was Dr. Austin Smith, the editor of the *Journal of the American Medical Association*. On 1 June 1950, Smith wrote a number of letters to prestigious doctors and medical societies urging them to make public statements against Dianetics. That same day, Smith also wrote to Oliver Field, director of the AMA's Bureau of Investigation, and suggested that the CIA ought to "look into" Dianetics. He also peppered his letter with negative innuendo about Dianetics and Hubbard, but cautioned that his material was "not for quoting until more facts are obtained." Field also distributed his virulent material to law enforcement agencies (FOIA documents, 1950). Dr. Houston Merritt, director of the Neurological Service at New York's Columbia Presbyterian Medical Center, responded to Smith's 1 June 1950 letter, conceding that he had had no personal experience with Dianetics, yet calling it "bizarre and unscientific" (FOIA Document, 1950).

13.   Daniel Blain, "Trends in Modern Psychiatry." Address given at the Annual Meeting, Canadian Medical Association, 21 June 1950, Halifax, N.S. reprinted in *The Canadian Medical Association Journal*.

14.   Significantly, the most vocal early critics of Dianetics and Scientology among the mental health community—Dr. Winfred Overholzer, Dr. Paul Hoch, and Dr. Louis J. West, among others—came from this group of psychiatrists and psychologists who participated in government mind control experiments; see Wiseman, *Psychiatry, the Ultimate Betrayal*.

15.   The two primary means by which Scientology is practiced are *auditing* and *training*. *Auditing*, which comes from the Latin word *audire*, meaning "to listen," is one-on-one counseling in which a trained Scientology minister utilizes Hubbard's discoveries to help guide a parishioner to new states of spiritual existence. *Training* is the study of Hubbard's works to learn to apply the principles they contain to improve conditions and to audit others. These two activities are the two primary practices of the Scientology religion. A wealth of material about these them is publicly available. [The bibliography includes a list of L. Ron Hubbard's books on the subjects, church publications, and Internet resources.]

16.   The Alaska Mental Health Act (HR 8009).

17.   In an interview in 1971, Dr. Zigmond Lebensohn stated that the opposition to the "Siberia bill" was a milestone in the psychiatric community's recognition of the intensity of the movement. Combating public opposition to the Alaska Mental Health Act was on the agenda of the 17 September 1956 meeting of the D.C. Mental Health Society. Attending this meeting were, among others, Dr. Zigmond Lebensohn, Dr. Winfred Overholzer, and Charlotte Murphy, a lawyer (FOIA Document, 1956).

Murphy came from the AMA and later went to the Internal Revenue Service and became a key figure in the IRS's attacks against Scientology.

18. FOIA Document, 1959.

19. Ibid.

20. Captain Earnest Jefferson of the D.C. Police Department (who was present at the 31 March 1959 meeting with the FDA and Assistant U.S. Attorney Edward Troxell mentioned above) sent his pregnant daughter into the Founding Church to try to get one of the staff to arrange for an illegal abortion. She failed.

21. FOIA Document, 1959. The Hubbard Electrometer (E-Meter) is a religious artifact used in Scientology and Dianetics counseling. It measures the minute changes in electronic resistance created by thoughts. Properly trained Scientology ministers use this meter in counseling to help guide the parishioners to areas of spiritual travail. The E-Meter is only available to Scientology ministers and ministers in training.

22. *Founding Church of Scientology v. United* States, 409 F.2d 1146, 1161 (D.C. Cir. 1969). Since then, a wealth of legal decisions have also affirmed the religiosity of Scientology, several of which are cited in Appendix 9 of Church of Scientology International, *What is Scientology* (Los Angeles, Calif.: Bridge Publications, 1998a); and *Scientology: Theology and Practice of a Contemporary Religion* (Los Angeles, Calif.: Bridge Publications, 1998b).

23. CCHR publishes an extensive library of materials documenting the social abuses of the psychiatric profession. The bibliography contains a partial list of these materials. These are also available at http://www.cchr.org.

24. The Special Agent's Report submitted by the Los Angeles CID in May of 1985 called for the "final halt" and "ultimate disintegration" of the church, even though the government's own evaluation of the CID's witnesses rated them in the most unreliable categories (Special Agent's Report released under the Freedom of Information Act).

25. Throughout their attacks, the FDA and the IRS utilized the media as a tool to forward their false reports and to create a public climate that would support their draconian measures against the Scientology churches. For example, in the 1950s, the FDA used *Saturday Evening Post* reporter James Phelan to write an article that was cleared with the FDA for publication. *Time* magazine filled this role numerous times over the years, such as with their May 1991 cover story for which the IRS was a prominent source of information. The use of the media in this manner is a common tactic.

26. See Bryan R. Wilson, *Scientology: An Analysis and Comparison of Its Religious Systems and Doctrine* (Oxford, England, 1995).

27. See http://www.scientology.org and related sites.

Christian Reconstructionism after Y2K: Gary North, the New Millennium, and Religious Freedom

ADAM C. ENGLISH

During the so-called Y2K crisis, many would-be techno-logical prophets and prognosticators predicted a computer meltdown on 1 January 2000. The reason? For the past three decades, programmers used the last two digits of the century instead of all four when installing the calendaring function on computers. Sometime in 1997, various programmers like Ed Yourdon began to suspect that when the date rolled to "00," computers would read it as "1900" and not "2000." It was con-jectured that such an error would result in widespread com-puter malfunction and/or shutdown. The thought of such an occurrence prompted some to consider the implications of a worldwide temporary computer failure. The results of such an occurrence were predicted to be dire. And perhaps no one was as fervent about the gravity of the circumstances as Gary North.

In 1997, Gary North launched a website, www.garynorth. com, warning the public of the imminent technological disas-ter. The site boasted over six thousand documents on Y2K as well as links to hundreds of other sites. It was even equipped with a "Doomsday Computer" simulator that calculated the probability of computer malfunction. According to the site:

At 12 midnight on January 1, 2000 (a Saturday morning), most of the world's mainframe computers will either shut down or begin spew-ing out bad data. Most of the world's desktop computers will also start spewing out bad data. Tens of millions—possibly hundreds of millions—of pre-programmed computer chips will begin to shut down the systems they automatically control. This will create a nightmare for every area of life, in every region of the industrialized world.[1]

Along with an uncounted number of governmental and busi-ness computers, perhaps as many as 300 million personal computers were noncompliant early in 1999 and would be subject to malfunctioning. What kind of turmoil would erupt with an unchecked Y2K crisis? According to North, months before 1 January, the world's stock markets will have crashed because everyone will have taken their money out of banks. After 1 January, all levels of orderly business both in the states and abroad will grind to a halt. Without their databases, governments will no longer be able to collect taxes because they will not be able to trace people and compel them to pay. Within a matter of time, governments will collapse due to lack of funding or anarchy, whichever comes first.[2]

A Premill or Postmill Crisis?

North's grim prophecies sound uncannily similar to the predictions of premillennial dispensationalists like Hal Lindsey who was popular in the 1970s. Indeed, North has always been drawn to the year 2000. As early as 1990, North had a premonition that something cataclysmic would happen at the turn of the millennium.[3] But, does that make him a date-setter? Is he just another doomsday premillennialist stoking the flames of fear and apocalyptic hype? Ironically, the answer must be "no." On first glance, it is often assumed that Reconstructionists like North are premillennialists (which involves the belief that Jesus Christ will rapture his church before a thousand-year reign of peace and final judgment). Nevertheless, Christian Reconstructionism is a staunchly postmillennial group. In fact, North often attacks premillennialists in his monthly newsletters and has even authored book-length exposés on them, including such titles as *Millennialism and Social Theory* and *Rapture Fever: Why Dispensationalism is Paralyzed*.[4] Why then was he so distressed about the Y2K situation? Why do his warnings have an end-of-the-world tenor? Y2K was to be a catastrophic event, but of the postmillennial, not premillennial type. What does this mean? Unlike the premillennialists of the past who were noted for their gloom-and-doom, end-of-the-world predictions and their mantra-like call to "Repent Now! The End is Near!," North did not see 2000 as "the end of the world."

North, and the overwhelming majority of Y2K pop-commentators, urged America to make preparations to *survive* Y2K. The question was not, "Will we still be here after 1 January?" but instead, "Will we be prepared to survive whatever is on the other side of 1 January?" A search of Amazon.com for books on Y2K turns up 209 titles, including *101 Ways to Survive the Y2K Crisis; 3 Steps to Y2K Readiness for the Home and Family; About Y2K Survival: Handbook and Guide to Practical Preparations for the Year 2000 and Beyond; Act Y2K Small Business Workbook; Action Y2K: A GrassRoots Guide to the Year 2000; Are You Ready? Y2K Challenge; Beat the Beast!–Y2K Preparedness Guidebook;* and *Building Your Ark: Your Personal Survival Guide to the Year 2000 Crisis.*[5] As is evident from this partial listing, most of the Y2K books are not pessimistic, gloom-and-doom farewells to life. They are pro-active, do-it-yourself survival manuals. As people took the advice of these manuals, they stockpiled canned food, water, guns, gasoline, and other supplies—determined to "beat the blackout." They did not, like the nineteenth-century Millerites, find a tall tree to sit in so that they would be closer to the Lord when he came out of heaven to rapture them on 1 January. It appears that the Y2K crisis, if nothing else, was certainly *not* a premillennialist crisis. Y2K never was the end of the world for North or any other Y2K prophet—far from it.

So what was the impetus behind North's Y2K scare? Besides feeling a genuine sense of responsibility to warn the world about the imminent technological, social, and political cataclysm, it seems that North envisioned the Y2K crisis as his chance for his lifelong project to reach fulfillment. It was a ray of hope for the establishment of God's theonomy (rule by biblical law) in America:

The Y2K crisis is systemic. It cannot possibly be fixed. . . . I think the U.S.A. will break up the way the U.S.S.R. did. Call me a dreamer. Call me an optimist. That's what I think. This will decentralize the social order. That is what I have wanted all of my adult life. In my view, Y2K is our deliverance.[6]

A Y2K disaster would provide the type of worldwide breakdown needed for Christians to step forward, take the reins of leadership, and establish a biblically-based society. Yet, the "reconstruction" of society would not be from the top-down, issuing from an autocratic or oligarchic Christian government. Instead, it would be "from the bottom-up: *self-government under God.*"[7] Millions of souls would have to be supernaturally transformed so that they would submit to the government of biblical law. In what manner would this occur? Another quotation from North is appropriate:

The postmillennialist is anti-apocalyptic. He knows that God breaks into history, but God does this by using the familiar processes of Church history: evangelism, the sacraments, Church discipline, civil justice, and family order. He will send the Holy Spirit to transform billions of individual hearts, and the regenerate then use the familiar tools of dominion to extend God's kingdom in history. This is *conquest by conversion*.[8]

Of course, 1 January 2000 came and went without the collapse of computers and government. The so-called "false prophets" of the millennium immediately became the objects of ridicule. Gary North was no exception, as illustrated by the Internet site entitled: "Gary North is a Big Fat Idiot."[9] Understandably, many questioned his "genuineness" and honesty concerning his Y2K warnings. Concerned Christians such as Steve Hewitt of *Christian Computing* magazine surmised that the Reconstructionists were making a profit from people's fears by selling Y2K videos and books.[10] It is not unimaginable that North benefited financially from the hype, but he could easily respond that the majority of his writings on Y2K were available for free on the Internet. Indeed, one of his websites is called www.freebooks.com.

Part of the difficulty in unraveling North's stance regarding Y2K revolves around the categories "postmillennialism" and "premillennialism" (not to mention a third category, "amillennialism"). Catherine Wessinger has attempted to resolve some of the confused terminology by suggesting the more descriptive labels: "catastrophic millennialism" and "progressive millennialism." Catastrophic millennialists (i.e. premillennial dispensationalists) hold a pessimistic view of humanity and believe that the current world order must be destroyed in order for a new, millennial kingdom to enter. Progressive millennialists (presumably North) have a more optimistic view of humanity and believe that social work and divine assistance will gradually usher in a utopian world order.[11] While Wessinger's tag describes fairly accurately the Reconstructionist position, there are two reasons to resist it. First, the Reconstructionists prefer the term "postmillennialist" because it locates them within a certain tradition. Thus, Greg Bahnsen called himself a "evangelical postmillennialist," Ray Sutton "covenantal postmillennialist," Kenneth Gentry "progressive postmillennialist," and North "judicial postmillennialist."[12] While different Reconstructionists adopt different adjectival qualifiers, all use the appellation, "postmillennialist." Second, unlike the progressive millennialists, the Reconstructionists do not have an optimistic view of humanity. They are strict Calvinists, believing above all else that people are totally depraved and will never progress without conversion. The progress toward the millennium reign of peace will not occur through social work, but rather through the divine work of the Holy Spirit on both individuals and institutions. Social and political progress in history depends upon divine, not human effort. Consequently, one way to explain North's obsession with the year 2000 is that he, like the premillennialists who look for signs of Christ's return, was looking for a sign of God's imminent "victory." Y2K was to be a sign that God was disrupting the social order to clear the ground for his theonomy (rule by biblical law).

Besides decoding the cumbersome categories of "postmillennial," "premillennial," and "amillennial," one must exegete the label "Christian Reconstructionism." This study will provide a brief sketch of Christian Reconstructionism's history and beliefs in order to set the stage for understanding North's views on the millennium and religious liberty.

A Short Historical Sketch of the Christian Reconstruction Movement

The most proper place to begin any history of Christian Reconstructionism (hereafter CR) is with the Westminster Seminary professor, Cornelius Van Til. Although he never condoned or affiliated with CR, he is in many ways the grandfather of the Reconstructionist project. Called the "demolition expert," Van Til systematically called into question the intellectual grounds of all aspects of modern secular society. In his books and lectures, he presented a rigorous apologetic for the Christian faith. The problem was that after he "detonated" the foundations of secularism, he did not leave "blueprints for the reconstruction of society."[13] Enter Rousas John Rushdoony, the father of the movement. While he appreciated the work of Van Til, he believed Christianity had to do more than simply dismantle secularism; it needed to offer a means to positively rebuild society according to biblical principles. Thus, in 1965, he started the Chalcedon Foundation[14] in Southern California that began publishing the monthly Chalcedon Report and hosting seminars and workshops. In 1973, the foundation began to gain momentum with the publication of Rushdoony's *Institutes of Biblical Law*. During the same year, Greg Bahnsen and Gary North joined the staff of Chalcedon. Rushdoony, Bahnsen, and North together formed the original triumvirate of the Reconstructionists.

All three share a Calvinistic Presbyterian background. All hold earned doctorate degrees: Rushdoony in educational philosophy, Bahnsen in philosophy, and North in history. All are prolific writers (over eighty books can be attributed to North and Rushdoony alone). All three are fiercely independent; they worked together until 1981 when North and Rushdoony clashed over a seemingly minor issue in one of North's articles. Although North is Rushdoony's son-in-law, the two men did not speak to each other for the final twenty years of Rushdoony's life. A permanent rift was generated within the movement between North and the Chalcedon group. The argument between the two camps became so vehement that in 1995 North and Chalcedon's Andrew Sandlin signed a "truce."[15] This is significant in our discussion of the Y2K crisis because the Chalcedon Foundation did not jump on the Y2K bandwagon like North but neither did it oppose it. Did they silently concur with North's analysis? Or, more likely, were they adhering to their agreement to avoid North altogether? Either way, any discussion of the millennial expectations of Christian Reconstructionists with regard to Y2K must be limited to North and others who openly advocate his position. As a consequence, this study will concentrate primarily on North, drawing upon other Reconstructionists as they either support or refute North.

At any rate, after the falling-out, North moved to Tyler, Texas and launched the Institute for Christian Economics, which publishes various monthly journals and books. North lived in Tyler until some months before the turn of the millennium when he relocated to a secluded location in Arkansas. Bahnsen moved to Orange County, California, where he pastored a small Orthodox Presbyterian church and served as dean of a teacher's college graduate school until his untimely death in 1999. His place among the leaders of the movement has been silently transferred to Gary DeMar, president of American Vision, an educational ministry out of Atlanta, Georgia. Although coming to the fore later than the others, DeMar has positioned himself as a spokesperson for Reconstructionism alongside North and Rushdoony by authoring such books as *The Debate over Christian Reconstruction* and co-authoring *Christian Reconstruction: What It Is, What It Isn't* with North. Meanwhile, Rushdoony continued to direct a twelve-member staff at the Chalcedon Foundation until his death in February 2001. Well before Rushdoony's death, most of the operational responsibilities had already been handed over to Andrew Sandlin, the foundation's executive vice president. Sandlin, author of *Christianity: Bulwark of Liberty*, continues to rise in stature among the second generation Reconstructionists.

Reconstructionism experienced its greatest flourish in the late 1980s. It became especially popular among Reformed and Orthodox Presbyterians, as well as others associated with the Presbyterian Church of America and, more broadly, Christian fundamentalism in general. Along with its popularity, major Christian publishers like Crossway and Thomas Nelson began to release Reconstructionist titles. Pat Robertson, Jerry Falwell, and Franky Schaeffer V read Reconstructionist books and endorsed the movement. Gary North estimated that between 25,000 and 40,000 names were on various Reconstructionist mailing lists during that time. It was not long until *Newsweek* had named the Chalcedon Foundation as the Religious Right "think tank." Articles about the CR began appearing in the *Christian Century*, *Christianity Today*, *Westminster Theological Journal*, and *First Things*.[16] Clearly, the movement was gaining recognition. But, as soon as it stepped into the spotlight, its popularity began to plateau and fade. And then, the Y2K crisis arrived.

What Is Christian Reconstructionism?

What do Reconstructionists believe? The big picture is rather complex for a number of reasons. First, a shroud of technical, "insider" jargon veils the heart of CR. Consider, for example, the boggled definition of Christian Reconstructionism given by Michael Gabbert:

Christian Reconstructionism is a complex movement of neo-Puritan scholars and evangelical Calvinist theology. Drawing history and the Scriptures together, Reconstructionists attempt to combine a dominion-oriented, postmillennial understanding of theonomy with various historical examples of anti-Erastian church-state structures. The goal of the movement is to integrate every aspect of American life into a consistent worldview based upon the abiding validity of the Old-Testament Law in exhaustive detail.[17]

Could this definition be any more convoluted? One reason why CR has been so often misunderstood is because it is hard

to define, as exemplified by Gabbert's good-natured attempt.
Yet, CR does not help its own case when it comes to intelligi-
bility. The movement makes some very radical claims on issues ranging from politics, economics, and sociology, to
education, historiography, and theology. Inevitably, these
claims are exaggerated by detractors and misunderstood by
analysts. As a result, the underlying seminal beliefs are neglected by all. Academia has yet to correct the problem of misunderstanding; the majority of academic reviews and
critiques of CR have capitalized on its eccentric and sometimes shocking pronouncements.[18] In essence, scholars have
repudiated and discarded CR as an extreme fundamentalist
fad.

Fortunately, Gary DeMar and Andrew Sandlin have
helped resolve the confusion by outlining CR's major tenets.
Each has independently composed lists of non-negotiable Reconstructionist beliefs. We will combine the lists of both
DeMar and Sandlin and propose five key tenets of CR. Hope-
fully, these will provide a framework for understanding the
movement.

1. Calvinism.[19] DeMar differs with Sandlin on the first
tenet. He suggests "Regeneration" is the primary belief of CR,
not Calvinism. Both in his 1988 and his 1991 definitions of CR,
regeneration is first. However, Calvinism remains the first
tenet here because it qualifies the type of regeneration that
occurs. When Reconstructionists speak of regeneration, they
are specifically referring to a Calvinistic understanding of the
event.[20] Calvinistic theology is a non-negotiable component of
Reconstructionism. Full adherence to the five points of the
TULIP[21] is expected of the Reconstructionist. Sandlin asserts
the true Reconstructionist "holds to historic, orthodox, Catholic Christianity and the great Reformed confessions. He believes God, not man, is the center of the universe and beyond;
God, not man, controls whatever comes to pass; God, not
man, must be pleased and obeyed."[22] Calvinism's emphasis
on correct dogma, biblical law, God's rule, and Christianized
government form an excellent theological foundation for the
advancement of Reconstructionist ideology. Not only is Calvinistic theology adhered to, even the failed historical instan-
tiations of Calvinism in Geneva and America become
authoritative exemplars of a Christian society.[23]

2. Biblical law. "The continuing validity and applicability
of the whole law of God, including, but not limited to, the
Mosaic case laws."[24] This "law" is the standard for individual,

familial, ecclesiastical, economic, and governmental conduct. It is alternatively known as "theonomy." Theonomy is the key term for a form of government characterized by God's direct and personal rule over society ("Reconstructionist" is often interchanged with "theonomist"). However, since the inerrancy debates of the 1980s, theonomy has come to mean more than just God's law; it means *biblical* law. Thus, Sandlin suggests that a more precise term is "biblionomy." He goes on to say:

> As a theological expression, it means the abiding authority of all the Bible's teachings, unless the Bible itself asserts that those teachings have been fulfilled or rescinded (for example, such distinctively Jewish practices as the national feasts and festivals, circumcision and the Passover). The law of the Old Testament as the authority for the believer and all of society has not been set aside.[25]

Bahnsen defended this idea in his 1985 seminal work, *By This Standard*, by saying that, "[W]e presume our obligation to obey any Old Testament commandment unless the New Testament indicates otherwise. We must assume continuity with the Old Testament."[26] Although many Christians would agree that a continuity exists between the Old and New Testaments, the continuity is normally defined as "spiritual" or religious, but not sociological or liturgical. Bahnsen, by contrast, believed that "the New Testament does not teach any radical change in God's law regarding the standards of *socio-political morality*."[27] The Pentateuch should be studied and applied by legislators and jurors in the same manner that the U.S. Constitution is studied and applied.[28] This is affirmed by Sandlin's statement in the declaration that the Old Testament laws remain valid not only for individual believers, but for "all of society." Those who reject such an approach are labeled "antinomian" in the same way that those who reject the authority of the Constitution are labeled "anti-American."

CR's idealistic affirmation of continuity quickly encounters trouble. Modern civility and humanity have disavowed such practices as slavery and stoning, which are discussed in the Old and New Testament. But, loyal to their convictions, the Reconstructionists uphold all of the Law, including some of the unsavory dictates of Pentateuchal law such as capital punishment[29] and slavery statutes.[30]

3. Presuppositional apologetics. Presuppositionalism is an idea that comes directly from Van Til, who argued that religious faith should not be established or debunked on the basis

of historical or scientific investigation. Rather, faith presupposes certain realities without proof. For instance, the Christian must presuppose God exists and that the Bible is true in order to come to faith in Christ because God's existence cannot be proved or disproved scientifically. Reconstructionists extend this idea to contend that every belief about reality, religious or not, is loaded with presuppositions. Modernity's confidence in impartiality and neutrality is a myth. Theonomists recognize that there is no such thing as an unbiased government, unbiased science, or unbiased education. Indeed, such institutions are biased—they are biased toward secularism. And on the other hand, theonomists admit that they are biased towards biblical law. So because North presupposes biblical law to be *the key* to Christianity and the world, he can claim, "The battle of the mind is between the Christian reconstruction movement, which alone among Protestant groups takes seriously the law of God, and everyone else."[31]

In the Van Tillian defense of the faith, the objective is not to prove the empirical validity of Christianity's claims. Rather, the argument proceeds along these lines: "Yes, as a Christian I assume certain realities by faith, but so does the non-Christian. They simply presuppose different realities by a similar leap of faith." What is significant about this form of apologetics is that it never lets an intellectual opponent have the upper hand. It simply asserts the superiority of the Christian faith based on biblical revelation. Furthermore, it provides a rationale for stances that are uncompromising and even intolerant.

4. Decentralized social order. This point is probably CR's most pragmatic and strategic. CR espouses a "minimal state." Reconstructionists seek to reduce the power of the state and give power to the individual, the family, the church, and various local structures.[32] They see that democracy is an unattainable hoax. In fact, Rushdoony has called democracy a "heresy."[33] Democracy, rule by the people, is a fantasy that will never be obtained and furthermore, it is not a form of government legitimized by the Bible. The solution: "self-government under biblical law." This will be further elaborated under the heading below on "Religious Liberty."

5. Postmillennialism. As mentioned earlier, postmillennialism is the belief that Christ will return after the thousand-year period of peace described in Revelation 20 (symbolically understood). It provides key motivation for Reconstructionist hope. According to DeMar, "A victorious view of the future

progress of the kingdom of God prior to the return of Christ is foundational for the building of a Christian civilization."[34] As mentioned earlier, a progressive view of history is central. Just seven months before the turn of the millennium, Gary North was emphatically insisting upon a linearly progressive understanding of history in his bimonthly newsletter, *Biblical Economics Today*.[35] At any rate, Reconstructionists intend to prepare the way for the eventual thousand-year reign of peace. Their goal is to get people ready to reinstitute biblical law in civic life. During this millennial reign, government will not be by democracy but by theonomy.

Here enters the genius of Y2K. Not only did 1 January 2000 signal the inauguration of a new millennium (at least in the popular mind), it also became the herald of potential worldwide disaster. A catastrophic collapse of life as we know it would actually prepare the world for a new world order—a millennial, theonomist world order. When the millennium begins, regenerated man (the masculine is used intentionally) will regain dominion over the earth, a dominion that was lost in Paradise. "Dominion" has become a key term for the belief that, during the millennium, Christians will be given authority over the entire world. It has become so important that Andrew Sandlin lists "Dominionism" as one of the five core beliefs of Reconstructionism.[36] Conveniently, in the millennium reign, Christians will be charged with the duty of enforcing God's law on those who do not submit. "Those who refuse to submit publicly to the eternal sanctions of God by submitting to His Church's public marks of the covenant— baptism and holy communion—must be denied citizenship, just as they were in ancient Israel."[37]

Religious Liberty: A Questionable Notion

So, what is to become of religious liberty? In the theonomist utopia, there will be no toleration for "pagan" religions. North asserts:

[W]e must use the doctrine of religious liberty to gain independence for Christian schools until we train up a generation of people who know that there is no religious neutrality, no neutral law, no neutral education, and no neutral civil government. Then they will get busy in constructing a Bible-based social, political and religious order which finally denies the religious liberty of the enemies of God.[38]

According to this quotation, religious liberty is a useful tool to Christians in the present world order, yet it is ultimately to be denied to anyone who is not Christian once Christians are in power. Such a position is not unique to North. Even Rushdoony, who was a vocal advocate of political, religious, and ecclesiastical liberty, as demonstrated in his books, *The Nature of the American System* and *This Independent Republic*, believed that religious liberty was ultimately a fantasy. He saw that every law is nothing more than "enacted morality" extracted from some sort of religious assumptions, whether theistic or non-theistic. In other words, there are no religiously neutral moral principles and thus there are no religiously neutral laws. According to Rushdoony, America operates out of humanism—a very real and definite religion disguised as nonreligious, objective neutrality.[39] So, the question is not, "Will government be religious or nonreligious?," but rather, "Which religion will the government follow?"[40] At this juncture one may wonder if the Reconstructionists are being paradoxical or are they inconsistent? They advocate the separation of church and state, yet long for the restoration of a "Christian America." They advocate the right to home-school, yet oppose prayer in school. They label democracy a heresy, yet champion political involvement and voting rights. They advocate religious liberty all the while denying the reality of the notion. Are they talking out of both sides of their mouths? Perhaps. Or maybe the situation is not as clear-cut as it appears.

True to their Reformed heritage, North, Rushdoony, and the other Reconstructionists do not understand "liberty" (political, religious, or otherwise) outside of a theological context. Authentic liberty is only found in a salvific encounter with Jesus Christ. Anyone outside of the Christian faith is in bondage. It is important to note that one of the most elemental presuppositions undergirding all Reconstructionist thought is the tripartite division of life: person, family, government. These are the three basic spheres of life. Each sphere has its own members, structure, rules, authority, and dominion. If Christians believe that God is lord over their person and their family, then why not their government? The Bible makes provision for each sphere of life and gives ultimate authority over all areas to God. Thus, if coming under the lordship of Christ on a personal level is not oppressive but rather liberating (as evangelical Christians claim), then similarly, government by rigorous theonomy is not oppressive but liberating. This is dramatized by the cover illustration on North's 1987 *Liberating Planet Earth: An Introduction to Biblical Blueprints*. Pictured on the cover is the earth encircled by chain links that are fastened together by a padlock with the inscription, "Adam Locks." Hovering above the keyhole of the lock is a silver key with an imprint of the cross. The message is clear: the problem with the world and its inhabitants is spiritual, not social, economic, political, or otherwise, and thus the solution is spiritual. North explains:

Liberty and God's law: the two are inseparable. He who preaches against the law of God preaches against liberty. Anyone who says that we can build our lives, our families, our churches, or our civil governments on any foundation other than the law of God, and still have liberty, is a liar. He is a deceiver. He is laying the foundation of tyranny.[41]

When Reconstructionists participate in public debates about society, education, and politics, they formulate the issues and answers in a spiritual (more specifically "biblical") vocabulary. They give no consideration to accommodationalist or politically correct jargon. If this consideration is lost, confusion about how to interpret CR quickly arises.

It is often assumed that Reconstructionists conspire to realize their millennial "dominion" through some version of the Holy Roman Empire or Constantinian Christianity (and certainly such an expectation would provide another rationale for CR's denial of pluralistic religious liberty). Yet, CR vigorously denies such suppositions. In a seminal article on "Covenantal Postmillennialism," Ray Sutton repudiates any top-down governmentally enforced religion (which he calls "Charlemagne's triumphalism"). He also rejects the rule of society by an institutional church (i.e. the Holy Roman Empire experiment). Sutton even foregoes the idea of a revivalistic postmillennialism (in this scenario there is no institutional expression of the millennium, but rather worldwide personal revivals). He refuses this option because the millennial reign must be institutional as well as personal. Sutton contends that any hope in a millennial reign of God over the nations must be peaceful, noncompulsory, initiated and guided by the Holy Spirit.[42] North fully agrees, realizing that none of his theonomistic and dominionistic designs will be put into practice without voluntary acceptance of biblical law, "when the Holy Spirit begins His visibly triumphant sweep of the nations."

Such a worldwide conversion and spiritual sanctification makes it evident how North can assert, "self-government under God's revealed law is the starting point for liberty."[43] As was stated earlier, "theonomy" means rule by God's law, not by an aristocracy of priests or even elected leaders. North best characterizes his vision as a "decentralized, international, theocratic *republic*."[44] The guiding document of this republic would not be the Declaration of Independence or the Constitution, but the Bible.

Conclusion

So, what has become of Reconstructionism after 2000? The Chalcedon Foundation continues to distribute its monthly publications and maintains an active web page. It continues to be involved in politics, especially regarding home-schooling and public education issues. North continues to publish—he released two large economic commentaries during the course of 2000.[45] He boasts a steady stream of books (12,000 to 20,000) being downloaded per month from his website, www. freebooks.com. When asked about the future of Reconstructionism after Y2K, North declares, "The future of Reconstructionism is the same as future of the kingdom of God on earth: complete victory."[46]

NOTES

1. Gary North, "Gary North's Y2K Links and Forums," accessed from Internet, 12 December 2000.
2. Ibid.
3. Referring to the Communist scheme for utopia, North writes, "the year 2000 . . . has been the target date for over 200 years." Gary North, "The Final Phase: East Side," *Remnant Review* 17 (19 January 1990): 1.
4. Gary North, *Millennialism and Social Theory* (Tyler, Tex.: ICE, 1990); Gary North, *Rapture Fever: Why Dispensationalism is Paralyzed* (Tyler, Tex.: ICE, 1993).
5. Amazon search for "Y2K" on the Internet site, accessed 8 January 2001.
6. Gary North, quoted in Rob Boston, "2000: Apocalypse Now?," *Church and State* (March 1999): 8.
7. Gary North, *Political Polytheism: The Myth of Pluralism* (Tyler, Tex.: ICE, 1989), 590, emphasis his.
8. North, *Millennialism*, 273.
9. "Gary North is a Big Fat Idiot," accessed 22 May 2000, www.gary north.shadowscape.net.

10. See Boston, "2000," 8-12.

11. Catherine Wessinger, *How the Millennium Comes Violently: From Jonestown to Heaven's Gate* (New York: Seven Bridges Press, 2000), 16-17.

12. Greg Bahnsen, "Postmillennialism and the Reformed Faith," accessed from the Internet 2 March 2001, forerunner.com/beast; Ray Sutton, "Covenantal Postmillennialism," *Covenant Renewal* 3 (February 1989): 1; Kenneth Gentry, "Whose Victory in History?" in *Theonomy: An Informed Response*, ed. Gary North (Tyler, Tex.: ICE, 1991), 213; North, *Millennialism*, 238.

13. Gary North, Preface, *Christian Reconstruction: What It Is, What It Isn't*, eds. Gary North and Gary DeMar (Tyler, Tex.: Institute for Christian Economics, 1991), xi.

14. The organization is named "Chalcedon" in reference to the A.D. 451 council, and the Chalcedonian creed is the keystone of Rushdoony's interpretation of orthodox Christianity.

15. Sandlin explains, "As a result of a series of fax exchanges between North and me, North agreed in a signed fax of April 28, 1995 to abandon any acrimonious criticism of Rushdoony and Chalcedon. In fact, he stated that, for the most part, he does not intend to criticize Rushdoony at all; when he does, he pledges that the criticism will occur in a context of reasoned academic discourse. He willingly called his statement a 'truce.' I had already stated in my April 27 fax to North: '[W]e want no trouble; we simply wish to be left alone. We did not start this fracas, we did not attack you, and we have never meant you harm. Aside from responding to specific views you address with which we disagree, we do not intend to mention you in the future. We expect you to act in kind.'" Andrew Sandlin, "Deconstructing Reconstruction: Review of Gary North's *Baptized Patriarchalism: The Cult of the Family*" [online article], accessed from the Internet 2 March 2001, chalcedon.edu/articles.

16. Anson Shupe, "The Reconstructionist Movement on the New Christian Right," *The Christian Century*, 4 October 1989, 880-82; Rodney Clapp, "Democracy as Heresy," *Christianity Today*, 20 February 1987, 17-23; Mark Karlberg, Review of *Covenant and Common Grace*, *Westminster Theological Journal* 50 (1988): 323-37. Richard John Neuhaus, "Why Wait for the Kingdom? The Theonomist Temptation," *First Things* 3 (May 1990): 14.

17. Michael Gabbert, "An Historical Overview of Christian Reconstructionism," *Criswell Theological Review* 6, no. 2 (1993): 281.

18. For instance, Rob Boston begins his 1988 article by stating, "The Reconstructionists' ideal is a country where a fierce God reigns supreme and government is based on the Law of Moses . . . [and] homosexuals, atheists, sabbath-breakers and 'infidels' face execution." Boston's presentation is biased from the start against the Reconstructionists. His article has not aided the public's understanding of the movement as much as it and other articles like it have instilled a fear of CR. Rob Boston, "Thy Kingdom Come," *Church & State* (September 1988): 6. Of course, not all publications are as brutal. Mark Karlberg's review of *Covenant and Common Grace* in the *Westminster Theological Journal* (1988): 323-37, is an exemplary work of respectability and scholarship.

19. While many are beginning to prefer the term "Reformed" to "Calvinist," the latter is used here because it is the term Sandlin chooses in his

"Creed of Christian Reconstruction" dated 1999-2000. Andrew Sandlin, "The Creed of Christian Reconstruction," accessed from the Internet 31 May 2000,

20. See Gary DeMar, *The Debate over Christian Reconstruction* (Fort Worth, Tex.: Dominion Press, 1988), 63-65.

21. Total depravity; Unconditional election; Limited atonement; Irresistible grace; Perseverance of the saints.

22. Sandlin, "Creed."

23. For instance, see Gary North, *Puritan Economic Experiments* (Tyler, Tex.: ICE, 1988).

24. Gary DeMar, "What is Christian Reconstruction?," in *Christian Reconstruction*, 81.

25. Andrew Sandlin, "Glossary of Frequently Used Terms," accessed from the Internet on 31 May 2000, www.chalcedon.edu.html.

26. Greg Bahnsen, *By This Standard* (Tyler, Tex.: ICE, 1985), 3.

27. Ibid.; italics his.

28. In fact, the analogy of the Constitution comes the closest to depicting the CR position. Reconstructionists believe that one day, the Bible will in fact replace the Constitution and that the legislative and judicial branches of the government will study the Bible, not the Constitution, for rulings.

29. Capital punishment is required for murder, striking or cursing a parent, kidnaping, adultery, incest, bestiality, sodomy or homosexuality, unchastity, rape of a betrothed virgin, witchcraft, offering human sacrifice, incorrigible delinquency, blasphemy, Sabbath desecration, propagation of false doctrines, sacrificing to false gods, refusing to abide by a court decision, and failing to restore the pledge or bail. In this penal system, prisons will not exist. A criminal will either repay his victim's loss, be exiled, or be executed.

30. Regarding slavery, David Chilton, in his *Productive Christians in an Age of Guilt Manipulators* (written in response to Ronald Sider's *Rich Christians in an Age of Hunger*), argues that resisting slavery is futile. Slavery has always existed and continues to exist everywhere, even in America, just not always in the forms historically associated with it. Furthermore, "If slavery were a sin, *God* would not have provided for it. Indeed, since God is the Standard of right and wrong, the fact that He gives rules for the proper management of slavery shows that to *disregard* the laws of slavery is a sin." David Chilton, *Productive Christians in an Age of Guilt Manipulators* (Tyler, Tex.: ICE, 1981), 60, italics his. Chilton argues that Christians should not attempt to abolish slavery wherever it may be found, but instead we should "follow God's laws for slavery." Ibid., 61. These laws, drawn directly from Exodus, Deuteronomy, and Leviticus, stipulate conditions for obtaining, caring for, and freeing slaves. The problem with American slavery in the South was that there was no process for gradually freeing the slaves. From a biblical perspective, people can be indentured for six-year stints, but had to be freed or hired as servants in the seventh year. Rushdoony agrees with Chilton's proposals and insists that because slavery was not outlawed, but indeed provided for under God's law, white Americans should not feel guilty for their ancestors' role in slavery in the states. He believes that historical distor-

tion has "systematically indoctrinated [the white man] into believing that he is guilty of enslaving and abusing the Negro." R. J. Rushdoony, *Politics of Guilt and Pity* (Fairfax, Va.: Thoburn Press, 1970), 3-4, 19, 25. At any rate, no debt could be imposed for more than six years. This is because alongside the hard-line approach to capital punishment and slavery is a hard-line approach to jubilee. Thus, long term mortgages would be a thing of the past in a reconstructed society.

31.   Gary North, *Backward Christian Soldiers? An Action Manual for Christian Reconstruction* (Tyler, Tex.: ICE, 1984), 66.

32.   In an effort to reduce state power, CR opposes almost all forms of tax. National tax should be a flat tax of no more than 10 percent or, even better, the church, which in turn would support the governmental agencies, should levy a tithe tax.

33.   R. J. Rushdoony, *The Institutes of Biblical Law* (Phillipsburg, N.J.: Presbyterian and Reformed, 1973), 747.

34.   DeMar, *Christian Reconstruction*, 82.

35.   In an extensive discussion on "The Idea of Progress and Inheritance," North says, "History is progressive because corporate sanctification is progressive. It is not simply that history is linear; it is also progressive." Gary North, "The Covenantal Ideal of Economic Growth," *Biblical Economics Today* 21 (April/May, 1999): 3-4.

36.   Sandlin, "Creed."

37.   North, *Political Polytheism*, 87.

38.   Gary North, "The Intellectual Schizophrenia of the New Christian Right," *Christianity and Civilization* 1 (Spring 1982): 25.

39.   North offers a full exposition on humanism, its evolution, and influence on American democracy in *Conspiracy: A Biblical View* (Tyler, Tex.: Dominion Press, 1996).

40.   See R. J. Rushdoony, "Publisher's Foreword: Can We Legislate Morality?," [online article] accessed on the Internet 2 March 2001, www.chalcedon.edu/report/2000jan.

41.   Gary North, *Liberating Planet Earth: An Introduction to Biblical Blueprints* (Tyler, Tex.: Dominion, 1987), 150-51. North infers that all parts are therefore equally normative. The preacher must not limit himself to "a chapter or two in Exodus, the Book of Amos, Acts 2 and 4, and 2 Corinthians 8. No, he must preach the whole law," 151.

42.   Ray Sutton, "Covenantal Postmillennialism" *Covenant Renewal* 3 (February 1989): 2-4.

43.   North, *Political Polytheism*, 67.

44.   Ibid., 590.

45.   Gary North, *Treasure and Dominion: An Economic Commentary on Luke* (Tyler, Tex.: ICE, 2000); and his *Cooperation and Dominion: An Economic Commentary on Romans* (Tyler, Tex.: ICE, 2000).

46.   Gary North to author (personal email), 30 May 2000.

A Not So Charitable Choice: New Religious Movements and President Bush's Plan for Faith-Based Social Services

DEREK H. DAVIS

Nearly three months after the initial winds of the election controversy began to blow and nine days after his inauguration as the forty-third president of the United States, President George W. Bush announced the creation of the White House Office of Faith-Based and Community Initiatives. This office, created by executive order and placed under the directorship of University of Pennsylvania political science professor John DiIulio, Jr., a professed Catholic and new Democrat, will work in conjunction with another new office, the Corporation for National Service, headed by former Jewish mayor of Indianapolis, Stephen Goldsmith, to coordinate partnerships between five departments of the federal government and religiously-based social service organizations. Departments involved include those of Justice, Health and Human Services, Housing and Urban Development, Labor, and Education. Such collaboration between the government and private charities will ostensibly level the playing field between government and faith-based charities and allow those charities to conduct their mission without stooping to a never-ending list of government regulations.

When he announced the creation of the new office, Bush pledged his support of a policy of nondiscrimination against any religion and referred to this collaboration initiative as one of the most important his administration will implement. "We will encourage faith-based and community programs without *changing their mission*. We will help *all* in their work to change hearts while keeping a commitment to pluralism."[1] Bush rightfully recognizes the limitations of government efforts to solve social ills; no secular agency that simply throws money at a problem can cure an illness that is the result of more serious internal problems than lack of resources. And exactly how some faith-based organizations will spend government resources is a subject of much controversy. Some churches and religious institutions that receive this money will undoubtedly zero in not on the outward needs of individuals that come to them for help, but on the inward, spiritual needs those individuals may or may not recognize. Herein lies a significant problem. Government then becomes an agent to transform the human soul. But under the American church-state separation principle, crafting the human soul is assigned to the spheres of religion and civil society, not government. The American founding fathers, fully aware of centuries of abuse of persons whose religious sentiments did not line up with the officially proclaimed doctrines issued by powerful church-state partnerships, sought to assign the business of soulcraft primarily to the private sphere, free from the corrupting influence of government. Alexander Hamilton properly delineated the roles of church and state when he wrote in Federalist 69 contrasting president and king: "The one has no particle of spiritual jurisdiction; the other is the supreme head and governor of the national church. What answer shall we give to those who would persuade us that things so unlike resemble each other? The same answer that ought to be given to those who tell us that a government, the whole power of which would be in the hands of the elective and periodical servants of the people, is an aristocracy, a monarchy, and a despotism."[2]

It was a prerogative of divine right monarchs to assume headship over their national church and to dictate what was and was not acceptable in terms of doctrine, practice, and belief. Such spiritual despotism was exactly the reason the Puritans sailed for New England to establish their own city on a hill where neither king nor prince nor royally appointed bishop could dictate what they could or could not do in their practice of religion. The spirit of man is best left under the jurisdiction of communities of faith, not the government. And, interestingly enough, it is this same acknowledgement that Bush makes by proposing that the government support faith-based charities *without* mandating strict religious conformity from every service provider. Religion must be kept vital and free of government restraint, he says.

So, does President Bush recognize the limitations of government in transforming society? Well, perhaps to some extent. He proposes to prohibit government from proselytizing by requiring that government money not be used for such purposes but rather only to administer the secular aspects of a program. But there is no limitation, nor could there be constitutionally, on a faith group using its own funds to proselytize—and to do it in a way that coordinates with the administration of the government-funded social program. Thus under the Bush plan government remains, at least indirectly, an agent to transform the human soul. It is the province of the religious community, not government, to provide services to the poor and needy in such a way that, through training in faith and practice, their innermost being is transformed spiritually.

Confusing the roles of church and state leads to another problem with the Bush plan. It is the proper place of the religious community to be a prophetic voice that speaks out against government encroachment upon freedom and justice. If religious institutions are to receive government handouts, even simply to provide social services, how can they exercise their prophetic voices effectively without lessening some of the sting that often accompanies such criticism? Government may expect a quid pro quo—we gave you money, now you lend us your moral support. How can religious communities dodge the control that inevitably follows the receipt of government money? How can religious institutions maintain their independence, preserve their right to proselytize and indoctrinate, and carry out their social functions in the manner their canons or rules mandate if they are dependent on government assistance from a government that is constitutionally prohibited from establishing any or all religions and prohibited from infringing the free exercise of religion? Will strictly religiously-based social services become the norm, thereby alienating the poor and needy atheist who has nowhere to turn for social services? There is a provision in current charitable choice law that a secular service provider has to be offered as an alternative to the religious services, but what if the secular service is too far away to make it reasonable that someone not wanting to go to the religious organization could travel there? A few miles for one person may seem like twenty-five or thirty miles without an automobile or some sort of reliable and affordable transportation. Would an atheist-based social program be considered religious so as to receive funds under the new program? Or would it be considered a secular alternative?

A number of critics have emerged, and surprisingly, several are from the conservative evangelical camps originally expected to be the most enthusiastic about the Bush program.

While these conservative critics are important to the debate over this issue and will be addressed in what follows, they are not the primary concern of this chapter. What is discussed here are the responses of the religious minorities, especially the so-called new religious movements, to Bush's plan—are they for it, against it, undecided? And what are the reasons behind their positions? Also, what are the constitutional issues that arise out of this new program that may aid or hinder participation by religious minorities? Will it be viewed as an establishment of religion? Will it be recognized to encroach upon the rights of religious minorities who have no social services provided by their own religious organizations? What will be the ethical concerns raised when the government is asked to fund contradictory social services such as abortion counseling in one institution and adoption counseling in another? Is it really the goal of some of these new religious movements to change the hearts of men and direct them to do good and succeed in the world? Can there be order amidst this seeming chaos?

Faith-Based Initiatives—An Overview

Before proceeding to the heart of the argument, it is first necessary to address the history and overall goals of Bush's plan for government and faith-based organization collaboration. Charitable choice, as a general concept of religious organizations receiving government funds, is not new. Beginning in the 1996 Welfare Reform Act, charitable choice was instituted to enable welfare clients to "choose" between secular providers and religiously based providers. Charitable choice has since been written into several pieces of federal legislation—for example, the 1997 Welfare-to-Work program, the Community Services Block Grant program of 1998, and the Substance Abuse and Mental Health Services Administration's drug treatment programs in 2000, all without much controversy. Several religious groups, of course, including Catholic Charities and Lutheran Social Services, have for many years received government funds to aid their secular social endeavors. These organizations accept government funding on the condition that they not discriminate on the basis of religion in their hiring or proselytize their clients. Such organizations operated effectively long before charitable choice sought to soften these rules, thereby making it possible for faith-based organizations to receive government contracts the best services with the highest success rates. All groups, regardless of religiosity, are equally eligible for federal money, but of course not all shall receive. Thus it is an equal opportunity initiative, and not an equality-in-reality that Bush's proposal creates. If there were true equality of funding, then the large First Church downtown would receive exactly the same provisions as the tiny rural Hindu Temple. That alone is not proportionally fair. Another way would be to give to all charities funding proportionate to the size of their parent religious organizations. This is problematic because membership totals for religious organizations are kept differently by different denominations and organizations, and given that there is only a limited supply of money to go around (Bush has proposed spending $8 billion in the first year, none of it "new" money, but all of it coming at the expense of existing programs), when that is divided amongst all organizations proportionally, there is hardly any benefit to receiving federal funds at all. Another problem would stem from the relative number of parties aided by the particular charity. Suppose a Buddhist charity in a large urban China Town is the most prominent in the area, but the total Buddhist population is a mere fraction of the whole. It would seem that the charity would be the victim of discrimination and would be disproportionately under-funded despite its size and services to the community. But it would not seem right, either for the large Buddhist charity and the much smaller Methodist charity to receive equal funding. In terms of gain, the Methodist charity would benefit more substantially than the Buddhist charity simply because of its smaller size. It could afford to spend more money on each person it helps and thereby offer better services to a more select community.

Detractors from charitable choice are from all parts of the spectrum. One would expect to find such groups as the American Civil Liberties Union, the Americans United for the Separation of Church and State, the Baptist Joint Committee, and the Coalition Against Religious Discrimination to be against charitable choice on constitutional grounds. Providing federal funds to religious charities, generally speaking, is an impermissible act under the Supreme Court's traditional interpretation of the Establishment Clause of the First Amendment. But their concern is also for the long-term health of religion in America after federal funding is made available. One compelling argument they make is that once religious organizations receive federal funding, dependence upon these funds will be the result and will eventually become a chronic illness of the system as it is in Europe and other parts of the world where church-state separation is less observed. When the charities receive government funds, they are ecstatic and believe they are then capable of expanding their social outreaches. The trouble with money is that it eventually is exhausted and more must be attained before further work can be conducted. Since money was given once to a religious institution by a state agency, it is highly possible that this state agency will be generous enough to write another check when the original money is exhausted. Once this happens, a cycle of receipt of government money by religious organizations, spending it, and then returning for more money becomes inevitable. This cycle further erodes the private citizen's perceived responsibility to fund these same religious organizations because he sees the government standing in for him and using his tax dollars in the process. Private funding eventually ceases or becomes negligible, and the religious organization is fully dependent upon the state money for survival. When this has occurred, the religious institutions are effectively subordinated to the state, lose their autonomy, and are compromised in their religious mission. The church becomes an arm of the state akin to any other bureaucratic agency, disrespected and reviled by the average citizen.

Another area of concern is that of discrimination in hiring and firing on the basis of religion. Is it right for any organization, regardless of its proclaimed mission, if it receives federal funds, to discriminate against otherwise qualified applicants on the basis of religion or sexual orientation? Senator Patrick Leahy (D-VT) has expressed concern that "religion [may be] used as a pretext to discriminate against homosexuals," and that "by allowing discrimination on the basis of religion, we may open the door to other forms of discrimination, including race."[6] Such fears are not unfounded. If a group such as the Ku Klux Klan could be considered a religious organization, then it would be eligible under Bush's plan for funds and would not have to compromise its tenets of racism and anti-Semitism. Bush claims that groups such as this that preach hate would not receive funds, but then observers ask whether this is not a discrimination against religion, even if it is offensive to the general public. For some faith communities, it would violate their core orthodoxy to be forced to consider homosexuals or members of certain races for employment. Would they not then cease to be a church if they violated these tenets simply to receive government funds? Can the government require churches to abandon the very foundational beliefs that constitute them as churches?

Another category of opponents to charitable choice, surprisingly, comes from the very ranks that would most likely spawn its proponents—evangelical Christians. Jerry Falwell and Pat Robertson have both gone on record to voice opposition to Bush's expanded charitable choice plan because they fear money going to religious groups with whom they fundamentally disagree. Such aberrant organizations would include the Church of Scientology, Wiccans, the Unification Church, the Hare Krishna, and the like. Said Robertson:

> I mean, the Moonies have been proscribed, if I can use that, for brainwashing techniques, sleep deprivation and all the rest of it that goes along with their usual proselytizing. The Hare Krishnas much the same thing. And it seems appalling to me that we're going to go for somebody like that, or the Church of Scientology, which was involved in an incredible campaign against the IRS. I mean, they were accused of all sorts of underhanded tactics.[7]

Robertson would promote, however, a system that, instead of direct cash payments, offered tax credits to persons and corporations that donated money to religious groups. He also advocates a government registry of participating religious organizations that track the participating groups and ensure that they segregate the funds they receive specifically for social services and not for religious indoctrination or proselytization. That appears neutral on the surface, but how would Robertson react to the government's telling him that he could use certain funds only in a specified manner and could not conduct social services with religious proselytization as a key component?

It is this group of opponents and its respective targets that are the subjects of this essay. What will follow is a study of how these and other new religious movements and religious minorities perceive the charitable choice proposals of the Bush administration and how they plan to use or not use the money offered to them. What are their reasons for accepting or rejecting these funds? Is it primarily theological, moral or ethical, or is it humanitarian or a fear of public backlash? The answers may prove surprising to some.

New Religious Movements and Charitable Choice

As previously noted, President Bush's plan theoretically opens the door for all religions offering social services to the community to participate equally in sharing federal funding. White House officials have been sending mixed messages to the public when asked whether fringe religious groups would be eligible to apply for federal aid for their social services. If America is to remain committed to a principle of freedom, whereby religion is a sacred right as much as a sacred rite, how far can and should the government go to ostensibly evenhandedly aid the multiplicity of religious sects in their quest to provide spiritual as well as social guidance to their constituencies and to the broader public? President Bush has several times emphasized that he is only concerned with the results the programs produce. Goldsmith seems to believe there are limitations. DiIulio, before he resigned his office in September 2001, appeared to advocate a performance model that may end up channeling money to groups that people do not like.

Are new religious movements clamoring to receive government recognition and aid, or are they content to remain where they are in the overall spectrum of religious diversity? By all indications, the community of new religious movements is as divided on the issue as the general public. Some, such as the Unification Church, are eager to feed at the government trough. Others, like the Church of Jesus Christ of Latter-day Saints, are issuing a staunch NO to government funds. The following shall address some of the major pros and cons as seen through the eyes of these new religious movements. It is not at all intended to be a rating or thorough examination of the theologies of each of these movements, nor can it be a complete examination of new religious movements and their opinions on the Bush initiative.

It is good to begin with the largest proponent of Bush's faith-based initiatives from the new religious movement spectrum—the Unification Church run by the Rev. Sun Myung Moon. Moon's official church was disbanded several years ago and replaced by the Family Federation for World Peace and Unification to lessen its unpalatable image in the eyes of conservative Christians. Few if any conservative Christians would openly and willingly channel funds to such a group that, among other controversial theological doctrines, hails its leader and his wife as the "True Parents," or the second messiah sent to complete the failed mission of Jesus Christ. Some critics have charged Moon with heresy or outright fraud. Nevertheless, several such religious conservatives as Jerry Falwell and top officials in Pat Robertson's Christian Coalition have joined Moon-sponsored efforts to promote family values and to create Christian unity against a hostile secular front. Moon appeals to the Christian Right often through the use of cash donations to certain organizations. Falwell's Christian Heritage Foundation, for example, received $3.5 million from a Moon group to offset some of the debt incurred by Liberty University. At another time, a Moon group gave gold wristwatches worth several thousands of dollars apiece to ministers who attended "We Will Stand" events that were part of a 50-state tour to promote family values and Bush's faith-based initiatives program.

By promoting Bush's plan for faith-based initiatives, Moon hopes to ingratiate himself to the leaders of the Republican Party. Moon could then easily win government funds for his teenage abstinence program. But that is not the whole of it by any means. Moon's theology teaches the unification of all religions under a Moon-headed theocratic state. It seems preposterous to most Americans to think that these goals could ever be realized, but that is not the concern of those who advocate separation of church and state. Why should the government and its supporting taxpayers channel money to an organization that is bent on taking over the world? It is a religious organization without a doubt. It has a theology, a charismatic leader, and organized structures. Under Bush's plan, it would only have to produce results with its social services to receive funds and would not have to alter its fundamental theology or its efforts at proselytizing. But is it morally acceptable for a government to fund an organization

Moon has also enlisted the support of several members of the African-American clergy as he has emphasized the renewal of the urban communities and the need for racial unity. The Rev. Donald Robinson of the office of Washington, D.C. Mayor Anthony Williams stated, "I don't see a conflict. I just see this as an opportunity for the city to align itself with like-minded people. We want the renewal and restoration of families, the renewal and revival of community. We want a sense of racial harmony."[8] If that is what they want, what is wrong with letting them have it? Moon has interests that run deeper than the family values, sexual abstinence, and Christian unity he appears to espouse.

that advocates its demise? That would be the equivalent of the government shooting itself in the foot. Many patriotic Americans would not want this sort of organization to use their tax dollars for pernicious ends. The doctrine of equality of all religions, given the plurality of sects and denominations in America, therefore demands that none receive government funds for any work that could remotely be connected to winning converts to their cause.

A far less radical take on charitable choice is that of the Sikhs. Concerns from the Sikh community include the possibility of government funds alienating religious minorities from mainstream acceptance since this could have a disproportionate impact upon Sikhism in the United States. For this reason, dialogue has been encouraged, but the community has been reluctant to make a commitment. According to the executive director of the Sikh Mediawatch and Resource Task Force (SMART), a Sikh advocacy organization, "We are not saying yes or no to this proposal by the Bush Administration, but we would like to hear more about how government funds could help social service programs in this country and we would like to participate in a dialogue that allows public funds to go towards non-proselytizing religious organizations."[9] Non-proselytizing provisions seem to be the key to Sikh acceptance of faith-based initiatives. But how can a faith-based charity that is truly *faith*-based be anything but an effort to proselytize those that come to it for help? If the charitable services are divorced from the parent religious organization, can that charity be said to be faith-based at all? Would it not then be simply another secular organization, only having a religious namesake instead of one from the government? This seems to be the concern of several who oppose the Bush initiative. Religion will have to be watered down in order to meet government funding standards. And with that, all parties lose out.

Other new religious movements have not been as sympathetic to the Bush program. Several such detractors come from the Neo-Pagan, Wicca, and earth religions traditions. In February 2001, a coalition of representatives from these diverse traditions sent a letter to Bush addressing their concerns about the Office of Faith-Based and Community Initiatives. Their concerns were twofold—fear of discrimination and fear of inequality. These fears require extended explanation.

According to the letter, for the government to fund faith-based organizations while at the same time withholding funding from secular alternatives is contrary to the principle of separation of church and state. (Remember, Bush has not allocated any new money for the faith-based initiatives he is proposing; all money will simply be redirected to faith-based charities rather than secular ones in one massive campaign of wealth redistribution). Federal funding of faith-based initiatives may inevitably lead to supplementing or fully paying the salaries of those "who may support and spread intolerance or violence based on religious, racial or ethnic supremacist ideals. They would be able to discriminate in hiring and firing persons with views not in sympathy with their own."[10] For them, it is not the government's place to promote or support individuals whose ideologies lend themselves to discrimination and exclusion. One difficulty with that, however, is that the definition of discriminatory and exclusionary is not as agreed upon as one would imagine it to be. Some, if not all, religions are discriminatory or exclusionary by their very nature. A religion that teaches one doctrine obviously discriminates against other doctrines that do not conform. And it will inevitably exclude someone from its rites and sacraments if that individual is not yet initiated into its fellowship. The definition of religion itself, therefore, would preclude faith-based organizations from receiving government funds. That may be what the earth/nature religions are driving at when they emphasize their concern that secular organizations will be forced to shut down when money begins flowing to faith-based groups.

Their concern with inequality is also high atop the list of problems with the faith-based initiatives. They assert that already some government officials have made derogatory and discriminatory comments about Wicca and other pagan religions. These officials have suggested that Wicca may be an inferior or substandard religion when put alongside more conventional religions. Of course, this "inferiority" would preclude them from receiving government funds. Because of their qualification for IRS tax exemption, state incorporation, and their recognition in the U.S. Army Handbook for Chaplains, Wiccans believe they deserve the respect of everyone else in the government as well. And in all due respect to the government officials' prerogative to decide who shall and shall not receive federal funding, the Wiccans have a valid argument. It is not likely that the IRS or the Army will back away from their stances, so why not press for further government recognition if the means are available? The next to last paragraph of the letter sums up the Wiccans and all neo-Pagan organizations' desires: "This country and its resources are for everyone regardless of race, religion, sex or age. We ask that our tax dollars be given to initiatives, programs and organizations that do not discriminate."[11]

It would seem the Wiccans have a legitimate claim against government officials in charge of the faith-based initiatives. When asked at a Congressional hearing in April 2001 whether Wiccans would be eligible for federal funding under Bush's plan, John DiIulio responded that he could not understand why anyone in Congress would focus on Wiccans as a point of concern. Said DiIulio: "It just baffled me."[12] DiIulio sidestepped the question and never clearly stated whether the Wiccan organizations would qualify for funding or not.

Some groups have been the targets of religious fundamentalists such as Jerry Falwell and Pat Robertson. Inevitably, the Church of Scientology is dragged into the debate as a religion that many fundamentalists are against providing funds for due to its unorthodox beliefs and practices. But surprisingly, not all of the animosity toward Scientology comes from the far right. In a survey conducted in the early months of the Bush administration, only 26 percent of the general public supported giving money to the Church of Scientology if it wanted to participate in the federal programs.[13] Scientologists themselves have been somewhat vague about whether they are willing and wanting to receive federal funds. To illustrate, it is good to cite a lengthy passage from the Vice President of the Church of Scientology International, Janet Weiland:

Government funding of social betterment activities is nothing new. Religious charities, such as Catholic Charities, Lutheran Services of America and the YMCA collect billions of dollars in federal money for their charitable programs. The organizations that sponsor these charitable activities happen to be affiliated with major religious movements. Up to now, this has not been controversial. When the programs are chosen based on the merits and effective results, then there are no reasons for complaint.

We support very effective drug rehabilitation and literacy programs that have always enjoyed excellent relations with the communities they serve, and they are open to people of all religions. These programs have freed more than 250,000 people from the ravages of drug addiction and have helped thousands more learn to read.

The religious leaders of this country should not be climbing over the backs of their brethren in a mad scramble for government coins.

Clergy of all faiths need to work together to solve the problems of escalating drug use, crime and illiteracy and the crashing moral values in this country. That is our traditional role in the community as religious institutions and it is a role we are uniquely designed to fulfill.[14]

On the one hand, they seem to be willing to accept government funds; on the other, they seem to say "no thank you" to the president's proposal. A February 20 *New York Times* article cited officials of the Church of Scientology as hoping to benefit from Bush's funding proposals, and already, Church of Scientology's drug rehabilitation program, Narconon, has in some instances received government funds for its services, even without the Bush program in place.[15] These programs, however, are devoid of religiosity and operate in much the same manner as Catholic Charities and Lutheran Social Services, divorced from the parent religious organization in all but name. The last lines of Weiland's statement above indicate the church's position on charitable choice that will fund religious charities without regard to their degree of religiosity: "Clergy of all faiths need to work together to solve the problems of escalating drug use, crime and illiteracy and the crashing moral values in this country. That is our traditional role in the community as religious institutions and it is a role that we are *uniquely* designed to fulfill." In other words, leave the religious social work and missions to the religious organizations, supported by their parishioners' generosity, not the government's handouts. Government-funded religious social services are simply secular bureaucracy in religious garb. It cannot let the religious community operate independently; and only in its independence is that community effective in transforming society. Furthermore, offering funds to seemingly desperate religious charities can only create animosity in an age when cooperation among religious leaders is needed more than ever. Many major wars in the history of the West were the results of religious competition. The beauty of America is its diversity and the harmony such diversity fosters. In the words of James Madison, "Whilst all authority in [the United States] will be derived from and dependent on the society, the society itself will be broken into so many parts, interests and classes of citizens, that the rights of individuals, or of the minority, will be in little danger from the interested combinations of the majority."[16] To keep the peace, government cannot offer to fund some religions and potentially discriminate against others. The Church of Scientology's answer to Bush's plan is apparently NO.

Another perennial target of religious critics is the Nation of Islam, the leader of which is the notorious Louis Farrakhan. This controversial organization has in the past received government funding, including money to fund Nation of Islam security guards at public housing projects in several major U.S. cities. The program was eventually terminated after two Republican congressional figures began making inquiries. However, the security guard programs had served to reduce crime and drug deals in their projects despite its effort to proselytize and distribute copies of its newspaper, *Final Call*, which many critics charge is laden with anti-Semitism and racism. While Bush had earlier publicly stated that the Nation of Islam would be ineligible for funding because it preached hate, this security guard program is an example of a successful faith-based program. If, as DiIulio maintained during his tenure, the federal money will go to those faith-based efforts that have the highest rates of success, then the Nation of Islam, at least in this instance, would undoubtedly qualify. However, despite its past cooperation with the federal government, Louis Farrakhan stated in February that he is no longer interested in receiving government money. "Bush is not foolish. He wants to win you, preacher."[17] According to Farrakhan, Bush's entire plan is an effort to coddle the nation's black clergy and to win favor from them in return—just another way to keep the black man enslaved to the whims of the white majority.

Another group, the Mormons, is more widely accepted in the American mainstream and is well known for its pro-family, pro-life agendas. Surprisingly, the Church of Jesus Christ of Latter-day Saints has rejected the Bush plan for faith-based charities. But this rejection does not stem from any particular ideology. Rather, the church has the resources to sustain itself and would rather not be tied down by government regulations. "We're neutral. That's not saying we think it's wrong for every organization, but we just don't need it," spokesman Dale Bills said.[18] The LDS has from the beginning prided itself on self-sufficiency. And in its social services, the church requires that all its recipients repay the charity in some way as they become self-reliant. By taking government money, the church could not insist upon this essential element to helping people become better citizens.

Mormon, Wiccan, Scientology, and Nation of Islam's rejection of federal money is a breath of fresh air to many, if not most in the American public. And undoubtedly, the efforts of Sun Myung Moon to gain credibility and funds is appalling to many. According to a March poll, the American public by a 2-1 margin rejected the idea of government funds going to the Nation of Islam, to Scientology, and to the Hare Krishnas.[19] If these controversial groups are not interested in receiving government money and the more generally accepted religious organizations are, what is the difficulty with Bush's proposals? Would not the requirements of religious neutrality have been met? The answers are not easily discerned, and the difficulties abound by the dozens.

Conclusion

President's Bush's creation of the Office of Faith-based and Community Initiatives unnecessarily invokes a host of church-state issues of fundamental importance. Congress could still steer clear of First Amendment problems if it limits the scope of potentially participating organizations to private organizations, including religiously affiliated organizations that have an organizational charter or bylaws establishing their secular function. Houses of worship and other religious groups, including the array of religious minorities across America, could then participate in the new social service programs, performing their contractual responsibilities with the state in a secular setting and without proselytization. This arrangement would be in keeping with Supreme Court precedent and would protect both church and state from encroachment by the other.

Many members of Congress seem convinced that meeting the needs of the nation's poor and needy can only be achieved by enlisting the aid of faith-based institutions. But why does this also require an infusion of government money, with all of the attendant problems, both practical and constitutional? If it is a lack of financial resources that hinders faith-based institutions from a full participation in social programs, Congress would do better to offer economic incentives (e.g., tax credits and multiple write-offs) to corporate America for donations that would enable faith-based institutions to administer needed social programs. The possibilities here are endless, but the notion of corporations adopting and providing the financial means for charities, churches, synagogues, and other faith-based organizations to administer social programs, in effect creating a new strain of partnerships across America to solve social problems that government cannot and should not be expected to solve, is an attractive prospect.

But apart from these possibilities, and even in the new world created by charitable choice, houses of worship and other religious organizations can still exercise the same option that was open to them even before the charitable choice provisions became law: assist the poor and needy on their own terms, with their own financial resources, in an expressly religious environment, and with complete freedom to proselytize and teach their own religious beliefs. America's tradition of religious liberty could never be more faithfully or effectively exercised.

NOTES

1. *The Baptist Standard,* vol. 113, no. 6 (5 February 2001): 1.
2. Clinton Rossiter, ed., *The Federalist Papers* (New York: Penguin Books, 1961), 422-23.
3. *Church and State,* vol. 54, no. 6 (June 2001): 5.
4. Executive Order: Establishment of White House Office of Faith-Based and Community Initiatives. 29 January 2001. Available at: http://www.tgci.com/faithbased/articles/eo012901.htm.
5. *Church and State,* vol. 54, no. 4 (April 2001): 5.
6. Baptist Joint Committee, *The Report from the Capitol,* vol. 56, no. 12 (13 June 2001): 1.
7. *Church and State,* vol. 54, no. 4 (April 2001): 5.
8. Quoted in *Church and State,* vol. 54, no. 6 (June 2001): 10.
9. SMART Press Release, 28 February 2001. Available at: http://www.sikhmediawatch.org/news_events/pr20010228.htm.
10. Letter to George W. Bush, Dick Cheney, and Honored Government Officials, available at *http://www.aren.org/lettersig.html.*
11. Ibid.
12. Laura Meckler, "Plan for Religious Groups Debated," AP Online, 6 May 2001.
13. Ibid.
14. Janet Weiland, "Scientology Responds to Faith-Based Accusations." Available at: http://www.beliefnet.com/story/74/story_7439_1.html.
15. *Church and State,* vol. 54. no. 4 (April 2001): 5.
16. Rossiter, "Federalist 51," James Madison, 324.
17. Ibid., 6.
18. Christy Karras, "Mormons Reject Bush Charity Plan," AP Online, 25 April 2001.
19. *Church and State,* vol. 54, no. 4 (April 2001): 6.

CONTRIBUTORS

Susan E. Darnell is the branch manager of a major bank in Portage, Indiana, has extensive financial management experience, and has authored or coauthored a wide variety of publications, including newspaper articles and columns, professional journal articles dealing with the sociology of religion and criminology, and various national professional conference papers. She most recently co-edited (with Anson Shupe and William A. Stacey) *Bad Pastors: Clergy Misconduct in Modern America* (New York University Press, 2001).

Derek H. Davis is a graduate of Baylor University School of Law and holds a Master of Arts in Church-State Studies from Baylor University and a Doctor of Philosophy in Humanities from the University of Texas at Dallas. He is the Director of the J.M. Dawson Institute of Church-State Studies, Baylor University, Waco, Texas. In addition to serving as Editor of the award-winning *Journal of Church and State*, Dr. Davis is an officer and Fellow of the International Academy for the Freedom of Religion and Belief, serves on the Advisory Council of the Interfaith Religious Liberty Foundation, and is a member of the Religious Liberty Council of the National Council of Churches U.S.A. He is the author of *Original Intent: Chief Justice Rehnquist & the Course of American Church-State Relations* (1991), *Religion and the Continental Congress, 1774-1789: Contributions to Original Intent* (2000), and editor or coeditor of twelve other books, including the *Legal Deskbook for Administrators of Independent Colleges and Universities* (1993). He has also published extensively in various law and academic journals.

Adam C. English is a Ph.D. candidate at Baylor University. He has forthcoming articles due to appear in *Perspectives in Religious Studies* and *Baptist History and Heritage*. Special interests include the relationship between faith and philosophy in the nineteenth and twentieth century as well as the postmodern situation in theology and philosophy. He is grateful to W.D. English and Bill Pitts for their assistance with earlier drafts of this essay.

Barry Hankins (B.A., M.A., Baylor University; Ph.D., Kansas State University) is associate professor of history and church-state studies in the J.M. Dawson Institute of Church-State Studies at Baylor University. He is author of *God's Rascal: J. Frank Norris and the Beginnings of Southern Fundamentalism* (1996); and *Uneasy in Babylon: Southern Baptist Conservatives and American Culture* (2002). He also co-edited with Derek Davis, *Welfare Reform and Faith-Based Organizations*. His articles have appeared in *Church History, Religion and American Culture, Fides et Historia, Journal of Church and State*, and other journals and magazines.

Heber C. Jentzsch, president of Church of Scientology International since 1982, has been a minister of the church for nearly thirty years. As a leading spokesperson for Church of Scientology International, he has lectured on Scientology at universities around the world, including Notre Dame and Oxford, and has spoken at international religious conferences in Italy, the United Kingdom, Germany, Canada, South Africa and the United States. In 1986, he received an honorary doctorate degree from St. Martin's College and Seminary in Wisconsin in recognition for his work to end drug abuse among young people and for his ongoing fight to expose psychiatric abuses among minorities. Reverend Jentzsch has been honored with the Nelson R. Mandela Multicultural Center's Humanitarian Award and the Roy Wilkins Outstanding Leadership Award from the National Association for the Advancement of Colored People for his human rights work.

J. Gordon Melton is director of the Institute for the Study of American Religion, a research facility in Santa Barbara, California. He is also a research specialist with the Department of Religious Studies at the University of California-Santa Barbara. He is the author of the *Encyclopedia of American Religions* (6th ed., 1999), the standard reference work on American religious bodies, and more than thirty other books in American religious history, including most recently *American Religion: An Illustrated History* (ABC-Clio, 2000). He has specialized in the study of America's minority religious traditions and produced two widely used textbooks, *The Cult Experience* and *The Encyclopedia Handbook of Cults in America*.

Timothy Miller is professor of religious studies at the University of Kansas. With research specialization in American religious history, new religious movements, and communal groups, Dr. Miller has authored or edited a number of books, including *The 60s Communes: Hippies and Beyond* (1999), *The Quest for Utopia in Twentieth-Century America* (vol. one, 1900-1960) (1998), and *American's Alternative Religions* (editor, 1995).

Kendrick Moxon received his B.A. in Anthropology from American University in 1972 and his Doctor of Jurisprudence from George Mason University in 1981. He has worked extensively in the areas of civil liberties and freedom of information/government litigation. He is currently a practicing attorney in Los Angeles, California.

Susan J. Palmer teaches religious studies at Dawson College in Montreal and is an adjunct professor at Concordia University, Montreal. She is the author of *Moon Sister, Krishna Mothers, Rajneesh Lovers* (Syracuse, 1994), *Aids as an Apocalyptic Metaphor*, and co-author of *The Rajneesh Papers* and *Children in New Religions* (with Charlotte Hardman) as well as many articles. She is associate producer on *The Endtime*, a documentary film on The Family.

James T. Richardson is a professor of sociology at the University of Nevada-Reno. He is the author of a number of journal and book articles on topics associated with new religious movements and the law. He also co-edited *The Satanism Scare* (1991, with Joel Best and David Bromley) and edited *Money and Power in the New Religions* (1988).

Anson Shupe is professor of sociology at the joint campus of Indiana University-Purdue University, Fort Wayne, and is a member of the graduate faculties of both universities. He has also held positions at Alfred University and the University of Texas at Arlington. Author of over two dozen books and over seventy journal/book articles (and numerous popular writings for such outlets as *The Wall Street Journal* and *The Philadelphia Inquirer*), most of his research has focused on religious movements, from the cult-sect type to televangelism, and their political implications. While he has continued to monitor these areas over the past twenty-eight years, his most recent research emphasis is clergy malfeasance. In studying this subject, he is attempting to marry the sub-disciplines of the sociology of religion and criminology in analyzing clergy misconduct. His most recent publications on the subject are *In the Name of All That's Holy: A Theory of Clergy Malfeasance* (1995, Praeger), *Wolves within the Fold: Religious Leadership and*

Abuses of Power (Edited, 1998, Rutgers University Press), and *Bad Pastors: Clergy Misconduct in Modern America* (co-edited with William A. Stacey and Susan E. Darnell, 2000, New York University Press).

Catherine Wessinger is professor of history of religions and women's studies, and chair of the religious studies department at Loyola University, New Orleans. She is a former chair of the New Religious Movements Group at the American Academy of Religion, and a member of the Executive Advisory Committee of *Nova Religio: The Journal of Alternative and Emergent Religions*. She was an adviser to the FBI during the Freemen standoff in 1996. She is the author of *Annie Besant and Progressive Messianism* (1988) and *How the Millennium Comes Violently: From Jonestown to Heaven's Gate* (2000). She is editor of *Women's Leadership in Marginal Religions: Explorations Outside the Mainstream* (1993) and of *Religious Institutions and Women's Leadership: New Roles Inside the Mainstream* (1996).

Stuart A. Wright is associate director of graduate studies and research and professor of sociology at Lamar University in Beaumont, Texas. Editor of *Armageddon in Waco*, he testified at the 1995 U.S. House of Representatives hearings on Waco and worked with the Senate Judiciary Committee on its Waco hearings later the same year. Portions of this essay appeared in Stuart A. Wright, "Justice Denied: The Waco Civil Trial," *Nova Religio: The Journal of Alternative and Emergent Religions* 5, no. 1 (October 2001): 143-51, and are reprinted with permission.

INDEX